SCHOLAR BOXER

SCHOLAR BOXER
儒拳師

Cháng Nâizhou's
Theory of Internal
Martial Arts and
the Evolution of
Tàijíquán

with complete translation
of the original writings (edited by Xú Zhèn, 1932)

Marnix Wells

North Atlantic Books
Berkeley, California

Published by
North Atlantic Books
P.O. Box 12327
Berkeley, California 94712
www.northatlanticbooks.com

Cover and book design by Susan Quasha
Printed in the United States of America
Distributed to the book trade by Publishers Group West

Scholar Boxer: Cháng Nâizhou's Theory of Internal Martial Arts and the Evolution of Tàijíquán is sponsored by the Society for the Study of Native Arts and Sciences, a nonprofit educational corporation whose goals are to develop an educational and crosscultural perspective linking various scientific, social, and artistic fields; to nurture a holistic view of arts, sciences, humanities, and healing; and to publish and distribute literature on the relationship of mind, body, and nature.

Library of Congress Cataloging-in-Publication Data
Wells, Marnix, 1945-
  Scholar boxer : Chang Naizhou's theory of internal martial arts and the evolution of Taijiquan / by Marnix Wells.
      p. cm.
  Contains a translation of: Chang shi wu ji shu.
  Includes bibliographical references.
  ISBN 1-55643-482-0 (pbk.)
  1. Martial arts--Religious aspects. 2. Martial arts--Psychological aspects. 3. T'ai chi. 4. Chang, Naizhou--Criticism and interpretation. I. Chang, Naizhou. Chang shi wu ji shu. English. II. Title.

GV1102.7.R44W45 2004
796.8'01--dc22

2004017144

1 2 3 4 5 6 7 UNITED 09 08 07 06 05

Dedication

*To my parents, Cháng Yìjun and family,
and the late Danny Connor, who said
a good technique should make you smile.*

Acknowledgments

I express my appreciation to Cháng Yìjun and Cháng Hóngjun for showing me the living tradition of Cháng Boxing in its home. Chén Wànqing, president of the Chángjia Boxing Research Association, and Cháng Songhuá, Chén Zengzhì, and Chén Wànlî, from nearby Xingyáng, were kind enough to advise me on the extent of Cháng Nâizhou's corpus, which I hope may soon be published in full.

I would like to thank old friends and fellow martial practitioners Bruce Kumar Frantzis, Barry Wicksman, and Allen Pittman for their support. Sinologist Dr. Ulrike Middendorf, of Heidelberg University, and Edward Lau gave valuable help in identifying literary sources.

Last and above all, I would like to express deep gratitude for the patient perseverance of my editors Kathy Glass, Adrienne Armstrong, and Paula Morrison who pulled it all together, designer Susan Quasha, Emily Boyd, and publishers Richard Grossinger and Lindy Hough.

Contents

List of Plates, Figures, and Diagrams

PLATE 1: CHÁNG NÂIZHOU IN BATTLE ARMOR

Painting inscribed: *Cháng Luòchén's portrait,* copy, repainted May 1975, photographed at Cháng family home in Hénán, Xingyáng, August 1, 1994. The subject's lively expression and whiskers fit the description of Cháng's portrait, in the mode of *Three Kingdoms* hero Zhang Fei, painted by Xú Quán (see below: biographies from *Sìshuî District Gazetteer,* in *Introduction: xii*).

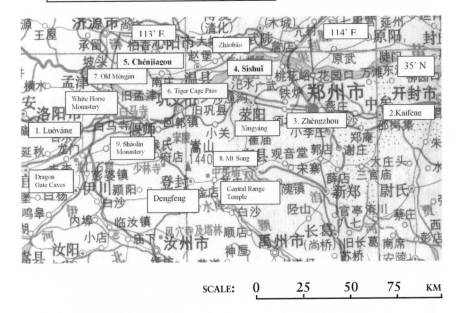

The Yellow River, Hénán Province

SCALE: 0 25 50 75 KM

PLATE 2: MAP OF HÉNÁN PROVINCE

The close-up of this modern map of Hénán Province shows the ancient capitals of 1) Lùoyáng to the west and 2) Kaifeng to the east, along the south bank of the Yellow River. In the center is 3) Zhèngzhou, provincial capital, and to its west 4) Sìshuî, home of Cháng Nâizhou, and 5) Mèngjin, home of his wife. Immediately across the Yellow River from Sìshuî on the north bank is Zhàobâo with neighboring 6) Chénjiagou, famed homes of Tàijíquán. 7) Tiger Cage Pass, Hŭlaóguan, is the home of renowned seventeenth-century martial expert Zhang Ba, a source of Cháng boxing and a possible fit for Jiâng Fa of Tàijíquán legend. Immediately to the south is 8) Mt. Song and to its west 9) Shàolín Monastery.

PLATE 3: CHÁNG DESCENDANTS IN ACTION

Present-day descendants of Cháng Nâizhou, Cháng Yìjun demonstrating Cháng Boxing (pictures 1–8) and younger brother Hóngjun demonstrating boxing and Monkey Pole (pictures 9–12), August 1994.

xvi

PLATE 4: DING HÓNGYÌ, EX-SHÀOLÍN MONK, WITH YOUNG SON AT RURAL HOME NEAR THE MONASTERY, ADOPTS A FIGHTING POSE, AUGUST 1994.

Ding Hóngyì, tonsured name Yônglì "Eternal Stance," living close by Shàolín with his wife and young son, strikes a wide-eyed fighting pose for the camera. Mr. Ding was photographed with the author by Barry Wicksman.

Format and Spelling

Chinese words are spelled in the official pinyin method. I utilize French accents for convenience to show speech tones. No accent means high tone (e.g. fa); acute accent means rising tone (e.g. fá); circumflex means falling-rising tone (e.g. fâ); grave accent means falling tone (e.g. fà).

The format of the translation is new. This includes paragraphing, indentation, alignment of verse, capitalization or italicization of key terms and phrases, boldfacing of titles, quotation marks, insertion of inter-textual notes or cross-referencing in square brackets, and source references in endnotes. The core Twenty-four Dynamics in section 69 are identified as "No. 1...." They are cross-referenced in other sections as *"[69:1...].*" These conventions are adopted to facilitate understanding of the work as a whole. The textual problems, and treatment of insertions by previous commentators, are discussed in detail at *Introduction: x,* below. Where the original text contains interpolated comments, these are in parentheses: "(xyz...)." My own remarks are italicized in square brackets [.....] or: *"Notes:"*

Translation, Numbering, and Sequence

Translations in this book aim for literalness and consistency of terminology, reproducing as well as possible the original word order. Word order is particularly important for parallel structured couplets, as in Chinese verse or prose. Wherever possible, I use the same English word for a given Chinese word. All this helps convey the flavor, rhythm, and stress patterns of the original. It also aids understanding of terms and their relationships without the wholesale importation of Chinese vocabulary. Trigrams and hexagrams from the *Change Classic* are shown here, for convenience, in binary of "1"s and "0"s for unbroken and broken lines.

I restore Cháng's titles and division of the work into *Part A: Nourishing Central Energy* and *Part B: Martial Defense,* which Xú Zhèn removed. I further retain Xú's six-chapter format *(I–VI),* which does not appear in Cháng's received table of contents.[1]

Serial numbering of articles and sub-items is now supplied to aid cross-reference. In the received text, only the Twenty-four Dynamics in 69 were serially numbered. Yet numerology underlies much of Cháng's structure. There are twelve acupuncture channels *[10],* twelve Joints *[19],* twenty-four Spear principles *[70],* forty-eight Monkey Pole *[71],* and thirty-six Double Swords *[72].* All are multiples of twelve, divisible by both two and three, characteristic of the Chinese farmer's calendar, with its fifteen 24-day periods and five 72-day "seasons," as Cháng explains in his cosmology *[30].* Xú Zhèn consolidates a total of seventy-four articles, from a received one hundred and thirty-one. It is perhaps fitting, whether coincidental or not, that the grand total of articles, which I now serially number, comes to exactly seventy-two. See comparative tables and notes in *Appendix V.*

Vocabulary of Key Terms

adamantine, steely, diamond body = jin'gangshen 金剛身, indestructible as the vajra club, or thunder-bolt, of Hinduism and Buddhism, ref. *Nirvana Sûtra: iv. [1; 25; 34; 69:17]* cf. Vajrapâni; Expansive Energy

blast, explode = pèng 硼, beng 崩 *[39; 41; 70:I-ii, -iii, II-ii, III-ii]* cf. uproot

body = shen, tî 身, 體

borrow Energy = jièqì 借氣

boxing, fist = quán 拳

breathing = huxí 呼吸, circular, reverse abdominal *[37; 48; 50; 52; 56; 62]* cf. Energy

broadsword, sabre = dao 刀

burst, surge = chong 衝, 沖

butt, resist, close-range strike, crown of head = ding 頂

compete = xiangjiao 相交 cf. cross hands

cross hands, fight, compete = jiaoshôu 交手 *[23; 26; 27; 54; 57]*

crown, top of head = dîng 頂 cf. butt

discharge and release, emit sound, shout = safàng 撒放 *[24; 28]*

double weighting = shuangzhòng 雙重, failure in Tàijíquán to divide weight into "empty and full" = xushí 虛實

drop, fall, ultimate contact point of Energy = luò 落 cf. point

dynamic, posture, movement = shì 勢

Elixir Field, "cinnabar field" = dantián 丹田; body's central point, just below navel elixir of longlife, "gold cinnabar" in Daoist alchemy = jindan 金丹 cf. vajra, adamantine

Energy, breath = qì 氣 cf. breathing

enter, begin, activate Energy, enter combat, penetrate defences = rù 入

entry and support, Cháng and support = Cháng 入扶

essence, sperm = jing 精, essential spirit = jingshén 精神

exercise, practiced skill = gong 功, gongfu 功夫

exertion = jîn 僅 = qín 勤

Expansive Energy = hàorán-zhi qì 浩然之氣 Mèng Zî (c. 300 B.C.): *iia-2 Gongsun Chôu*: "extremely great, extremely hard" and courageous. *[32; 58; 70:I-ii, III-i]*

Fate's Gate, acupoint between kidneys = Mìngmén 命門 *[1; 17; 34; 35; 37; 49]*

Finish, smash, ultimate exertion phase of Energy = jìn 盡, 儘, or ji 木 + 齏 = sa 搔 *[15; 17; 18; 19; 22; 50; 54; 57; 69:9, pass.; 70:I-iii, II:ii]* cf. Power

Five Actions, five elements = wû-xíng 五行

flexion/extension = qushen 曲伸

force, effort = lì 力; natural force = zìrán-zhi lì 自然之力 *[30; 35; 36; 52]*

form/shape (physical body) = xíng 形

ghosts, demons = guî 鬼

god, divine, spirit = shén 神 cf. essence, essential spirit

Gold Elixir = jindan 金丹 cf. elixir of longlife; adamantine, vajra *[1; 69:4]*

Grand Polarity/Pole = Tàijí 太極 interactive unity of Shady and Sunny cf. Grand Unity, below *[1; 12; 15; 30; 34]*

grapple = qínná 擒拿

hard and soft mutually complement = gangróu xiangjì 剛柔相濟 *[13; 18; 30; 39; 57; 70:I-iii, II-i]* hit = dâ 打

immortal, Dàoist fairy, saint = xian 仙

law, method, dharma = fâ 法

magic, sensitive, soul = ling 靈; sensitive perception = língtong 靈通 *[70:I-ii]*

martial = wû 武

martial defense and preparation = wûbèi 武備

moment, pivot point, crucial timing = ji 機

point of contact, to ignite (of fire, or Energy) cf. skip = diân 點 cf. drop

pole, staff = bàng 棒

pounce, catch, knock over, throw in wrestling = pu 撲

power, "intrinsic energy," strength = jìng, jìn 勁, 觔 = 斤/秦 + 力. N.B. Lî Yìyú: *Five Word Maxims* writes "pound" jin 斤 + "force" lì 力; Chén Xin writes it interchangeably with 筋. *[57]*

prone (face-up)/supine (face-down) = yâng/fû 仰俯 cf. flexion/extension, shady/sunny

random skipping, on toe-point, ball of foot = luàndiân/dian 亂點/顛 *[10; 13; 19; 64]*

reeling silk power = chánsijìng 纏絲勁

refine, forge, train = liàn 煉

release, set down = fang 放

shady/sunny = yinyáng 陰陽 cf. prone/supine, flexion/extension

shoot = fa 發

skip, step on ball of foot, cf. random skipping, 點/顛 *[10; 13; 29; 64]*

slice, side-kick = cè 策

spear = qiang 槍

stick and link/follow = niánlián/suí 黏連/隨 *[23; 26; 27; 69:17, 18; 70:I-ii, II-ii, III-i]*

Supreme Vehicle, Vajrayâna = Shàngchéng 上乘 of Tibetan Buddhism
  [1]

sword, double-edged and pointed straight-sword = jiàn 劍

tally-stick, broken into two parts, "sunny" and "shady," fitted
  together to prove credentials; magic talisman or charm = fú 符

thrust, stab = cha, cì 插, 刺

tip, pointed peripheral = jian 尖

touch, contact = zhan 沾, jie 接

Triple Tip Alignment = san-jian zhào 三尖照 *[16; 20; 21; 30; 31;
  46; 57; 70:II-i]*

tug and drag, inefficient force = qianchè 牽扯

uproot, bounce, ward-off = pêng 掤; proffer = pêng 捧 *[12; 69:5,
  10, 17]* cf. blast

urge = cui 催 cf. destroy = cuî 摧; push = tui 推

vajra, diamond, indestructible, steely, literally "gold hard" = jingang.
  Cf. Vajrapâni (below); adamantine, elixir, (above). *[1; 69:4, 17]*

Personal Names and Sources

Avalokiteshvara, Guanyin 觀音 *[69:19, 22]*, bodhisattva of mercy. ref. *Lotus Sûtra: xxv.*

Ban Chao 班超 (First century B.C.) *[69:8, 20]*, conqueror of the Western Regions of Central Asia under early Hàn.

Bîng Jí 丙吉 (d. 55 B.C.) *[69:2]*, guardian and later premier to Hàn Emperor Xuan.

Bodhidharma (c. 530), pioneer of Dhyâna sect in the Far East, reputedly meditated nine years in a Shàolín cave, and composed the apocryphal *Change Sinews Classic.* qv.

Buddha (c. 500 B.C.), Amitâbha 阿彌陀佛 *[69:22]*, "Buddha of Infinite Light."

Cantóngqì 參同契, *Triple Correlation*, by (Hàn) Wèi Bóyáng 魏伯陽, who used fire and water trigrams of *Change* as symbols of alchemic physiology. *[1; 18; 62]*

Cáo Cao 曹操 (155–220) *[72:25, 27]*, military genius and dictator at the close of Hàn. His son founded Wèi, with capital at (Hénán) Luòyáng, one of the Three Kingdoms.

Chán (Japanese: Zen) Buddhism, Dhyâna sect (zong) 禪宗. *Pointing to the Moon Record* (1602), *Zhîyuè Lù* 指月錄 *VII-7.* A monk asks about the lion using full force, whether seizing a rabbit or an elephant, and a senior monk replies that it describes "the force of not cheating." *[60]*

Cháng Nâizhou, Luòchén, Chúnchéng 萇乃周, 洛臣, 純誠, 三宅 (1724–1783?), of (Hénán) Sìshuî 汜水, the "scholar boxer," rúquánshi 儒拳師, the author.

Cháng Shìzhou, Mùtíng 萇仕周, 穆亭, elder brother of Nâizhou, 1742 graduate, served as prefect of (Shânxi) Yíjun 宜君, and authored *Change Classic Lectures, Yijing Jiângyì*, in eight chapters, analyzing hexagrams by their component halves.[2]

Cháng Yìjun "Resolute Army" 萇毅軍, and brother Hóngjun "Red Army," living descendents of the Scholar Boxer.

Change Classic, Yì Jing 易經. *[1; 12; 15; 28; 68:19; 69:9, 11, 18, 20]*

Change Sinews Classic, Yìjîn Jing 易筋經 to train body "hard and rigid." *[1; 19; 24; 34; 50]*

Chén Xin, Pînsan 陳鑫, 品三 (1849–1929) of (Hénán) Chénjiagou, authored first book on Chén Tàijíquán.

Chéng Chongdôu, Zongyóu 程沖斗 (1561–c. 1630?), of Anhui, author of *Shàolín Staff* and works on other weapons that he studied at the Temple. *[27; 29; 50; 69:14, 20]*

Chéng Hào 程顥 (1032–1085) of Luòyáng, with his brother Chéng Yí, pioneers of neo-Confucian learning and meditation. *[34]*

Chénxiang Rescues Mother, Chénxiang Jiùmû 沉/陳香救母, folk legend and play of the "Giant Soul" who chops open Mt. Huá to free his mother, imprisoned inside. *[69:20]*

Confucius, "The Master," Kông Zî/Fuzî 孔子/夫子 (551–471 B.C.). *[68; 69:4]: Analects, Lúnyû [26; 68:1, 23; 69:8]; Change Classic: Appendix a-5 [69:18]; "Central Norm," Zhongyong [68:25]*

Dongfang Shuò 東方朔 (160–? B.C.) *[69:1],* court jester to Martial Emperor of Hàn.

(Táng) Dù Yòu 杜祐 (d. 812): *Tongdiân* encyclopedia (c. 800), with important commentary on Sun Zî: *Arms' Laws. [70:II-ii]*

Grand Mountain (Shandong) = Tàishan 泰山. *[30; 68:4; 69:14, 19]*

Grand Unity, Tàiyi 太一/乙, monist deity, linked to Heavenly Unity (Tianyi 天一) and Mysterious Martial (qv.), the element of water and north pole. Cf. Grand Polarity, above.

Guan Yû 關羽 (d. 219), of Shanxi, commonly called Guan Gong "the Duke," halberd-wielding hero of the Three Kingdoms wars, was canonized by the emperor as Guan Dì, god of war, after he appeared to Chinese troops helping Korea repel a Japanese invasion (1592–1598), at the retaking of Peongyang. He is never named here, just his weapon—the "Spring-Autumns Halberd."

Hán Xiang Zî 韓湘子 (ninth century) *[69:4]*, one of popular Daoism's Eight Immortals, reputed nephew of Táng statesman and poet Hán Yù (768–824).

Hú Xû 胡煦 (1655–1736), of Guangshan, Hénán. Leading expert on the *Change Classic*, who may have influenced Tàijíquán.

Huá Yuán 華元 *[69:2]*, general of Sòng, defeated by Zhèng in 607 B.C.

Huáng Zongxi 黃宗羲 (1610–1695) of Yúyáo (Zhèjiang), and his son Huáng Bâijia, wrote an epitaph for Internal School boxer Wáng Zhengnán, and a detailed account of his martial arts, regretfully without illustrations.

Huángshí Gong 黃石公, "Yellow Rock Duke" (c. 200 B.C.), teacher of Zhang Liáng 張良, strategist to Liú Bang, founder of Hàn, *Three Stratagems, Sanlyuè* 三略. *[27:4; 33]*

Iron Fan Princess, Tiêshan Gonzhû 鐵扇公主 *[69:8, 14; 70:III-vi]*, *Westward Travelogue*, wife of ten-headed Bull Demon, mother of fiery Red Boy; see Sudhâna.

(Qing) Jî Yún 紀昀 (1724–1805), *"Examine the Subtle" Cottage Notebook, Yuèwei Câotáng Bîjì* 閲微草堂筆記, a collection of supernatural tales. *[28]*

Jiâng Fa, Ba/Bâshì/shí 蔣發, 八/把式/拾 legendary patriarch of Tàijíquán, displaying some affinity to Zhang Ba q.v. *(FIGURE 7)*

Lâo Zî 老子 "Old Lord/Ancestor," Lâojun/zû (c. 400? B.C.) *[69:2, 3, 4]*, author of *Way Virtue Classic. [1]*

Lî Yìyú 李亦畬 (1832–1892), first dated compiler of the *Tàijíquán Classic*.

Liú Bang 劉邦 (247–195 B.C.) *[10; 14; 70:II-ii; 72:23]*, founder emperor of the Hàn dynasty who overcame Xiàng Yû, Chû Bàwáng, Hegemon King of Chû.

Liú Bèi 劉備 "First Master," Xianzhû (162–223) *[69:12]*, founder King of Latter Hàn in Sìchuan (Shû) and *Three Kingdoms* epic hero.

Liú Hâi 劉海 *[69:1b]*, Daoist immortal saint, depicted in art from the Yuán period as overgrown child playing with giant toad and string of cash.

Liù-Tao 六韜, *Six Satchels*, attr. (Zhou) Tàigong 太公望, 呂尙, military adviser to King Wû who founded Zhou, in 1122 B.C. (trad.). *[27]*

Lyû Dòngbin 呂洞賓 (tenth century) *[69:4]*, scholar swordsman, one of Daoism's Eight Immortals.

Mèng Zî, Ke 孟子, 軻 Mencius (fl. 310 B.C.), Confucian philosopher who linked martial prowess to morality. Quoted here is his *Gongsun Chôu* chapter on Expansive Energy and courageous valour. *[29; 32; 34; 58; 69:21b; 70:I-ii, III-i]*

Mysterious Martial, Dark Warrior, see Xuánwû, Grand Unity.

Nirvâna Sûtra, allegedly preached by the Buddha on his entry into extinction. Cf. adamantine body. *[1]*

Qi Jìguang 戚繼光 (1528–1587) of Shandong, general and conqueror of the Japanese pirates, author of the first illustrated training manual on tactics and martial arts, including the *Boxing Classic* with thirty-two dynamics illustrated.

Râkshasa, or Yaksha demon guardian of Hindu-Buddhist mythology *[69:8, 9, 14, 22; 72:29]*.

Shady Tally Classic, Yinfú Jing 陰符經, attr. Yellow Emperor (attr. c. 2000 B.C.), commentary by Zhugé Liàng (181–234) et al. *[68: 20]*

South Forest Virgin, Nánlín Chù 南林處女 (c. 500 B.C.). *[25; 45]* cf. *Wú-Yuè Chunqiu.*

Spring-Autumns, Chunqiu 春秋, annals of Lû, 722–477 B.C., edited by Confucius; with *Zuôzhuàn* commentary. *[69:8]*

Su Qín 蘇秦 (d. 219 B.C.) *[69:3, 12; 71:9, 26]*, diplomat swordsman who brokered an alliance against Qín.

Sudhâna, "Goodly giver," Shàncái 善財 *[69:22]*, the demonic Red Boy converted by Avalokiteshvara, into pilgrim hero of *Avatamsaka "Garland" Sûtra*. See *Westward Travelogue: Iron Fan Princess.* Fiery Red Boy has affinity with the Hindu Skanda, son of Shiva.

Sun Dàniáng, "Madame Sun" 孫大娘 *[72]* whose spectacular sword dance was celebrated by Táng poet Dù Fû (712–770).

Sun Quán 孫權 (181–253) *[69:12],* founder of southern Wú kingdom, on the Yangtze, one of the Three Kingdoms.

Sun Zî, Wû 孫子 (c. 500 B.C.), strategist and author of *Arms Laws, The Art of War, Bingfâ. [23; 27; 28; 31; 35; 38; 46; 53; 54; 70:II-ii]*

Three Kingdoms Romance, San-Guó Yânyì 三國演義 *[69:12, 14, 18–19, 22b; 70:II-i, -ii; 71:21; 72:8, 25]* Heroic saga of failed endeavor to re-establish the fallen Hàn dynasty.

Three Stratagems, Sanlyuè 三略, see Huángshí Gong.

True Martial, see Zhenwû.

Vajrapâni, Jingang Lìshì 金剛力士, are Buddhism's gate guardian deities, of amazing ferocity and strength. Of similar appearance are the Four Kings who guard the cardinal compass points whose statues are often venerated in the entrance to temples. Cf. vajra (above). *[69:18]*

(Jìn) Wáng Xizhi 王羲之 (306–365) of Zhèjiang, "Right Army General" *[69:7],* supreme calligrapher and swordsman.

Wáng Zongyuè, "Lineage of Yuè (Fei)" 王宗岳, "of Shanxi," enigmatic figure, ascribed author of Tàijíquán Theory.

(Jìn) Wen Jiào 溫嶠 (288–329) *[69:2],* general who allegedly saw into the watery underworld with a rhinoceros tusk torch.

Westward Travelogue, Xiyóujì 西游記, a humorous romance based on the adventures of Táng monk Xuánzàng, who travelled overland to India. Its definitive version is attributed to (Míng) Wú Chéng'en. *[69:1, 5, 10b, 13–14b, 22, 24b]*

(Yuán) Wú Chéng, canonized as Wénzhèng "Culture Correct" 吳澄, 文正 (1249–1333) *[12],* neo-Confucian philosopher of Línchuan (Jiangxi) under the Mongol Yuán dynasty.

Wú-Yuè Chunqiu 吳越春秋, (Hàn) Zhào Yè 趙曄. An historical romance that details South Forest Virgin's instruction in martial arts of Goujiàn of Yuè (Zhèjiang) who used them to regain his throne.

Xiàng Yû 項羽 (233–202 B.C.), "Hegemon King" Bàwáng 楚霸王 *[69:10, 12, 14; 70:I-ii; 72:23]* of Chû (Anhui), overthrower of Qín in 208 B.C., but defeated by Liú Bang of Hàn.

Xú Panguì (eighteenth century) 徐攀桂, "Governor of Hénán," evidently Xú Ji 徐積 (served 1774–1778), who composed a eulogy for Cháng Nâizhou.

Xú Zhèn, Zhédong 徐震 哲東 (1898–1967) of Wûjìn, Jiangsu, martial researcher who edited and published Cháng's works in 1936, prefaced 1932.

Xuánwû 玄武, Mysterious Martial, or Dark Warrior; Xuándì, Mysterious Emperor; god of the North. See Zhenwû.

Yán Shèngdào 閻聖道 [33], teacher of Cháng Nâizhou.

Yáng Family Sixth Lad, Yángjia Liù-láng, Yáng Yánzhao 楊延昭 [70:I-ii] of Shanxi, lancer general, son of Yáng Yè (d. 986) who died heroically fighting the Khitans.

Yâng Yóuji 養由基, and Panwâng Dâng, of Chû, in 575 B.C., could shoot an arrow through seven layers of armor.[3] [28]

Yellow Court Classic, Huángtíng Jing 黃庭經, attr. Lady Wèi 衛夫人 (c. 300). [1; 25; 34; 62; 69:7]

Yellow Emperor's Internal Classic: Soul Trunk, Huángdì Nèijing Língshu 黃帝內經靈樞. [10]

Yì Jing, see *Change Classic.*

Yìjîn Jing, see *Change Sinews Classic.*

Yinfú Jing, see *Shady Tally Classic.*

(Míng) Yú Dàyóu 俞大猷 (1503–1579), of (Fújiàn) Jînjiang, victorious general against Japanese pirates: *Sword Classic, Jiànjing* 劍經. [32; 69:4, 15]

Yû Ràng 禹讓, allegedly a teacher of Cháng Nâizhou. Cháng's unpublished "Thirty-six Spear tablature" (1780) records that the fifth generation spear of "Zhang of Hûlâo" had been transmitted to the Yû family.[4] Cf. Zhang Ba.

Yuè Fei "the flying" 岳飛 (1103–1141) [69:14], a general of Southern Sòng, executed by the appeasement party, but later canonized "Martial Reverence" Wûmù 武穆, the patriot hero who defeated Jurchen invaders. Qing dynasty lore links him to boxing, notably Xíngyìquán, *Change Sinews Classic,* and *Double Push Hands.*[5]

Zen, see Chán Buddhism, above.

Zhang Ba 張八 *[33]*, "Divine Hand" (Shénshôu), probably identical to "Zhang Flying God" (Zhang Feishén), sixteenth century martial artist who lived near the home of Cháng Nâizhou. Cf. Jiâng Fa, Yû Ràng.

Zhang Fei "the flying" 張飛 *[69:12, 22b; 70:II-i; 71:21; 72:8, 25]*, enfiefed as baron Huánhóu 桓侯, lancer hero of the *Three Kingdoms.*

Zhang Sengyóu 張僧繇 (sixth century) *[69:9]*, renowned Buddhist painter under the southern Liáng dynasty.

Zhào Yún, Zîlóng 趙雲, 龍 *[69:14; 70:II-ii]*, lancer hero of the *Three Kingdoms.*

Zhenwû 真武, "True Martial" Daoist God of Wûdang *[72]*. The name occurs in the *Chang Classic* appendices, and was used as a taboo substitution (c. 1008–1016) for "Mystic Martial," Xuánwû q.v.[6] Cf. Guan Yû. *(FIGURE 28)*

Zhongyong 中庸, *Central Norm,* attributed to Zî Si 子思, disciple of Confucius q.v.

Zhou Dunyí 周敦頤 (1012–1073): *Tàijí Diagram* theory. *[15; 30]* Zhou's diagram divided the circle into three bands of alternating black and white halves, not the familiar black and white swirls that first appeared under the Míng (1368–1644).[7]

Zhu Xi 朱羲 (1130–1200), of Southern Sòng, supreme neo-Confucian philosopher of the Tàijí monad, later criticized for entrenching yinyáng, logos-energy (lî-qì) dualism.

Zhuang Zî, Zhou 莊子, 周 (third century B.C.) *[69:23]*, Daoist philosopher and satirist, butterfly dream. *[30; 32; 69:18, 22]*

Zhugé Liàng, Kông Míng 諸葛亮, 孔明 (181–234) *[66]*, supreme strategist of Later Hàn, in the Three Kingdoms wars. *[69:19]*

Introduction:
TOWARDS A MARTIAL PHILOSOPHY

i. Cháng Nâizhou's Legacy

Neither the massive Daoist temple to the god of war on (Húbêi) Mt. Wûdang, built in 1418 by usurper Míng emperor Yônglè, nor the Buddhist Shàolín Monastery, willfully set ablaze by warlord Shí Yôusan in 1928, preserve a comprehensive martial philosophy. For this, we turn to the few cryptic pages of the *Tàijíquán Classic*, edited by Lî Yìyú in 1881.[8] *[Appendix II]* Yet there is a more complete source, from a century earlier, that anticipates and elaborates more fully many of the same ideas. This is the writings of Cháng Nâizhou (1724–1783?), the "scholar boxer" (rúquánshi).[9]

Cháng Nâizhou was a native of Sìshuî, in Hénán Province, on the south bank of the Yellow River. To its south, less than fifty miles away as the crow flies, lie Tiger Cage Pass (Hûláoguan) and the slopes of Mt. Song, "central" mountain of China, on which stands the Shàolín Monastery. Northwards, over the Yellow River, still in Hénán, is Chénjiagou, the village now famous as the home of Tàijíquán. Westwards, there is Luòyáng, "capital of nine dynasties," while to the east are Zhèngzhou, a royal city of the Shang, and farther along the south bank Kaifeng, capital of Northern Sòng. This was the home of Cháng Nâizhou, the "scholar boxer."

Here, in the central cradle of Chinese history, the mid-eighteenth century, and peak of Qing imperial power under the sixty-year reign of Qiánlóng (1736–1795), we stand at the cross-roads of internal and external martial arts; of Shàolín and Tàijíquán, Xíngyìquán and Baguàzhâng; Confucianism, Daoism, Buddhism, and a hint of shamanism. Yet this is a world of political repression and a region known for famine and banditry.

1

In 1727, the Manchu Qing Emperor Yongzhèng (r. 1723–1735) issued an edict to suppress ethnic Chinese martial arts and boxing. The government's particular concern was the involvement of subversive sects. Books on martial arts could be published again in China only after the fall of the Qing Empire in 1911. As a result, between the flourishing of martial arts in the sixteenth and seventeenth centuries, and their progressive gradual reappearance with loosening imperial control from the nineteenth, there is a black hole of detailed information. Cháng's writings open a window into the eighteenth century. They should help to fill the crucial gap between the account of the "Internal School" of boxing from Zhèjiang, left by Huáng Zongxi (1610–1695) and son Bâijia, and the *Tàijíquán Classic* manuscripts of Lî Yìyú (1832–1892) from Hébêi.[10]

Cháng makes the earliest dateable attempt to explain martial arts in terms of Tàijí, the "Grand Pole," with its opposing forces of yinyáng, "Shady and Sunny." The reader will find here a system of physiology, *qìgong* Energy cultivation, and explosive application in practical self-defense, against a background of alchemy, arts, ethics, history, humor, medicine, mythology, philosophy, poetry, religion, and strategy. Its dynamic postures are illustrated by lively sketches. Breathing, qì Energy, and body alignments are analyzed in detail. Open-handed boxing techniques and weaponry, solo practice and competitive combat, are all closely integrated.

Cháng's Central Energy is a synthesis of flexion and extension, hard and soft, vacuous and substantial, yinyáng, "Shady and Sunny." Cháng emphasizes Shady and Sunny as prone (down-facing) and supine (up-facing) in the vertical plane, ducking down and leaning back like a boxer, rather than the horizontal turns to left and right characteristic of Tàijíquán. Yet Tàijíquán Theory, in an adaption of Confucius' *Analects,* has the lines: "Prone (looking down), it is deeper; supine (looking up), it is higher."[11] Nevertheless Yáng Family Forty Chapters, transmitted by Yáng Banhóu (1837–1892) and translated by Douglas Wile, discuss prone and supine bending as advanced faults, breaks in flow to be reconnected before achieving true "understanding power." Cháng's 15: *Shady and Sunny, Rotation and Resolution Theory* also emphasizes continuity and connection. There is a shared concern to deploy energy smoothly and without obstruction, or in Cháng's words, without "tugging and dragging"(qianchè).

Cháng's relationship to Tàijíquán is close in the realm of theory, sources, and language. The system of martial movements that he collated is quite differently based but contains many of the same elements. Thus, two of Cháng's Twenty-four Dynamics boxing titles, White Swan (Crane) Displays Wings and Twin Peaks (Yáng: Winds), are near-variants of Tàijíquán names. Eight techniques named by Cháng—Gold Cock on One Leg, Seven Stars, Cross-sign Hands, Bestride Tiger, Single Whip, Bend Bow, Cannon Fist, Tiger Hold Head (Chén's Beast Head), and Hold Head, Push Mountain (Yáng's Carry Tiger Back to Mountain)—match moves in both Qi Jiguang's (1528–1587) *Boxing Classic* and Tàijíquán. Five correspond to Huáng Zongxi's Internal School: Cross-sign Hands, Bend Bow, Gold Cock on One Leg, Wield Whip, and Tiger Hold Head.

There are visual and technical Tàijíquán parallels in Cháng's Crab Closes Pincers with Yáng Tàijíquán's Twin Winds Through Ears; and the spin-turns in the closing number Gold Cat Catches Rat, matching Yáng's Swing Lotus Legs *[69]*. Among Cháng weapons, we see other Tàijíquán images: Jade Girl Threads Shuttles from Monkey Pole *[71:33]*; and White Snake Spits Out from Double Swords *[72:18]*.

The martial writings of Cháng Nâizhou, including weaponry, as published by Xú Zhèn (1898–1967) after Yuán Yûhuá 1921, are presented here in their entirety for the first time in English. They are one of the most complete pre-modern treatments of martial arts theory in any language. Yet Cháng's complete martial manuscripts have still not been published, even in Chinese. Chén Wànqing, president of the Cháng Family Boxing Research Association, with Chén Zengzhì and Chén Wànlî, have been active in the work of editing. They point out that Cháng's prefaces bear precise dates, omitted from Xú Zhèn's edition. "Twenty-four Fist tablature: introduction" (33, below) is dated 1777. Four other dates that Xú

Zhèn does not include are attached. They attest to precise moments in Cháng life:[11]

a) *Twenty-four Pole tablature.* Cháng relates how he chanced to meet itinerant master Liáng Dào from Sìchuan, on the 9th of the ninth month, 1756, while enjoying the Autumn Festival with his friend Yû Hóngqî. Cháng learned these pole techniques from Liáng in just over ten days.[12] *(cf. FIGURES 32, 33)*

b) *Thirty-six Spear tablature,* dated 20th of the sixth month, 1780. Cháng traces it to Mr. Zhang of Hûlâo, the late Míng expert at spear, whose technique was transmitted in the fifth generation to the Yû clan (cf. Yû Ràng, below). Cháng from youth desired to learn it, but on reaching adulthood was able to find few traces of it. Subsequently, he encountered only the Twenty-one Spear but, finding it deficient, strove to correct and improve it. (cf. *xii*, below, Chái Rúguì)

c) *Double Sword against Spear,* dated fourth month, 1781. Cháng confesses that he secreted it for twenty years, since learning it from Wáng Xinxiàng from Gûsuí, but now decided to share this treasure out of concern for his students.[13] *(cf. FIGURES 32, 33)*

d) *Twenty-four Great Dynamic Fists,* dated tenth month, 1781.

FIGURE 1: QI JÌGUANG'S CHARGE MAIN GATE SPEAR

Charge Main Gate, at the end (bottom left-hand corner of the page) of Qi Jìguang's spear, changes long- for short-range direct attack.[16] *[27; 31; 69:15; 70:I-ii]* The copy at Chénjiagou bore a remark, attributing the spear tablature to "Zhang Flying God," via the "Yû and Cháng clans."

Cháng's above attribution of spear to "Mr. Zhang of Hûlâo" via the Yû clan, adds confirmation to the Chénjiagou archives in which Xú Zhèn noticed that the old Wénxiutáng manuscript at Chénjiagou had spear techniques of Míng general Qi Jìguang. By "Charge Main Gate" was an inserted note:[17]

> These spear law pictures are Sìshuî district Yû the Spear Master's transmission from Zhang Feishén ["Flying God"] to the Cháng and Yû clans. (He was Cháng clan's son-in-law.)

Collating this evidence, we may posit a transmission of Qi Jìguang spear:

> Zhang of Hûlâo c. 1640 > Yû c. 1740 > Cháng > Chén Family.

The authorship of Qi Jǐguang's work was evidently no longer known, but its use by Zhang "the Flying God" is signifcant. Chén Tàijíquán's boxing moves are also largely those of Qi Jǐguang. "Yû the Spear Master," who apparently married into the Cháng clan, is presumably the master Yû Ràng, a senior near-contemporary of Cháng. Zhang "the Flying God," five generations earlier (c. 1640), is surely "Divine Hand" Zhang Ba, the renowned late Míng spearman and boxer. If so, Zhang Ba provides a remote but documented link between Chén and Cháng traditions and illustrates the milieu they shared.

Furthermore, Zhang Ba in person may even be considered a candidate for the mystery role of "Jiâng Fa/Ba," reputed bodyguard and instructor of commander Chén Wángtíng (c. 1600–1680), who founded Chénjiagou's martial lineage *(see FIGURE 7)*.[18] Both are outstanding martial artists reported active in the area during late Míng. Given the orthographical and phonetic variants in the manuscript notes, it is not difficult to see how "Zhang Ba" could transmogrify into "Jiâng Fa." A further point in common between Chénjiagou and Zhang is their use of Qi Jǐguang's spear system. *[See Zhang Ba's biography in xii, below.]*

ii. Internal Boxing and the Shady Tally Spear

By the early twentieth century, the origin of Tàijíquán, first propagated at Bêijíng by Yáng Lùchán (1799–1872), had become generally ascribed to Zhang Sanfeng. According to Huáng Zongxi, Internal School Boxing was received in a dream from the "Dark/ Mysterious Emperor (Xuándì)," alias god of war, on Mt. Wûdang by Daoist saint Zhang Sanfeng, during the reign of Emperor Huizong of Northern Sòng (reigned 1101–1125). Zhang is usually dated around three centuries later, though this is not a problem for believers in Daoist longevity. This legend was recorded by anti-Manchu patriot Huáng Zongxi in his epitaph of Wáng Zhengnán (1610–1669) of Zhèjiang, a master of this art, described in detail by his son Huáng Bâijia, who had been Wáng's student. This style of boxing was characterized by short-range direct attacks, "using stillness to control motion," by which it was reported easily able to defeat Shàolín. *[cf. 27; 31; 69:15; 70:I-ii]* Yet these records of Internal School Boxing show scarce affinity with Tàijíquán writings, though Wáng Zhengnán's boxing shares some techniques with Qi Jìguang, Cháng, and Tàijíquán.

Qi Jìguang's boxing, the major source of Tàijíquán techniques, and the Internal School Boxing of Wáng Zhengnán are both traceable to maritime Zhèjiang in the early sixteenth century. Its city of Níngbo had been the official port for Japanese missions. After their forced termination in 1549, its off-shore Zhoushan Island became a base for Japanese and local pirates. It was there that Qi Jìguang describes learning the practical art of boxing in Major Liú's thatched hall.[19] Manuals by generals Qi Jìguang, and his mentor Yú Dàyóu, leaders against Japanese pirate attacks, provide us with the first detailed knowledge of Chinese fencing and boxing.

Lâo Zî's philosophy is famed for its advocacy of the soft and gentle, the feminine principle, and the recurrent metaphor of water. Strange to relate, Huáng Zongxi's detailed description of the "Daoist" Internal School has not a word on the "soft" aspect. Conspicuous by its absence from the *Tàijíquán Classic,* as from Cháng's writings, is any quotation from founder of Daoism Lâo Zî's *Way Virtue Classic.* Belatedly, among Wile's 1996 *Lost T'ai-chi Classics from the Late Ch'ing Dynasty,* translating recently released documents, is a postscript by Wû Chénqing (c. 1810–?) that cites parallels to Tàijíquán from both Zhuang Zî and Lâo Zî by name. Yet these are Wû Chéngqing's own interpretations of Tàijíquán, whose theory he attributes to an enigmatic Wáng Zongyuè, without mention of Zhang Sanfeng. Wú Chéngqing, like the *Tàijíquán Classic* and Cháng, speaks rather of blending hard and soft.[20]

Ironically, in view of the stereotype of Shàolín as the epitome of hard "external" martial arts, it is from Shàolín that we first hear of martial arts that blend hard and soft. "Soft can overcome hard" is affirmed by seventeenth-century Shàolín boxer, Reverend Xuánji. Wú Shu (1611–1695) of Jiangsu asserts in his 1678 preface to *Hand and Arm Record* on spear technique that Chéng Chongdôu's (1616)

Shàolín Staff chose only the hard, whereas in true Shàolín technique "hard and soft mutually complement."[21] The phrase, much exploited by Cháng, describes the intermix of hard under soft lines in hexagram 63 (Jìjì: ䷾) of the *Change Classic*. Its earliest practical use is in a pre-battle warning, from military dictator and strategist Cáo Cao (155–220):[22] [13; 18; 30; 41; 57; 70:I-iii, II-i]

> Always, if you wish to be a general, let *hard and soft mutually complement.* You may not simply rely on your courage. If you simply rely on courage, then you are one fellow's match.

Lî Yìyú (1832–1892) of Guângpíng city, Yôngnián County in Hébêi, in 1881 conceded that the origin of Tàijíquán is unknown, yet subscribes Tàijíquán Theory to a "Wáng Zongyuè of Shanxi."[23] The name Zongyuè, "lineage of Yuè," recalls patriot general Yuè Fei (1103–1141). In 1930, researcher Táng Háo (1897–1959) of Wúxiàn, Jiangsu, discovered, in a Bêipíng bookstall, the manuscript of a brief collection of spear aphorisms entitled *Shady Tally Spear* by a "Mr. Wáng of Shanxi," who was "at Luòyáng in 1791." The aphorisms were bound with the *Tàijíquán Classic* and a fragmentary *Spring-Autumns Halberd,* very similar to that of the Chén Family, then still unpublished. "Spring-Autumns Halberd" is named after deified Three Kingdoms war-hero Guan Yû. Guan's favorite reading was the *Spring-Autumns Annals* (771–481 B.C.), which chronicle the disintegration of the Zhou dynasty, and whose chosen weapon was the great halberd ("big knife").[24]

An anonymous scholar tells us that, in 1795 while at Kaifeng to sit for government examinations, he composed the preface to Mr. Wáng's *Shady Tally Spear.* This preface links the spear to the one logic of the Grand Pole (Tàijí), and its constant sub-division into Shady and Sunny. He complains of commonplace spearmen: "They speak of dynamics, but don't speak of logic. They only know force, and do not know there is skill. They are not expert in technique." Mr. Wáng, on the other hand, is a student of the Way, who from youth up, in addition to the prescribed classics, learned "the Yellow Emperor and Lâo Zî's books with strategists' sayings."

Mr. Wáng's spear technique demonstrated: "Hard and soft's were mutual exchange, yet in conclusion he returned to "Shady, one word. This in sincerity is what is meant by "Shady Tally Spear'."

An extant style is called "Shady Spear" (yinqiang) because it uses the shady hands' down-facing grip, with thumbs towards each other for greater power.[25] Although the preface states that Mr. Wáng did not desire a written "tablature," he nevertheless "took spear laws and assembled them as 'maxims' of instruction."[26] Notable are the phrases "vacuous and substantial" together with "sticking and following," common to Tàijíquán and to Cháng.[27]

All this, in the absence of a likelier candidate, led Táng Háo to argue that this Shanxi Wáng is Wáng Zongyuè. If so, the evidence for his contribution to Tàijíquán philosophy is slight compared to Cháng Nâizhou.

iii: The Tàijíquán Classic

I take as standard the *Tàijíquán Classic,* copied by Lî Yìyú in 1881, which consists of a short essay entitled Tàijíquán Theory of "(Shanxi) Wáng Zongyuè" and the Thirteen Dynamics Exercise: Heart/Mind Interpretation. In addition, the techniques listed are: the Thirteen Dynamics Set of thirty-two (fifty-three with repeats) moves; Ten Principles of "body-law" posture; Four Broadsword laws; Four Spear laws; and Thirteen Dynamics of pushing hands and dàlyû. Finally there are the songs: Thirteen Dynamics Exercise's Song Maxims; Hitting Hands' Important Words with Interpretation, to which Wû Yûxiang co-signed; Hitting Hands Song; and Hitting Hands: Discharge and Release.[28] "Hitting hands"(dâshôu) is now called "pushing hands" (tuishôu).

The above physical techniques, solo and partnered, mostly match the Chén tradition at their home in Chénjiagou, in Hénán just north of the Yellow River. Yet the theoretical essays Tàijíquán Theory and Thirteen Dynamics Exercise were unrecorded there. The only line of Tàijíquán discursive theory in the Chén Qing dynasty archive is: "Tug in motion four ounces to deflect a thousand pounds, from the Hitting Hands Song.[29]

The first dissemination of Tàijíquán is described in detail only by Lî Yìyú. Lî's accounts are found in his postscript of 1881, mid autumn, third day, and preface of the sixth day, to his own *Five-Word Secrets* and redaction of Tàijíquán materials.[30] Lî recognized Chénjiagou, home of the Chén family, as the immediate source from whence the practical art of Tàijíquán was propagated. Indeed, Chén family records evidence a tradition of boxing, credited to their ancestor, early seventeenth-century Míng commander Chén Wángtíng. Chén archives list various boxing and weapons sets. Yet the term "Tàijíquán" itself occurs only twice there, as an alternative name for their now famous main boxing set, which appears strongly influenced by Míng general Qi Jìguang. The name "Thirteen Dynamics" there appears to pre-date the name "Tàijíquán," and this auspicious number thirteen recurs in Chén spear and broadsword set names.

Lî tells us that, aged over twenty, he began to receive oral instruction from his uncle Wû Yûxiang in 1853, who had studied with Chén Qingpíng (1795–1868) at Zhàobâo, near Chénjiagou, while on a business trip. The "tablature" (pû) itself was obtained in a "salt shop" at Wûyáng.[31] In 1852, Wû Yûxiang's brother Chéngqing had been appointed magistrate of Wûyáng, near the path of the Tàipíng Rebellion's 1853 northern expedition and within the area of the Moslem Niân insurgency. *Guângpíng Gazetteer* records that Wû Chéngqing trained a militia that saved Wûyáng from a hundred thousand rebel "bandits." *Wûyáng County Gazetteer* incidentally records a tradition of Wûyáng being the birthplace of Zhang Sanfeng, who is enshrined on Mt. Wûdang, in neighboring Húbêi Province. Thus, Wile concludes that Wû Chéngqing, while posted to Wûyáng, may have recovered boxing writings there, presumed they were linked to Zhang Sanfeng, and then passed them to Wû Yûxiang.[32]

Lî Yìyú attests that Tàijíquán Theory was composed by Wáng Zongyuè, who passed the art to Hénán's Chénjiagou, where it was transmitted by masters for generations. There, a "Yáng person, evidently Yáng Lùchán (1799–1872), from Yôngnián County went to learn it, and trained diligently for more than ten years. This suggests that Lî believed Wáng Zongyuè to be a remote historical figure, and hence not the Mr. Wáng of *Shady Tally Spear.* Yet if Tàijíquán Theory was indeed found in a "salt shop" (yándiàn), or perhaps "opium den" (yandiàn), then in vogue, the manuscripts are unlikely to have been of great age.[33]

Hometown tradition asserts that Yáng Lùchán was "purchased as a youth" (i.e., about 1810) by the Chén family, who owned Tàihé Táng Pharmacy, which had a branch in (Hébêi) Guângpíng. He was sent to Chénjiagou head office, where he was indentured as a bond servant.[34] Pharmacy businesses in China customarily promote martial arts to advertise medicines and tonics. If Yáng went to Chénjiagou expressly to acquire this art, as Lî alleges, martial instruction may have been part of his apprenticeship. Chén Chángxing (1771–1853), a family member, was employed as instructor at the pharmacy. Propagation of Tàijíquán was the direct result of Yáng's service in the Chén medicine shop, his return to Yôngnián, and subsequent introduction to high society in the capital. Lî tells us that, after returning to Yôngnián, Yáng "competed skills" with Wû Yûxiang, Lî's maternal uncle, but was willing to divulge only an outline of what he learned.

The Wû family, landlords of the Guângpíng pharmacy, appreciated the value of this martial art. Yet Wile suggests that a rift between Wû and Yáng may appear in Lî's failure to give Yáng's personal name, and his remark that Yáng was reluctant to teach Wû Yûxiang. Wile notes that the *Yôngnián Gazetteer,* to which Wû family members were contributors, omits mention of Yáng Lùchán, as of Tàijíquán itself.[35] Yáng himself was uneducated and largely illiterate.

The 1867 manuscript of *Tàijíquán Classic,* signed by Lî Yìyú, implies that Wû Yûxiang promoted the idea of Zhang Sanfeng as founder of the art.[36] Yet in 1881, after Wû's death, Lî felt free to query this, calling the founder "unknown." Tàijíquán Theory is composed in a highly polished and compressed style, replete with classical Confucian allusions, which suggests that a scholar such as Wû Yûxiang is responsible for its present form. More songs and fragments entered the canon in the twentieth century.[37] Their origin and age are uncertain, but they may represent elements of the martial arts culture in central Hénán from which Tàijíquán crystalized.

iv. Polar Dialectics and the South Forest Virgin

Cháng Nâizhou's intellectual resources, like those embedded in the *Tàijíquán Classic,* are the Confucian *Change Classic* and Four Books: *Analects, Mèng Zî, Great Learning,* and *Central Norm.* This is hardly surprising since neo-Confucianism formed the educational curriculum. It was the neo-Confucian logicist (lîxué) movement in the Sòng dynasty that developed the concept of Tàijí as the underlying principle of all phenomena and made it into the governing ideology of the past millennium in China. It is this grand unification theory that underpins Tàijíquán philosophy.

The concept of Tàijí, the "Grand Pole," is first defined in Appendix I-10 to the *Change Classic,* dateable to approximately the third century B.C. There it is a primal monad that divides itself continually into halves, in quasi-cellular reproduction: 1 > 2 > 4 > 8 > 16 > 32 > 64 ad infinitum. This principle of division means that all phenomena evolve from the binary, or are thus combinations of 1 and 0, as in Leibniz's theory, or "Shady-Sunny," negative and positive, yinyáng. With the introduction of Buddhism from India to Hàn China at the start of the first millennium, the idea of Void (sunyata), allied to Lâo Zî's Non-Being (wú), came to dominate cosmogony. A need arose for the re-assertion of a positive physical principle, coupled with a Confucian native national identity. Tàijí unitary theory provided the answer.

Zhou Dunyí (1012–1073), under Northern Sòng, interpreted this old idea of a subdividing ancestral monad as both infinite void and prime mover, and further linked the Tàijí concept to elemental Five Action theory. The Chéng brothers of Luòyáng, one of whose verses is quoted below [34], adopted it as corner-stone into a streamlined neo-Confucian education system, based on the Four Books. After Northern China fell to the Jurchen, Zhu Xi (1130–1200) consolidated the new learning in the unconquered South.

The Grand Pole posited an absolute unitary ideal and center, manifesting a "logos" (lî) and "Energy" (qì) in creation. This Confucian principle, directing a world of practical politics and material things, could counter the other-worldly religions of Buddhist and Daoist monasticism. Yet, despite Zhu Xi's Grand Pole ideal, the system settled into a static dualism, reflecting the entrenched social division between educated scholar class and illiterate peasantry. The ultimate Grand Pole of the emperor became increasingly remote from the infinite No Pole of the masses. Wú Chéng (1249–1333) objected:[38]

> Therefore, Master Zhu combines "No Pole" Wújí and "Grand Pole" Tàijí into One, and says: "It is not that at the Grand Pole's exterior there is a separate No Pole."

Efforts were made to revitalize the system, pre-eminently by Wáng Yángmíng (1472–1529), a military Confucian, who pacified the southeastern aborigines, teaching "innate knowledge" (liángzhi) and "sincerity" (chéng) in action. In the Qing dynasty Gù Yánwù (1613–1682) advocated practical learning, while Dài Zhèn (1724–1777) asserted the immanence of rational logos in material Energy. In 1757 a compendium was published on Zhou Dunyî's Tàijí theory, containing a line by Hú Xû (1655–1736): "Shady and Sunny do not leave each other: they have mutual need and mutual interchange's marvels."[39] Táng Háo sees this as the source of Tàijíquán Theory's "Sunny does not leave Shady, Shady does not leave Sunny. When Shady and Sunny mutually complement, only then do they contrive 'understanding power'."[40]

Cháng's elder brother Shìzhou authored a study on the philosophy of the *Change Classic,* presented to court by Governor of Hénán. An abstract was included by Jî Yún, editor-in-chief, in Emperor Qiánlóng's encyclopedia *Sì-kù Quánshu,* begun in 1772.[41] Cháng Nâizhou himself went on to apply *Change Classic* theory to practical physiology, as a means to both health and defense through martial arts. Thus, Cháng employs the line "Shady and Sunny mutually complement," which we just saw in Tàijíquán Theory, or a variant on seven occasions. *[13; 18; 30; 41; 57; 70:I-iii, II-i]* I have shown above that the phrase using "hard and soft" was attributed to Cáo Cao (155–220).[42] Only in spear *[70:I-iii]* does Cháng use "Shady and Sunny, and applying the phrase to footwork, Cháng uses "Vacuous and Substantial" for weighted and unweighted, as in Tàijíquán Theory. *[13]*

Cháng explains the function of thumb within the hand as Grand Pole, citing the above cited Yuán philosopher Wú Chéng (though I fail to trace the quote in Wú's collected works). Within the human body, Cháng identifies the "Elixir Field," dantián—the point just below the navel—as Grand Pole, the source of Central Energy. Cháng extends this unifying concept to his detailed analysis of the interactive forces of Shady and Sunny, in the dialectics of limb flexion and extension, whose resolutions govern the generation of force.

Cháng explains the actions of the fingers as pivoting or twisting around the thumb, and the actions of the five elements as spirals of clockwise and anti-clockwise action within the Nine-Palace grid of *Change Classic* diagrams. This helps us understand the conventional "double-fish" Tàijí circle of yin and yáng, an image current only from the Míng. It resembles the double helix or "figure eight"-shaped infinity sign. It is perhaps a sublimination of the snake twirling back on itself round the earth tortoise, like the wobble in the rotation of the terrestrial axis, in the emblem sacred to the Mysterious Martial deity of the North Pole. *[46]* A related image, from Táng esoteric Buddhism, is of two dragons fighting for a flaming pearl, the cintâmani, "wish-fulfilling gem."[43] *[69:4; 72:7]* Such contending dragons are carved on a great stone lintel, inscribed 1555, outside the Shàolín Temple.

These images illustrate the unity of opposites, an empirical law of practical physics, not speculative meta-physics. Action and reaction as in Newton's law are equal and opposite. When the back of the hand is turned up, it is called Shady because its inside energy is suppressed and thus holds the dynamic potential. When the inside of the hand is turned up, it is called Sunny because the back is suppressed and now in turn holds the dynamic potential. As with a spring, depression stores the bounce-back. Lâo Zî, never quoted here, said: the Way works by reversal!

A significant quotation, shared by Cháng and Tàijíquán's Thirteen Dynamics Exercise, is:

> Inwardly consolidate the spirit,
> outwardly demonstrate peaceful ease. *[25; 45]*

Whereas Cháng acknowledges his source, the *Tàijíquán Classic* simply borrows. The lines encapsulate martial teachings of the "South Forest Virgin," related by Zhào Yè (c. A.D. 150) of Zhèjiang. His *Wú and Yuè Spring-Autumns* details instructions in "hand-combat" that she imparted to Goujiàn of Yùe, aiding him to overthrow Wú in 473 B.C. and briefly become a superpower. On her return to the forest, she defeats a White Ape in human form who challenged her. Local traditions of coastal Zhèjiang, home of swordsman-calligrapher Wáng Xizhi (306–365) and later renowned for "internal" boxing skills, evidently underlie this tale.[44] Even more remarkable is the sharing by Cháng and Tàijíquán's Thirteen Dynamics Exercise of the unique, unprecedented couplet:

> If he does not move, I do not move.
> When he is about to move, I first move.

This is used and developed with variation in three separate places by Cháng. *[23; 44; 47]* It occurs just once, without elaboration, in the *Tàijíquán Classic*. When assessing textual borrowing, it is important to consider the rarity, or uniqueness, of unacknowledged quotations. The above couplets do not appear, to my knowledge, in any other earlier text. In summing up, it must be said that, apart from the classics, Cháng Nâizhou provides the only known comprehensive antecedent to *Tàijíquán Classic* theory.

v. Shàolín and Japanese Pirates

Cháng is frankly eclectic in his approach to sources and makes no claims to exclusive lineage. There is no reliance on a secret transmission or supernatural revelation. Cháng appeals rather for common sense, earnest seeking, and diligent practice. He does, nonetheless, speak of enlightenment experiences and awesome powers. Cháng freely mixes elements of Confucianism, Daoist alchemy, and Buddhism, without sectarian bias. He equates Confucian Sagehood with the Daoist alchemic Elixir, conflated in turn with the "adamantine" vajra body of the Supreme Vehicle (Vajrayâna) in esoteric Buddhism. The common goals are health and self-defense.

Cháng relates how he studied with teachers of different schools and synthesized the best of them. In eclecticism he is no different from (Míng) General Qi Jiguang (1528–1587), conqueror of the Japanese pirate raiders. Qi Jiguang explains how he assembled a set of thirty-two boxing moves, selecting the best from different schools for his *Boxing Classic*. Many were later incorporated into Tàijíquán and (Shanxi) Hóngtóng Tòngbeìquán, as well as Cháng's system. Xú Zhèn's 1936 publication of Chén martial archives shows them to contain varied styles of boxing and weaponry, some associated with Shàolín, such as Red Boxing and the monks' "Prajna Pole" of Shàolín, disguised as "Shàolíng."[45] The varied styles of Tàijíquán—spawned and disseminated from Chénjiagou following Yáng Lùchán's (1799–1872) youthful sojourn there and in nearby Zhàobâo—show additions such as Twin Winds Pierce Ears. *[69:20, 21]*

All this serves to question the authenticity, and indeed practical viability, of supposedly "pure" lineages in the world of martial arts. Cháng gives an unassuming account of both his various teachers and the process whereby he digested their teachings to summarize them and create his own Twenty-four Dynamics. He shows no awareness of the Internal School Boxing that Huáng Zongxi attributed to Daoist recluse Zhang Sanfeng. He speaks much of the Grand Pole, Tàijí, but does not show any consciousness of it as a school of boxing.

It may be for political reasons that Cháng never refers to the Míng dynasty, or its martial writings. Yet Cháng uses nomenclature that often echoes Qi Jiguang's "Twenty-four Long Spear" *[69:14, 16,*

19, 24; 72:29, 31, 34] and "Eight Rattan Shield and Broadsword." *[69:3; 71:37; 72:16]* Even more striking is Cháng's use of General Yú Dàyóu's (1503–1579) *Sword Classic,* from which he borrows six maxims. *[32]* Two of Yú's fourteen fencing titles appear as Cháng boxing's "Twenty-four Dynamics." *[69:4, 15]*

Yú Dàyóu of Fújiàn was a mentor to Qi Jiguang, and a key leader in the defeat of Japanese pirates. Yú personally trained two Shàolín Temple monks, whom he took on campaign with him against Japanese pirates in 1560. Yú was concerned by the loss of practical realism in the monks' martial skills. In 1571, he helped found the Ten Directions Hall at Shàolín Temple for itinerant monks to foster martial training.[46] Doubtless, the memory of Yú persisted there.

Yet under the Manchu Qing—particularly Emperor Yongzhèng (r. 1723–1735), a Buddhist adherent who believed himself enlightened—unorthodox practices and martial arts at Shàolín and elsewhere suffered severe repression. This may explain why Cháng, despite his evident Buddhist interest, never refers to neighboring Shàolín. The first sentence of Cháng's *Part B: Martial Defense* begins with a rebuke to the supernaturalism, hinted at by Chéng Chongdôu's (1616) *Shàolín Staff. [29]* Chéng's martial publications never depict monks, but in 1930 Xú Hèlíng published a "secret" version that shows a monk's staff training. *(FIGURE 20)*

Cháng mentions neither Bodhidharma of Shàolín nor Zhang Sanfeng of Wûdang, nor does he betray any knowledge of their legendary opposing Daoist "Internal" and Buddhist "External" schools. The pugilistic and weapons arts described by Cháng Nâizhou are the first on record to comprehensively synthesize "internal" and "external" arts, in the sense of combining internal human physiology and external defense. Both the generation and deployment of Energy within the body, and its various applications in striking the opponent at different points, are meticulously analyzed. In this Cháng conforms to the pattern of the *Change Sinews Classic,* associated with Shàolín, which describes training in both "Internal" and "External Strength," though the "battles" therein envisaged are evidently to take place in the bedroom with the aim of impregnation. No martial arts techniques are detailed there, though martial strength and valor are promised.

Cháng's text altogether makes one direct and four indirect references to *Change Sinews Classic,* which describes how to forge an invulnerable body with the aid of massage, pommeling, meditational breathing, medicaments, and exercises. This work bears an implausible attribution to Bodhidharma (c. 530 A.D.), the Chán monk from India famous for meditating "nine years facing a wall" in a cave at Shàolín; it is translated by Paramiti, a Táng monk from India, and includes an equally dubious preface by Niúgao, a subordinate of General Yuè Fei. Both Bodhidharma and Yuè Fei are commonly revered in Xíngyìquán's legendary lineage.

The earliest reliably dateable testimonies to *Change Sinews Classic* occur paradoxically in fiction, close to the time of Cháng's birth. The first is the strange tale by Pú Songlíng (c. 1640–1715) from Shandong, of a Moslem expert in "Iron Shirt law," which quotes but does not name it: "Bunched fingers can pierce an ox's stomach; lateral palm can sever an ox's head." Slightly later, the satirical novel *Scholars' Forest: an Unofficial History* by Wú Jìngzî (1701–1754) cites its title and quotes, omitting the above first line and adding from a different version: "Clasped fist can smash a tiger's brains."[47] Such short tales spawned the increasingly fantastic flying swordsmen and -women in Qing dynasty martial arts fiction, generating the kung-fu movies of modern times.

vi. Xíngyìquán's Six Coordinates

At first sight, Cháng's set of twenty-four movements reveals little in common with the Tàijíquán forms now known, in nomenclature or posture. They resemble rather a style of Xíngyìquán or Baguàzhâng, with forward body posture, low kicks, and leaps.

An early name for Xíngyìquán is "Mind Idea: Six Co-ordinate Boxing," Xinyì Liùhéquán. It is a genre linked to Shàolín's Zhànjû Dharma Master, the "Mind-Idea Grappling King," said to be depicted in the Temple's Báiyidiàn fresco of the monks' boxing display before Qing Court visitor Lín Qìng in 1828.[48] *(FIGURE 2)*

Táng Háo, at Chénjiagou in 1932, saw a handwritten copy by Chén Xin of the "Three-three Boxing Tablature" but was permitted to copy only its preface and contents, which include "Six Co-ordinates" with "Change Sinews Classic: Connected Energy Maxims."[49]

Xíngyìquán lineage is documented back to "Divine Spear" Ji Lóngfeng (c. 1600–c. 1680) of Púzhou in Shanxi.[50] Its core theory of Six Coordinates has a close relationship to spear work. Spear in Qi Jìguang's (c. 1562) training manual uses the title "Six Coordinates" in the sense of a six-fold series of encounters, as opposed to the body and mind coordinates of Xíngyìquán. Nevertheless, Qi Jìguang does record the Triple Tip Alignment (san-jian zhào) of nose, spear, and foot.[51] Alignment of Triple Tips recurs in the alleged "Shady Tally Spear" maxims of "Shanxi Wáng," present at Luòyáng in 1791.[52]

The Six Coordinates of Xíngyìquán are precisely shared by Cháng, both in boxing and spear. *[68:11; 70:II-i]* They are as follows:[53] "Feet and hands coordinate, hands and eyes coordinate, eyes and mind coordinate; mind and spirit coordinate, spirit and Energy coordinate, Energy and body coordinate." The first three of these coordinates, feet-hands-eyes, correspond effectively to the Triple Tip Alignment of nose-spear-foot, or hand-head-foot. This underlies Xíngyìquán's basic "Triple Body Posture" (san-tîshì) and the triplet form that typifies many of its maxims. Shàolín martial arts also have a triple principle, as in "strike and link three" (jí, -zé liánsan) consecutive hits.[54]

Triple Tip Alignment of hand-head-foot is a fundamental principle that runs throughout Cháng Energy, boxing, and spear arts. It governs not only posture but Energy production and direction through Essence, Spirit, and Energy, as in Daoist metaphysics, and as described by Yáng Tàijíquán's Forty Chapters.[55] Triple chains are further developed in the Triple Urgings and Triple Arrivals, as well as the reaction of "Triple Joints," root > mid > peripheral (shoulder-elbow-wrist). *[18; 19; 50]* "Urging" of connected joints is also described in Xíngyìquán canons such as the "Seven Compliances": "Shoulders should urge elbows, and elbows not oppose shoulders; elbows should urge hands, and hands not oppose elbows...."[56]

Cháng compares the "release" (fang) and "shooting" (fa) of explosive energy from the Triple Urgings to the loading, ramming tight the powder and ball, and firing of a musket. "Power" (jìng) is described as lightning striking the body. *[57]* Cháng describes emissions of sounds ha and yi, like the Japanese martial kiai, and Discharge and Release, safàng, sounds in the *Tàijíquán Classic*. *[24; 28]*

vii. Drunken Monkey Shaman

Each dynamic image in Cháng's boxing is related to specific techniques and applications. Yet they are illustrated with a vivid imagination. Metaphors for Energy are taken from fire, and even gunpowder. The poems appended to each illustration of Twenty-four Dynamics are an unparalleled tour-de-force, firing the imagination with a panorama of images from myth and legend, heroes and ladies from history as well as popular imagination, mixed with supernatural beings from Daoist and Buddhist lore, monsters, the beauties of nature, and a bestiary of fauna. It combines elements of creative fantasy projection with therapeutic role-playing.

Archetypal animal imagery permeates the martial arts, including Tàijíquán. The Twelve Animal Forms of Xíngyìquán are a clear formulation. In an early version, preserved in Hénán-style Xíngyìquán, there were only ten forms, namely dragon, horse, tiger, monkey, swallow, cat, cock, eagle, hawk, and snake.[57] Of these, all are represented in Cháng's system. Dragon, tiger, monkey, eagle, swallow, and cat are especially prominent in Cháng's Twenty-four Dynamics. Rhinoceros, crab, geese, ducks, dragonflies, and butterflies are the more unusual animals introduced by Cháng. There is even reference to a scorpion tail, and to the Bactrian camel, tuó, similar in writing and sound to the inscrutable tái, or the tuó (ostrich, an animal alien to China), of Xíngyìquán's twelve animals.[58]

The boxer warrior assimilates qualities of the shaman wizard; like Sherlock Holmes he is "the master of disguise." He metamorphoses into different animals, taking on their special qualities, portrayed in masks or tattoos. James Fraser's *Golden Bough* (1922) evidences how shamans throughout the world claim animal doubles as "external souls" or emanations of "familiar spirits."[59] Esoteric Buddhism has a similar doctrine of emanation. Animal dances, totems, or mascots link the martial world to that of spirit-possession and trance. Zhongkuí, demon-catcher and exorcist, who in his contorted action, usually balanced on one leg, is identified with the Dipper Constellation, and thus appears to reflect the hopping dance on the seven starpoints of the Dipper of the lame shaman and Daoist priest. *(FIGURE 32)* [69:17; 72:36] Ascend to Pace Seven Stars is a familiar move in Tàijíquán. Daoist priests, like ancient Chinese shamans (wu), ritually pace the stars of the Northern Dipper. Another figure that might suggest the "wounded healer" of shamanism is Kuí, the one-legged monitor-lizard dragon, who leads the ancient dance of the Hundred Beasts, and also appears as the unicorn-rhinoceros.[60] [69:2]

On the heavenly plane, triple honors are shared by Lâo Zî, Confucius, and the Buddha. Of a singular, supreme godhead, nothing is said until the opening of the final Double Sword section. There at last True Martial, alias "Mysterious Martial" or "Dark Warrior," appears. [72] This deity is pictured in the Cháng manuscript of Monkey Pole, with the inscription: *(FIGURE 21)*

> Heavenly Unity Producing Water, North Pole's True
>   Martial,
> Both hands press swords: Myriad Things all submit.

"Heavenly" or "Grand Unity" is traditionally identified with the North Pole star, palace of the Heavenly Ruler. He may be considered the personification of the Grand Polarity, Tàijí. The line, "Heavenly Unity (One) Produces Water" is traceable to the Hàn dynasty.[61] [12] Amazingly, this idea of genesis from Water matches the text "Grand Unity Produces Water" from a Chû tomb from c. 300 B.C., uncovered in 1993 at Guodiàn, Húbêi. The work, painted on bamboo strips together with the earliest known Lâo Zî fragments, was lost over two millennia, preserved in water-logged deposit.[62] Thus the concepts of dark mystery (xuán), warlike prowess, and life-giving water are all attributed to the most high, resident above the pole.

More accessible to humankind is the young god, or divine child, a Jungian archetype, prominent in world mythology and in spirit-medium cults.[63] In Hindu-Buddhist iconography the cosmic ruler is identified with Indra (later Shiva or Vishnu), or Vaishrâvana, on axial Mt. Meru, deputized by his son Nata (Nuózhá), the valiant Third Prince with his fiery wheel.

Of this ilk are the fiery Red Boy, who is converted, with his cannibal mother Hârîtî who becomes protectress of children, into Sudhâna, the devoted pilgrim. [69:22] Chénxiang, like Buddha's disciple Maudgalyâna who saves his mother from Hell, splits open Mt. Huá to free her. [69:20]; Daoist trickster Dongfang Shuò steals the peaches of immortality [69:1], a feat emulated by the impish Monkey King himself [69:5, 13; 71:34].

Monkey, as "Great Sage Equal to Heaven," is both a favorite of the theatre and a folk deity, revealed in spirit-medium cults.[64] Such cults inspired adherents of the "Righteous Harmony Fist" boxers, whose uprising ended with the siege of the Peking Legations in 1900. Embodying the common shamanic roots of religion, dance, and martial arts, they could easily beguile the simple with delusions of invulnerability.

The monkey is a Buddhist symbol of the unruly human mind. In the epic novel *Westward Travelogue*, Monkey, Sun Wùkong, invades Heaven and becomes drunk at the birthday party of the Queen Mother. The Drunken Monkey style of boxing, inspired by this episode, is characterized by spontaneous movements as if possessed, wild swaying motions, and mimicry of drinking actions, imbibing Energy from the air [cf. 10]. Once Monkey has been subdued by the power of the Buddha, he is confined but released to aid the historical Táng pilgrim Xuánzàng "Tripitaka" (599–664) in reaching India and obtaining the Buddhist scriptures. Thus he becomes the magic monkey, wielding his amazing wand-pole and overcoming all demons.

As in the time-honored strategy of using barbarians to control barbarians, the erstwhile monster monkey is now enlisted as a defender of the peace. A similar role is played in Hindu-Buddhist mythology by Nâga dragons, Râkshasa temptresses, and fierce Yaksha demons, converted to protectors of the dharma, who figure in both Shàolín and Cháng boxing and stave fighting. *[69:9, 14, 22; 72:29]* In India Hanuman, the mythic monkey who led monkey armies to support Râma in his attack on Sri Lankâ, also figures on the war banner of the righteous Pandava brothers in the *Mahâ Bhâratâ* epic. He remains patron of wrestlers in Varanâsi.

According to ancient Chinese tradition, monkeys' arms are continuous through the back, and slide from one side of the shoulders to the other.[65] This tale gave rise to the name "Interconnected Arm Boxing," Tongbeìquán, for a style of "White Monkey" boxing that is practiced at Shàolín.[66] Tòngbèi Boxing of Hóngtóng district in Shanxi preserves records that relate this style to both Qi Jiguang's *Boxing Classic* and Tàijíquán's old name of "Long Boxing."[67] One Tàijíquán technique, not from Qi Jiguang, is shân tongbèi, which may be understood as "Dodge Interconnected Arms."

(Míng) Wáng Shìxìng (1547–1598) in his travel diary of Mt. Song describes a display at Shàolín Monastery:

> Martial monks again each came to present skills. With fists and staves contending, they struck as if flying. Their teacher with folded hands looked on. Among them was a monkey striker, spinning and leaping, just like a monkey....[68]

FIGURE 2A: MARTIAL DISPLAY AT SHÀOLÍN

A high Manchu visitor, Lín Qìng, a dignitary, requested the Sháolín Abbot to put on a display of the monks' martial arts, then officially banned. We see here sparring rather than solo sets. A statue of "Kinnara," Shàolín's guardian deity, with his staff is seen in the background shrine, and the two faces peering through the window of the courtyard wall. This woodprint is from Lín's travelogue of 1828.[69]

FIGURE 2B: Táng Háo 1930:43 reproduces an evident Míng antecedent of this picture, probably of Hénán governor Chéng Shào's 1625 visit.

The monkey plays a major part in both Cháng's boxing, typically presenting a cup [69:5], and his Monkey Pole [71]. Cháng's "Drunken Form" (zuìxíng) and its "random points" (luàndiân) recall the uninhibited movement of "bobbing and weaving" in international boxing footwork, focused like that of Cháng on the toes. [10; 13; 29; 64] "Feet are purple swallows entering the forest, swooping and dodging. [31; 49; 69:6, 7, 11b] Drunken Eight Immortals, Crazy Boxing (Míquán and Mízongquán), and Monkey feature in the *Boxing Classic* of seventeenth-century Shàolín monk Xuánji.[70]

viii. Central Energy, according to Cháng and Chén

Cháng's writings may help elucidate a key concept, hinted at in the *Tàijíquán Classic*. This is the function of yì, "ideation" or imagination. In addition to inspirational imagery borrowed from myth and legend, Cháng explains how idea directs Energy in the body, in a manner remarkably like that in Tàijíquán Theory. *[17]* He names the precise targets to which techniques are directed and emphasizes the importance of the practitioner visualizing possible enemy attacks and the best method of dealing with them. He recommends that the student experiment and vary the prescribed set of dynamics, rather than spend years learning ever more formal sets. *[30]*

Among all traditional writers, Cháng gives the most complete account of qì, "breath-Energy," in relation to the physics of martial arts and internal organs. I interpret his alchemic prescription as a definition of reverse abdominal breathing, as practiced in Tàijíquán today. *[37]* In terms of mechanical Energy, the interdependence of opposing forces in Tàijíquán Theory, "Shady does not leave Sunny" (yin –bùlí yáng), is physically demonstrated by Newton's law of motion: "action and reaction are equal and opposite." Force is concentrated by opposition. Thirteen Dynamics Exercise declares:

> Should your idea be upward,
> First lodge a downward idea.
> It is like, on scooping up an object,
> To add the idea of crushing it,
> So that its root will automatically be broken.
> Then its destruction will be speedy and without doubt.

We noted numerous coincidences between the unprovenanced *Tàijíquán Classic*, undocumented at Chénjiagou, and the work of Cháng Nâizhou. In a different way, as Wile observes, the voluminous 1919 publication by Chén Xin, the earliest on Chén Tàijíquán, also contains significant parallels to Cháng's writings.[71] Cháng and Chén's shared objective is longevity, physical health, and spiritual realization, and both link "outer" self-defense applications and competitive practice to "inner"-cultivation of Energy, in a mutually supportive manner. Like Chén Xin, Cháng does not make extravagant claims. Both speak of striking acupuncture points, but in terms of practical anatomy rather than secret death-touches.[72]

Most notable of all is the Central Energy theory that is at the heart of Chén Xin and Cháng Nâizhou's systems. It is virtually inconceivable that Chén was unaware of his famous neighboring predecessor's work on this same topic. Both Cháng and Chén base their theory on the ancient *Change Classic* and its concept of the Tàijí principle and the interaction of Shady and Sunny forces. Cháng uses the Tàijí principle to explain the interaction of Shady and Sunny Energy channels, which run along the front and back, respectively, of limbs and torso. I observe that these respective positions generally correspond to those of flexor and extensor antagonist muscle pairs. Cháng analyzes their interaction in terms of "entry and support" (rùfú), "urging" (cui), and final "exertion" (jìn).

Chén uses the Tàijí principle to develop his own not-dissimilar theory of Central Energy through "reeling-silk power," (chánsijìng), which generates dynamic tension between muscle pairs by total body twisting action. It is this intrinsic power of "reeling silk" that allows you to "shoot power" (fajìng) effortlessly, while maintaining a bowed configuration of the limbs. Chén uses "essence," jing, and "power," jìng, interchangeably.[73] He inserts an unusual poem on White Goose Displays Wings (now known as White Crane Spreads Wings), with limbs curved like crescent brows, in the half-bent limb "uproot" pêng dynamic that typifies Táijíquán and the "unbendable arm" of Aikidô:[74]

> Is not the "moth-eyebrow moon" imitated in likeness true?
> When the bow is bent why not shoot? If you shoot, you double essential spirit!

Chén explains "reeling silk energy" in terms of the convoluted spirals of the *Change*'s Luó and Yellow River Diagram. His exposition is dominated by terms (hardly used elsewhere in his writing) that are typical of Cháng, such as: hands "supine" (yâng) and "prone" (fû); "twisting" (niûpiào), as in reeling silk; "dropping to a point" (luòdiân); head, hands, and feet as triple points; "tugged and dragged" (qianchè).[75]

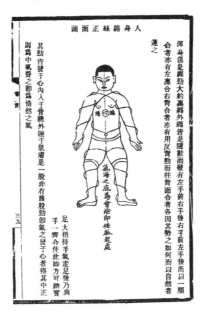

FIGURE 3: CENTRAL ENERGY AND REELING SILK POWER

Chén Xin's diagram shows coiling body lines of force, which correspond to interaction of flexor and extensor muscle pairs, with the comment: "Get their Central Correctness, then their Central Energy..." (Chén Xin 1919: 95)

Chén, and Tàijíquán in general, differ from Cháng in their emphasis on erect posture. Chén Xin makes exceptions to the vertical stance, provided that the spine itself is straight. Chén's self-composed *Tàijíquán Classic* speaks, like Cháng, of moveable body law:[76]

> Forward prone, backward supine, extraordinary and
>   correct mutually generate:
> Turning spins, sideways leans, jumps and leaps are all on
>   center.

ix. "Crossing Hands": Combat and Competition

The pictures found in Cháng's Twenty-four Dynamics show the boxer is stripped to the waist, bare-headed and wearing straw-shoes, rather than head-cloth and floppy boots, as in Míng boxing woodcuts. The bare head seems to have close-cropped hair, suggestive of the lax tonsure of a Shàolín martial monk, with no sign of the pigtail that Manchu law required for all male adult laity.

Another curious feature in Cháng's pictures is what appear to be bangles worn on both arms, as seen on Buddhist-style guardian-gods, but these may represent the rims of boxing gloves. An old woodcut, in the possession of Cháng Yìjun, eighth-generation descendant of Cháng Nâizhou, of which I was able to photograph just one page in 1994 (and reportedly no longer extant), gives the impression of mittens.

Figure 4: Monkey Tugs Rope, with boxing gloves

Engraving of Cháng's Twenty-four Dynamics: no. 13, Monkey Tugs Rope, showing what appear to be boxing mittens. *[69:13]* It is from a type-set edition of Cháng's work, probably that of Yuán Yûhuá 1921.

Cháng's figures in their vibrant attitudes resemble international boxers or sumô wrestlers more than conventional wûshù exponents. Cháng's exposition makes clear that his system is not merely for exhibition or solo cultivation purposes. Interactive contact and combative competition are explicitly analyzed. We see marks of affinity with the pushing-hands (tuishôu) of Tàijíquán, particularly in "borrowing energy" and "sticking and following." [23; 26; 27; 69:17, 18; 70:I-ii, II-ii, III-i]

Japanese sumô wrestling bears the name and something of the style of the ancient Chinese sport of "mutual pounding," xiangpu. Like traditional Chinese "drubbing platform," lêitái, sumô differs from wrestling or jûdô, which aim to throw, or from punching and kicking arts, in that it centers on control of a defined spatial area. The victor is the one who remains in control of the space. Its roots are ancient, and the sport relates more closely to courtship battles in nature, where the object is not to kill but rather to see off challengers. Sumô similarly seeks to secure and defend territory.

FIGURE 5: XIANGPU WRESTLERS C. 220 B.C.

Lacquer painting of xiangpu wrestling on a wooden comb from a Qín dynasty (221–207 B.C.) tomb at Fènghuángshan, Húbéi, discovered in 1975. (Xí Yúntài 1985:62; Lî Chéng 1991:40)

Tàijíquán "pushing hands" may likewise be explained in this light. Strikes, kicks, or throws are not excluded, but the body itself is the main weapon. Xíngyìquán's "seven fists" include all seven joints of feet, knees, hips, hands, elbows, shoulders, and head. Chén gives a variant "Pushing Hands Song":[77]

Uproot, Pull-back, Squeeze, and Press must be in earnest:
Draw him to advance, drop into void, let men invade.
Entire body mutually following, opponents cannot
  approach:
Four ounces transform in motion eight thousand pounds.

This is the only part of the *Tàijíquán Classic* documented at Chénjiagou. Uproot, Pull-back, Squeeze, and Press (pêng, lyû, jî, àn/nà) are the four cardinal dynamics in pushing hands. Instead of "pushing hands," Chén terms competition "contest running" (zhengzôu), and, like Cháng, speaks of "crossing hands," jiaoshôu.[78] "Crossing hands," translated by Wile as "sparring," is likewise the term used by Wû Rûqing (c. 1810–?) in his discussion of competitive Tàijíquán partner practice.[79]

Chén Xin explains that winning depends on control of position, "getting moment, getting dynamic," as in "encircling chess" (wéiqí, go in Japanese). Describing the High Reach Horse dynamic, Chén explains how to kick and use shoulder barge to strike an assailant's chest while his hands are constrained:[80]

Mountains are exhausted, waters finished, you think
  there is no road:
Prone shoulder, with one barge, breaks a bronze wall.
If you do not arrive at body with body mutually to
  barge,
Though you have treasured pearls, they hardly emit
  radiance.

"Barge," kào, is one of Tàijíquán's eight trigram dynamics. These are close-range techniques, based on using an opponent's force, as in the saying "four ounces deflect a thousand pounds." Most remarkable is the Chén-family "seven-inch barge," qi-cùn kào, in which the shoulder is only seven inches above the ground, and the "back-bend barge," bèizhékào, using whole-body "power."[81] Shàolín features such short-range weapons as "elbow law," "iron-head work," and "iron-barge."[82] Cháng gives ample evidence of full-body work at close quarters, entering within the triple gate of wrists, elbows, and shoulders. *[26; 54]* Close body strikes and low kicks are evident.

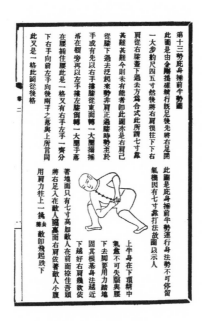

FIGURE 6: SEVEN-INCH BARGE

The low shoulder-stroke from Chén Tàijíquán. (Chén Xin 1919: 251)

Cháng's footwork emphasizes mobility, and weight is placed towards the toe or ball of the foot (Bubbling Spring acupoint) rather than the heel as seen in many modern Tàijíquán practitioners. Cháng's theory directly describes the interaction of Shady and Sunny energies, but neither Cháng nor indeed the *Tàijíquán Classic* explicitly relates these to weighting of the feet, though it is implied in right and left alternation. Wile points out that Cháng prescribes weight to be evenly distributed between the feet, yet the *Tàijíquán Classic* likewise prescribes a "central stance." I would not necessarily equate this with a prescription for "double-weighting." Division into weighted and unweighted, Sunny and Shady, is said by the *Tàijíquán Classic* to occur in motion. The feet at the resting position, at the start of the Tàijíquán exercise, are undivided in weighting. Cháng details dynamic weighting on one leg. *[13]* A detailed exposition of dynamic single-weighting theory is given, as applied to the resolution of forces in Crossing Hands: "Energy takes one side." *[23]*

x. Textual Diagnostics and a Tale of the Occult

Douglas Wile (1999) holds the distinction of publishing the first English translation of Cháng's neglected masterpiece, though Wile excludes Cháng's writings on weaponry. He also was the first in English (1996) to draw attention to the many mirrorings of Cháng in the *Tàijíquán Classic*.[83] Wile indeed opened the way for further study and evaluation. Thus, given the obvious importance of Cháng's work to an understanding of Chinese martial and energy culture, I feel that a full and exclusive treatment is due.

Works on martial arts in China were mostly suppressed by the Manchu Qing dynasty (1644–1910) for fear of subversion. It was not until after its overthrow that such censorship was lifted. Xú Zhèn, whose preface is dated 1932, published Cháng's *Martial Arts: Complete Book* in 1936, and first re-issued at Táiběi in 1969. Xú based his edition on Yuán Yûhuá's 1921 publication, but remarks that he used the original illustrations for accuracy. I saw in 1994, courtesy Cháng Yìjun, an early type-set edition that seemed to correspond to that of Yuán. Cháng Yìjun later showed me old illustrated manuscripts of qìgong and weapon sets that have affinities with, but do not correspond to, the present text. In the absence of sustained access to earlier sources, I have relied on Xú Zhèn as the primary source in making this present translation.

Xú remarks on problems with the text, including orthography, sequence, and repetitions. I accept most of Xú's proposed textual corrections. As explained, I have restored the sequence of Cháng's articles from the received table of contents, which Xú thoughtfully appended, rather than accept Xú's re-arrangement. *[See* Translation, Numbering, and Sequence, *above.]* While the received sequence is not without problems, I do not consider the tentative advantages of Xú's arrangement sufficient to outweigh sacrifice of the old order. Above all, I consider the old division into two parts (here A and B: Central Energy and Martial Defense) too important to discard.

The text contains numerous classical quotations, mostly unmarked, many of which I have successfully identified. As mentioned above, six maxims are listed, without attribution, which I traced to Yú Dàyóu's *Sword Classic*. *[32]* This raises the question of how much of the work is by Cháng himself. It is likely that some of the previously unknown materials here may derive directly from Cháng's teachers. There is also the question of editing and possible interpolation. As Xú Zhèn noted, the received text contained obvious orthographic errors and non-standard forms, lacunae, duplications, and at least one obvious misplacement.

The text edited by Xú Zhèn, on which I base my translation, bears signs of earlier editorial attention. The authorship and standpoint of these anonymous commentators appear to vary. Some notes may be by Cháng himself; others attempt to clarify meaning. There are a few brief notes in smaller writing, within the columns of the received text, which I place inside parentheses. In two cases, there are longer commentaries, prefaced by the word àn, which I translate as "Comment" and place entirely in italics. *[57]* Xú's editorial preface tells us that he converted received upper-margin notes into indented postscripts at the end of articles. I mark these as "indented commentary." Such comments mostly concern Energy and trigrams from the *Change Classic,* in which the author's elder brother Cháng Shìzhou was an acknowledged expert.

A paragraph, on para-normal qì power, seems to have been added as an unannounced postscript at the end of *Part A* (after *28: Ignition Energy*). The source was identified for me by Dr. Ulrike Middendorf of Heidelberg University. Its text is borrowed verbatim, but unacknowledged, from a collection of weird tales published in 1800 by encyclopedist Jì Yún, who perhaps turned to the supernormal for light relief. This story's parapsychology appears inconsistent with Cháng's practical martial philosophy. It recalls the legend of the stone from a cave by the Shàolín Monastery upon which Bodhidharma, who sat facing it for nine years, imprinted his visage,[84] or the Japanese Kabuki play about a calligrapher whose intense brush-writing penetrated a stone slab. Such "psycho-phenomena" were explained as physical proofs of "sincere intention" (chéngyì), a key concept of the Confucian Great Learning.[85]

If Cháng Nâizhou's dates are as purported, 1724–1783, this paragraph can hardly be his own. Cháng did warn us against obfuscation by "decadent scholiasts" (fûrú), the reactionary Confucian gentry. *[68:16]* Researcher Chén Wànqing advised me that Cháng's date of death is uncertain, and has been deduced from his latest recorded date as 1783.[86] This date fits Xú Panguì, evidently Xú Ji who served as governor of Hénán 1774–1778, and reportedly composed an epitaph for Cháng. (see: *xii*, below) Xú Ji, evidently a martial arts enthusiast, was reproved by orthodox Emperor Qiánlóng in 1775 for employing a Shàolín monk to train troops in spear technique.[87]

To demonstrate the subtleties of Cháng's physiology, I insert acupuncture channel diagrams from Chén Xin's 1919 work on Chén-family Tàijíquán, with notes on their relevance to the antagonistic muscle pairs of flexion and extension. Furthermore, I supply additional background detail, translating biographies from local histories and Cháng's weapons arts, in particular spear, which lies at the root of Chinese martial arts, not least Tàijíquán.

I strive to preserve Cháng's metaphors, with their historical and poetic associations, and above all the Chinese word order, with its structured parallel patterns. This literal approach, with scientific transliteration of Chinese words showing speech-tones, it is hoped will bring the reader closer to the authentic world of evolving Chinese martial arts in their genuine cultural matrix. The work provides valuable insights for students of Chinese civilization in general, as well as for practitioners of martial and health arts alike. It cuts a microcosmic cross-section of Chinese history, literature, and religion.

The underlying metaphor in Cháng's physical refinement is taken from Daoist alchemy, which aimed to "refine" (liàn) the base metal of lead with mercury by smelting it in a "cauldron" at the center of a "furnace" and thereby producing the magic "gold cinnabar" (jindan), the "elixir" of long life and immortality. "Refinement" means physical training of the bodily "Form" (xíng). Internally this is achieved by cultivation of breathing and circulation of "Energy" (qì). Externally it is by practice of the described martial actions or "dynamics" (shì). The two, internal and external, are complementary. Health is attained by learning self-defense, and vice versa. The "elixir" is outer health and inner strength.

Wile makes a case that martial literature be recognized for its due place in Chinese culture studies. He boldly inquires, with good reason, why researchers have merely sought to locate Cháng inside the Tàijíquán tradition, rather than vice versa.[88] The factual history of the Chinese martial arts, and its wider cultural implications, is a story still unfolding.

xi. Cháng Family Boxing Today

Today, Cháng's blood and boxing lineages continue. In 1994, as related below, I visited his family, which continues to flourish in his ancestral village in Hénán, near Sìshuî in Xingyáng district. There I witnessed their faithful perpetuation of the traditions of Cháng boxing, which is gradually becoming more widely taught and recognized.

According to his home-town gazetteer, Cháng Nâizhou took up the practice of martial arts for health reasons (namely, nocturnal emissions), yet he never ceased to pursue practical fighting applications in the techniques. Cháng's writings detail an unprecedented vision of unity among spiritual, physical, and martial aspects that has been unsurpassed, even today. He acknowledges his teachers by name and explains how he creatively consolidated and developed their art.

A leading contemporary exponent and teacher of Cháng-Style Boxing is Liú Yìmíng (1943–) of (Hénán) Sìshuî. At the age of sixteen, Liú became the disciple of seventh-generation Cháng Style master Gao Qinglián. In 1986, Liú received a special award for a demonstration in a national competition. Japanese martial historian Matsuda Ryûchi interviewed him in 1993 and published an essay by Liú, with Lî Chéng and Chén Shàowû, on the nature of Cháng-Style Boxing in a major Japanese martial arts periodical.[89]

Douglas Wile's 1999 *T'ai Ch'i's Ancestors: The Making of an Internal Martial Art* included a first English translation of Cháng's theory on energy and boxing, but not his weaponry. Though readable, it does not probe into Cháng's underlying sense. In 2002, Jarek Szymanski at Shànghâi introduced Cháng boxing on his website *FromInsideChina.* He visited Cháng Yìjun's home and translated a part of Cháng's opus.

I will now describe my experiences of Cháng-Style Boxing, in its home environment, gained on brief visits in 1994, 2002, and 2003.

On July 29, 1994, with Barry Wicksman, ex-fellow student of Chén Pànlîng Tàijíquán under master Zhang Yìzhong in Tôkyô (1968–1971), I visited Zhèngzhou Shàolín Martial Arts Academy, headed by Zhu Tianxî, who had trained under Shàolín monk master Shì Dégen (1914–1968). There we met Chéng Rìmào, teacher of Cháng-Style Boxing, who gave a brief demonstration of Cháng-Style qìgong breathing. Next morning we watched the students train in the clear dirt space under the trees. His wielding of the heavy halberd "big knife," dàdao—a weapon linked to Guan Gong, hero of the Three Kingdoms wars—was particularly impressive.[90]

We then proceeded to the Shàolín Temple itself, with an introduction to senior monk Shì Déjiàn, lay name Xú Yi. Monks Shì Xíngjia and Shì Xíngtao gave us a tour of the stele courtyard. Hearing that we practiced Tàijíquán, they asked us to adopt the opening stance then told me to press my knees more out and to the side. They told us of an older martial monk named Yônglì, "Eternal Stance," lay name Ding Hóngyì, "Red Justice," secularized during the Cultural Revolution and rusticated nearby. Early the following morning, July 31, we set off by bicycle along dirt tracks, led by Shì Xíngxìng. Yônglì lived with his wife and young son in a small farm house, with high packed-earth walls, guarded by a cockerel. He agreed to demonstrate for us a few postures of Drunken Monkey boxing.[91]

On August 1, 1994, with the aid of a reluctant taxi driver, anxious about making it safe back to Zhèngzhou before nightfall, we finally located the ancestral village home of the Cháng family, at Xingyáng between (Hénán) Sìshuî and Zhèngzhou. We were warmly welcomed by Cháng Yìjun, "Resolute Army," and younger brother Cháng "Red Army" Hóngjun, sons of Cháng

"Mountain Forest" Shanlín (1932–1991), living descendants of Cháng Nâizhou, with their mother.[92] I photographed their impromptu display of their lineage "fists and poles," which resembles Drunken Monkey style, of which the retired Shàolín monk had given us a sample the day before. On the wall hung a 1975 copy of a badly damaged original, whose fragments also I was permitted to photograph. The image recalls the description of the life portrait of Cháng painted by his artist friend Xú Quán. *[See biographies, Introduction: xii.]*

I also photographed an engraved illustrated page *[FIGURE 4]* of an early printed edition of Cháng's boxing work, possibly that of Yuán Yûhuá c. 1921. Surprisingly, what appear in Xú Zhèn's reproduction of the drawings as wrist bangles are here apparently revealed as mittens. This may be the earliest extant evidence for use of gloves in Chinese boxing. From my own observation, Hong Kong Wú-style Tàijíquán master Zhèng Tianxióng used international boxing gloves in sparring at his rooftop gym in Kowloon in the 1970s. At Táibêi in 1982, Allen Pittman and I witnessed Baguàzhâng master Hóng Yìmián use light boxing mittens for applications training in the park outside the Dànshuî River floodwall. Earlier, William Chen in New York published a book showing use of boxing gloves in Yáng-style Tàijíquán practical training.[93]

On August 14, 2002, I again visited Cháng Yìjun, still at Xingyáng, now in modern housing. He allowed me to photograph old manuscript booklets, including illustrated qìgong, Monkey and Demon Pole, and Double Sword against Spear. He reported that the old edition of Cháng Boxing, a page of which I had photographed in 1994, had since been destroyed. He disagreed that it showed use of boxing mittens. *[FIGURE 4]*

On August 21, 2003, I met Chén Wànqing, president of the Chángjia Boxing Research Association, Cháng Songhuá, Chén Zengzhì, and Chén Wànlî, who shared with me some of their research into Cháng Boxing, still mostly unpublished. Early the following morning I was shown demonstrations of Cháng Boxing, including the Twenty-four Fists, and weaponry in the main square of Xingyáng.

xii. Local Histories

The Chén family of Chénjiagou, Hénán Province, who perfected the art now known to the world as Tàijíquán, has the following record, said to refer to Cháng Nâizhou by the alternative name Cháng Sanzhâi:

> Chén Jìxià, who lived in the latter part of the Qiánlóng reign (1736–1796) "was painting a Buddha in the Ancient Sage Temple, to the east of the [Chén Jiagou] village, when a man pushed him from behind. He threw the man down in front of him and asked his name. It was Cháng Sanzhâi of Hénán [lit. "south of the Yellow River"], a man famous in the art."[94]

This anecdote indicates direct contact between Cháng Nâizhou and Chénjiagou across the Yellow River (long before it was bridged). Chén Jìxià would have been much younger than Cháng Nâizhou. Chén Pànlíng (Jùnfeng, 1892–1967), martial arts expert and native of Xipíng in Hénán, attested that Cháng-Style Boxing was famous in Hénán martial circles, where Cháng Nâizhou was commonly known as "Cháng Sanzhâi." Chén admired Cháng Boxing's "Green Dragon Exits Water," whose "movements are soft, as if having no bones." This technique does not occur in the present book, though it is present in Chén Boxing.[95]

(Qing) Sìshuî District Gazetteer records the following biographical notice for the brilliant portrait painter Xú Quán of "Zhào village" (possibly Zhàobâo, next to Chénjiagou) who:

> ... with Cháng Nâizhou, had deep friendship. Cháng frequently asked him for a portrait, but he did not assent. One day passing by, Cháng grabbed his robe, saying: Today if you do not paint my portrait, I won't let you go. Xú ran off, but, looking around, saw Cháng's beard and hair all outstretched, just like a picture of Zhang Fei ("Baron Huán").[96] He immediately returned, and at one sweep finished it. Delighted he said: Your honor's talent, combining the civil and martial, is extremely hard to depict. Now I've got it![97]

In 1994 Cháng Yìjun allowed me to photograph a copy of a painted portrait of "Cháng Luòchén," copied in 1975 from a badly decayed original, that I was also allowed to examine. This portrait closely resembles the above description. *[PLATE 1]*

Sìshuî District Gazetteer has several martial biographies. I translate those most relevant, beginning with Zhang Ba, who is cited by Cháng Nâizhou. The name Zhang Ba is phonetically close to "Jiâng Fa."[98] Chén Xin 1919 relates a tale of Chén Wángtîng, reputed founder of Chén Boxing, which may be relevant. Chén Wángtîng was friendly with Lî Jìyù, a military graduate of Dengfeng adjacent to Shàolín in the late Míng (1628–1644). However, when Lî led a popular revolt against official extortion, Chén Wángtîng opposed him. On this occasion, Chén chased one bandit three times round the Imperial Mountain-fort, by Shàolín, but could not overtake him. Later, Chén Wángtîng learned that this man was Jiâng, who "could catch a hare at a hundred paces and excelled at boxing." Jiâng then became Chén Wángtîng's retainer.[99] In 1928, at the age of eighty, Chén Xin, concerned to uphold family honor, wrote a formal denial that his ancestor Chén Wángtîng had learned from "Mr Jiâng," alleging (without evidence) that the Chén clan had become famed for boxing centuries earlier, in the Yuán dynasty. Chén Xin noted that "Jiâng Bâshí" lived during the reign of Qiánlóng (1736–1796). Interestingly, the name "Bâshì," literally "hold posture," can simply mean the "boxer."[100]

Yáng family boxing lineage holds Jiâng Fa to be intermediary between the undated Wáng Zongyuè,' and Chén Chángxing (1771–1853), teacher of Yáng Lùchán. If Chén Chángxing revered Wáng Zongyuè and Jiâng Fa as ultimate progenitors of Chén family boxing, rather than his own teachers, there is no reason to make Jiâng Fa eighteenth rather than seventeenth century. Chén Zîmíng, of the Yáng school, possessed an antique portrait that, he claimed, represents Chén Wángtíng and his retainer Jiâng Fa holding the halberd.[101]

FIGURE 7: CHÉN WÁNGTÎNG WITH BODYGUARD JIÂNG FA (TRAD.)

Táng Háo reports this antique painting was brought south during the Japanese war from the Chén ancestral shrine by Chén Zîmíng. It is believed to portray General Chén Wángtîng (c. 1650), progenitor of the Chén family martial tradition, with retainer Jiâng Fa. (Xú Zhèn 1936, book cover)

a) ZHANG BA

Zhang Ba was a man of Hûláo Pass *[just west of Sìshuî, guarding the road to Luòyáng and Shàolín].* In youth he studied the sword. Nearing thirty, he was expert in martial arts. His Divine Boxing's Twenty-nine Laws under Heaven were invincible. He was known as Divine Hand Zhang Ba.

At the time *[late Míng, c. 1630]*, Shandong's giant outlaw Liú Si had practiced rapine for forty years, and often
defeated official troops. When three provinces pooled
troops to capture him, he ran to Wèishì district *[Hénán,
about 100 km east of Shàolín]*, at once killing seven men.
No one dared anything. Zhang Ba met him and all alone
went directly ahead. Pointing to the sword at his waist he
asked: Can you use this or not? The bandit cursed, saying:
Do you dare compete with me in skill? Then they fought
each other. Zhang Ba with a short spear pierced his elbow
and took him prisoner.

When Zhang Ba was living at home, a monk from
the South came, whirling two whips (flails). He ordered
a man to splash water, but the man could not wet him.
Laying a hundred pieces of gold on the ground, the monk
said: "If anyone can come and compete with me, I'll give
it to him." Zhang Ba took indigo and, having dyed a staff
[to mark strikes], instantly entered. The monk in aston-
ishment submitted, saying: "While you, sir, are at Sìshuî,
there will be no burglaries." This man was surely a major
outlaw. *(Old Records)*

Impregnating a staff with dye or soot was an old method of mark-
ing hits, preferably on white clothing, in staff-fighting competitions.
A similar tale occurs in Cháng's own biography, following. A comparable method is used in a type of Chinese jousting, a horseback
spear contest described by the Yuán dynasty *Water Margin* epic.
Spear-points are replaced by felt daubed with chalk, while contes-
tants wear black clothing, to mark strikes.[102]

b) CHÁNG NÂIZHOU

Also called Luòchén ("Luòyáng citizen"), Cháng Nâizhou
was an annual stipendiary scholar living in "Cháng village,"
Chángcun. When over thirty, he suffered from "loss of

semen syndrome," so he took up meditation, practicing fists and staves. He took private lessons with Zhang Ba of Hûláo *[Pass, near Shàolín]* and obtained all his techniques. *[N.B. Zhang Ba lived a century earlier, as recorded in his biography above. Cháng himself informs us he took lessons from Yán Shèngdào of Luòyáng.]*

He further submerged his mind in the Zhou Changes *[Change Classic]*, profoundly penetrating Shady and Sunny (yinyáng), rise and drop principles. Then he edited the ancients' boxing tablatures of facing and backing, exit and entrance, analyzing and arranging them in the minutest detail.

He further composed the *Central Energy Theory* to elucidate its scope. Among this, his refining Energy technique of upward and downward, opening and closing marvels, were all things no one previous had discovered. Xingyáng Cáolî Village Lî clan was his wife's family. *[cf. Appendix III, below: Xú Zhèn's 1932 preface, which says Qín clan of Mèngjin]* In front of their gate, stones had been laid to make a road. When Cháng Nâizhou trod on them, they all broke.

There was an expert in staff technique who, hearing of his reputation, came to call. Cháng Nâizhou clothed him in a long shirt of white color and, having dyed it *[his staff]* in soot water, whirled his staff, so that his *[opponent's]* whole body was like ink *[from being hit]*.

Once, when drinking tea on a stone table, he used the cup to lightly strike the stone. The stone split in two. At the time his fist and staff technique was most developed. Cháng Nâizhou's name was known to the Four Seas. Heroes jostled to visit him. Cháng Nâizhou competed with them, becoming ever more extraordinary. No one could defeat him.

Cháng Nâizhou was an accomplished poet and essayist. He taught the classics, and disciples were numerous. In spare time, he gave instruction in fists and staves. Men, expert in one art, all achieved spiritual marvels. Chái

Rúguì, Gao Liùgeng, and Lî Fawén [possibly identical to Lî Gentú, below] are the most famous.

Hénán provincial Governor, Xú Panguì [Xú Ji], paid him the utmost respect. On Cháng Nâizhou's death, he mourned him with an ode, as follows:

South I travelled to Chû and Shû,
    west travelled to Qín:
Never did I see the like of Cháng Luòchén.
Turning the head within rafters and walls,
    everything is a dream: [death comes suddenly]
Filling the gate, peach and plum trees [his sons]
    are all like gods.

His Fists took as master Yuè Wûmù [Yuè Fei],
    root and source correct; [103]
His Spear succeeded Baron Huán [Zhang Fei],
    cassock and bowl true. [104]
In the whole world, heroes are now scarce indeed!
Ascending the hall and entering the chamber,
    there are Three Men. [inner disciples]

Surely this is a factual record. Chái Rúguì has a separate biography. Gao Gengjian and Chái Rúguì were equal in reputation—Chái Rúguì in Fists, and Gao Gengjian in Spear. At that time both were called "Invincible."

There was Gao Tínglín, an imperial Academician, who attended his mother with utmost filialty and studied martial arts from Gao Liùgeng. Gao Liùgeng told him: My way was obtained from Mr. Cháng. Now I give it all to you! [Gao Liùgeng's brief separate biography writes simply: "He obtained Mr. Cháng's true tradition." He may be identical with Gao Gengjian.]

Within the Cháng gate, apart from the Three Disciples, there were Yáo Lâojiû and Zhang Yùlín, whose art was extremely expert and extraordinary. There was also Fû Xiâodé, of a different school from Cháng Nâizhou, but the same achievement.

Also, Pan Yuèsong in the five weapons [probably saber, spear, archery, sword, and staff] was acclaimed for outstanding skill.

Notes: Pan "Yuèsong" seems to be identical with Pan "Bingsong" "whose martial technique was renowned. He authored Spear forms, Fist forms, and Staff forms." Two other martial disciples of Cháng Nâizhou named are: Wáng Guóxiáng of Húgù Village, and Lî Gentú of Xiâowáng Village, expert in boxing and poles.

c) Chái Rúguì

Also called Tíngfang, Chái [*a leading disciple of Cháng Nâizhou*] lived to the west at "Ten Lî Store," Shílîpu.[105] His four elder and younger brothers had already settled elsewhere, and, on the death of his parents, he alone arranged their funeral. He was expert in fists and staves, and especially expert in Twenty-one Gate Spear laws. [*attributed to "Zhang (Ba?) of Hûláo" by Cháng. See i. b, above.*]

At the time [1795–1804], White Lotus Religion bandits [*White Lotus Religion, Báiliánjiào, mixing magic with martial arts, was a quasi-Buddhist apocalyptic movement, and precursor to the Boxer Uprising of 1900*] had one Zhang Cháohàn, who seized Díjia, gathering over ten thousand men in revolt. Hénán Governor Mâ invited Chái as Trainer of Troops Deputy. Chái taught them Chop-Mountain Staff law. In three months they were fluent. (Hénán) Wûzhì's prefect Lín Làn led them to battle. There was not one of them that could not match a hundred. The bandits were subsequently pacified.

Next, Jiangnán (south of the Yangtze) River Affairs Chief Commissioner Wú Jing summoned and appointed Chái to his camp. At (Anhui) Xúzhou wicked people had seized the city and sacked it. When the government army arrived at the city gate, they opened it, deceptively displaying a vacuum. Among the multitude, none dared advance. Chái, grasping a long spear, courageously charged in. The crowd followed him, and the wicked people were all arrested.

d) CHÉN TIANJUÀN

This man of Anshàng got strength from Cháng Nâizhou's Central Energy Theory.[106] In fists and staves he was
most expert. His son Zhènwàn, and grandson Yùshu,
were able in their generations to carry on the enterprise.

e) CHÁNG KÈJIÂN

A practitioner of *[Cháng Nâizhou's]* Central Energy
Theory, his martial arts surpassed men.[107] He once followed his father and younger brother and others to
Guângwû *[near Zhèngzhou]*, where they defeated the
(Muslim) Niân rebels (active 1853–1868). Together with
his younger brother Kèjùn, both used their martial techniques to teach men. Their students were very numerous.

In the early twentieth century, Yuán Yûhuá of Sìshuî learned the
art from fifth-generation descendant Cháng Dépû.[108] In 1921 Yuán
became military trainer of the army stationed on Mt. Song, near
Shàolín Temple, and published the first book of Cháng's Martial
Skills in Shânxi. Martial historian Xú Zhèn further edited and
published this at Shànghâi in 1936. The present translation is based
on Xú's text.

From information received on my third visit to Cháng Yìjun, on
August 14, 2002 regarding recent Cháng genealogy, plus the *Sìshuî
Gazetteer* data, I reconstruct a tentative outline of Cháng Nâizhou's
lineage by generation, as follows:

> Zhang Ba, "Flying God," of Hûláo, Jiâng Fa, Chén
>   Wángtîng of Chénjiagou c. 1650
>
> Yû Ràng, spear master, of Sìshuî c. 1730
>
> Yán Shèngdào of Kaifeng, teacher of Cháng
>   Nâizhou, c. 1750
>
> Cháng Nâizhou of Sìshuî (1724–1783?), Chén Jìxià

i-ii. Chái Rúguì c. 1800, Gao Gengjian (=Liùgeng?),
Lî Fawén, spear master "Shanxi Wáng"
(=Wáng Zongyuè of Tàijíquán fame?)

iii-iv. Cháng Kèjiân c. 1860, Chén Chángxing
(1771–1853), Yáng Lùchán (1799–1872), Wû
Yûxiang (c. 1812–1880) of Tàijíquán

v-vi. Cháng Dépû c. 1910, Yuán Yûhuá c. 1921

vii. Cháng Shanlín 1932–1991

viii. Cháng Yìjun, 1955–, Cháng Hóngjun

ix. Cháng Míngjiâ, 1985–

Cháng Nâizhou's Writings
PART A
Nourishing Central Energy
培養中氣 *Péiyâng Zhongqì*

I

1. Central Energy theory
中氣論 **Zhongqì lùn**

Central Energy is what *Immortals' Classics* call the Primal Sunny (yuányáng), what in medicine is called Primal Energy (yuánqì). Because it occupies the body center, martial defense (wûbèi, "martial preparedness") names it Central Energy. This Energy is pre-heavenly [pre-natal] True Unity Energy. Through civil refinement, it contrives the Internal elixir (nèidan). Through martial refinement, it contrives the External elixir. Internal elixir invariably borrows External elixir to be completed.

> *Notes: "Primal" (yuán) developed as an imperial taboo substitution for "Mysterious" (xuán). This central acupoint is an inch below the navel, in the lower abdomen. In acupuncture it is called "Energy Sea" (qìhâi), and "Elixir Field" (dantián) in mystic alchemy, equivalent to an Indian chakra, as in Tàijíquán Theory. [2; 22]*

Overall, motion and stillness are mutually rooted. Warmed and nourished by their coordinated laws, they naturally have "conceived embryo" and "return to Prime" marvels. Vulgar students, uninitiated into Central Energy's root and source, just strive at hands dancing and feet stamping. They desire to enter the Primal Orifice, but of necessity are unable.

Men from birth onward are endowed with pre-heavenly Spirit to convert to Energy. They accumulate Energy to convert to Essence (sperms/ova). Father and mother copulate essences, which first congeal at Vacuous and Perilous (Xu, Wéi) acupoints' interior. Vacuous and Perilous in front face the navel, and behind face the kidneys. They fly up, fly down; fly left, fly right. They are not in front nor behind; "not partial nor leaning': correctly abiding in every human body's center. They are termed Heaven's Root, or called Fate's Gate. What the *Change Classic* calls Grand Polarity, Tàijí, is this.[109] True Shady, yin, and True Sunny, yáng, are both stored in this center. Spirit depends on it.

> *Notes: Cháng boldly links Daoist alchemy to Confucian classics, equating the body's energy center with that of embryonic conception, and the celestial north pole. Tàijíquán Theory states: "Energy sinks to the Elixir Field, not partial nor leaning." "Not partial nor leaning" (bùpian, bùyî) is a quotation from philosopher Zhu Xi of Southern Sòng.[110] A commentary on the* Daoist Yellow Court Classic *by Liú Yimíng (of possible Qing dynasty date) applies this phrase to the body center: "centrality is neither partial nor leaning, not going too far nor falling short."[111] [4; 9; 11; 28; 36]*

> *Vacuous and Perilous are adjacent constellations, at due north in the Chinese zodiac of Twenty-eight Constellations. A late Hàn dynasty alchemical work,* Cantóngqì, *"Three Together Joined," gives them a sexual sense as of conception: "Containing the Primal, Vacuous and Perilous discharge Essences at midnight."[112] Lâo Zî said: "The Mysterious Female's Gate is Heaven and Earth's Root."[113] "True Shady and Sunny" designate "pre-natal," absolute negative and positive charge in Daoist medicine.*

This Energy's efficacious brilliance shoots forth to contrive the Five Organs' spirits. Heart-mind's Spirit, liver's Soul, spleen's Idea, lungs' Anima, kidney's Essence and Will: rely on this rulership. Exhalation and inhalation depend on it. Inhalation garners Heaven and Earth's Energy. Exhalation expels the Five Organs' Energy. Exhalation goes from Fate's Gate to kidneys, liver, spleen, heart, and lungs. Inhalation goes from lungs to heart, spleen, liver, kidneys, and

Fate's Gate. The Twelve Channels' (nerves) and Fifteen Blood-vessels' interflow are tied to it. Channels and Blood-vessels are Energy and blood's ways and roads.

When man once exhales Energy, blood flows three inches. At exhalation and inhalation's complete breath, it moves six inches. Man, in one day and one night, has 13,500 breaths. Day and night it moves 81,000 inches *[6 × 13,500]*. Sunny moves 25 times, Shady also moves 25 times. Altogether day and night 50 times, they circulate around the entire body.[114] *[body circuit of 1,620 inches (2 × 810) × 50 circulations = 81,000 inches.]*

> Notes: Body height is taken as 810 "inches," in Chinese ten-inch feet: "eight foot, one inch."

From the visceral organs, it issues to meridians and Blood-vessels; from the meridians and Blood-vessels, it enters visceral organs. From these, it generates Two Indicators *[sun and moon = yinyáng]*, which generate Five Actions.[115]

Metal can generate Water; Kidneys belong to Water's organ and generate bones.

1. (Kidneys have left Shady and right Sunny.)
2. Water can generate Wood; Liver belongs to Wood's organ and generates sinews.
3. Wood can generate Fire; Heart belongs to Fire's organ and generates blood's pulse.
4. Fire can generate Earth; Spleen belongs to Earth's organ and generates sinews and muscle.
5. Earth can generate Metal; Lungs belong to Metal's organ and generate skin and hair.

The Five Organs in turn grow; Six Viscera in turn are generated. This is Form's (physique's) completion. Adapting True Unity's Energy, they marvellously coordinate and are completed. Energy concentration from the hundred joints integrally lodges. It is one, yet two; two, yet one. From the source, it may not for an instant be separated.

Martial defense is like this: refine the Form to coordinate externals; refine Energy to solidify internals. "Hard and tough as iron" [*Change Sinews Classic*], [16] you will naturally complete a "Gold Elixir [*jindan = jingang, vajra*] indestructible body." [*Nirvâna Sûtra*][117] You then transcend laity and enter Sagehood. The Supreme Vehicle [*Vajrayâna*] may be attained. To speak of "facing men fearlessly" is the least of it.

> Notes: Here we see the combination of the vajra or diamond body from Buddhist transcendental meditation, physical immortality from Daoist internal alchemy, and the conditioning by exercise from the Change Sinews Classic, Yìjîn Jing, dubiously attributed to Bodhidharma. [19; 24; 34; 50] Mencius derives courage and his own "immoveable mind" from cultivation of the Expansive Energy (hàorán-zhi qì) of innate human goodness. He cites knight Mèng Shìshè who declared: "How can I, Shè, contrive necessarily to be victorious? I can contrive to be without fear, that's all."[118]

2. Shady and Sunny, Entry and Support theory
陰陽入扶論 **Yinyáng rùfú lùn**

Refinement of Form (physique) does not exceed Shady and Sunny. If Shady and Sunny are not clarified, from where does one begin to refine?

> Notes: Cháng's "entry and support" theory is based on the counter-action of Sunny and Shady channels, which I interpret as extensor and flexor muscle forces. In a stabilized static posture, isometric tension between muscle pairs ensures that "entry" as the prime mover is counter-balanced by an antagonist "support" muscle. This state of dynamic equilibrium is held until the antagonist muscle relaxes, releasing energy to shoot in a given direction.

a) The *Immortal Classics'* Governor Meridian (Dumài) moves from the posterior center, directing the various Sunny channels.

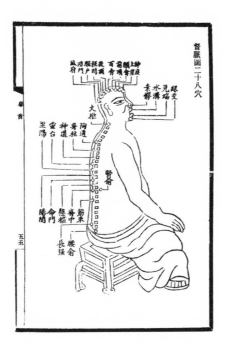

FIGURE 8: GOVERNOR MERIDIAN

Governor Meridian (Dumài) runs along the center line of the post-vertebral muscles, the head, and face. (Chén Xin 1919: 127)

> *Notes: Governor Meridian runs along the posterior central line of the spine and its post-vertebral muscles, between extensor muscles such as the erector spinae, latissimus dorsi, teres major. Fate's Gate (Mìngmén), behind the kidneys, is sixth from the bottom; Hundred Assembly (Bâihuì), here called Cut Communication (Duànjiao), is on the top. This and the following acupuncture charts are from Chén Xin, who in 1919 prefaced the first book on Tàijíquán.*

b) Deputy Meridian (Rènmài) moves from the abdomen's center, controlling the various Shady channels.

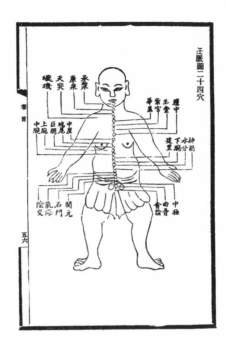

Figure 9: Deputy Meridian

Deputy Meridian (Rènmài) runs along the center line of the pre-vertebral muscles to the perineum between the legs. (Chén Xīn 1919: 129)

> *Notes: Deputy Meridian runs along the anterior center line, between flexor muscles such as the pectoralis and rectus abdomini. Assembled Shady (Huìyin) is at the perineum. Energy Sea (Qìhâi), i.e. Elixir Field (Dantián), is below the navel and Pit of Stomach (Zhongguàn).*

So, **the back is Sunny, the abdomen Shady.** The two channels interact below at Assembled Shady (huìyin, perineum) and above at Cut Communications (duànjiao, the crown). One is north *[abdomen]*, one south *[head]*, like midnight and noon matching. Again, they are like Abyss Trigram *[water ☵]* in the north, and Shining Trigram *[fire ☲]* in the south, fixed and unchanging.

[The body's antagonistically paired musculature consists of "Shady" flexors inside and "Sunny" extensors outside.]

Prone dynamics are Shady dynamics, yet enter Sunny Energy to reinforce the Governor Meridian. They lead all Sunny-channel Energy home to the upper anterior.

Supine dynamics are Sunny dynamics, yet enter Shady Energy to reinforce the Deputy Meridian. They lead all Shady-channel Energy home to the lower posterior.[119]

3. Entering Sunny, adhere to Shady;
Entering Shady, adhere to Sunny theory
入陽附陰入陰附陽論 **Rùyáng fùyin, Rùyin fùyáng lùn**

The back is Sunny. If you are excessively prone and flexed, then Governor Meridian interacts with Deputy: excess Sunny enters Shady. Sunny to Shady adheres and combines.

The abdomen is Shady. If you are excessively supine and extended, then Deputy Meridian interacts with Governor: excess Shady enters Sunny. Shady to Sunny adheres and combines.

Shady urges Sunny, or Sunny urges Shady: pursuing a circle without a break. All somersault and spinning dynamics employ it.

Notes: Circular motion results when supporting and restraining antagonist muscles urge in the direction of a prime-mover muscle force that goes beyond the point of balance.

4. Entering Sunny, support with Shady;
Entering Shady, support with Sunny theory
入陽扶陰入陰扶陽論 **Rùyáng fúyin, Rùyin fúyáng lùn**

When prone dynamics enter Sunny Energy and do not get Shady Energy support, then they are partial to Sunny. You will necessarily have, led and pulled, forward planting disasters.

When supine dynamics enter Shady Energy and do not get Sunny Energy support, then they are partial to Shady. You will necessarily have, lifted and pushed, backward toppling worries.

Notes: Without the restraint of a "supporting" force, you are liable to overbalance and fall. Tàijíquán Theory introduces these same interactive oppositions: Shady-Sunny, Prone-Supine, Forward-Backward.

So, when a supine dynamic issues forth, dropping to a point, quickly reverse it with a prone[120] dynamic, causing you not to be partial to Shady:

When Shady comes, Sunny counters;
When Sunny comes, Shady counters.
"Not partial nor leaning;
Without excess or insufficiency." [Zhu Xi][121] [1; 4; 9; 11; 28; 36]

Notes: When isometric tension is released and force issued to a given point, it should be reversed before balance is lost. This rhymed couplet, from leading Sòng Confucian philosopher Zhu Xi, is exploited both by Tàijíquán Theory (each line separately), and by Chén Xīn.[122]

"Dropping to the point, return to the Prime [center]": then is this Law. When pushed to flexion, return it with extension; if extended, return it with flexion; when high, return it with low; if low, return it with high; when lateral, return it with face-on; if face-on, return it with lateral: until obliquely twisting, revolving back and forth, without exception are all thus.

Progressively, by each dynamic, refine onwards until Shady and Sunny interact and resolve. Naturally, you will get Mind responsive to hands, marvellously never missing a move!

Notes: Tàijíquán Theory: "Following flexion, proceed to extend." Thirteen Dynamics Exercise: "Up, down, forward, backward, left, and right are all thus."

5. Shady and Sunny joint entry, Shady and Sunny joint support explained

陰陽并入陰陽并扶說 **Yīnyáng bìngrù, Yīnyáng bìngfú shuo**

These are laterally oblique dynamics. In lateral dynamics, Shady and Sunny each occupy their half. So, left dynamics laterally, with right-side Shady and Sunny, jointly enter, left-side Shady and Sunny supporting them. Right dynamics laterally, with left-side Shady and Sunny jointly enter, right-side Shady and Sunny supporting them.

Notes: To move the torso to the right, left-adductor muscle pulls left hip towards the center of the two legs, while right-abductor muscle pulls right hip away from the center. Front and back muscles remain in equilibrium, keeping the torso erect.

6. Shady and Sunny separate entry,
Shady and Sunny separate support explained
陰陽分入陰陽分扶說 **Yinyáng fenrù, Yinyáng fenfú shuo**

These are level arms' opening and closing dynamics. When opening the chest and closing shoulders, Shady Energy's portion enters the Sunny portion. When opening the back and closing the chest, Sunny Energy's portion enters the Shady portion.

The dynamics separate to the two sides. So, Energy from the center splits apart: separately entering and separately supported.

> *Notes: Here shoulder flexors oppose each other; and, then, shoulder extensors oppose each other. Thus: left-pectoral flexor pulls right-pectoral flexor in front to expand the back; left-deltoid extensor pushes right-deltoid extensor behind to expand the chest.*

7. Shady and Sunny rotational entry,
Shady and Sunny rotational support explained
陰陽旋入陰陽分旋扶說 **Yinyáng xuánrù, Yinyáng xuánfú shuo**

These are level wheeling dynamics, twisting dynamics, swinging and shaking dynamics. When dynamics revolve and rotate without stop, Energy also follows it without rest. Shady enters the Sunny portion, Sunny enters the Shady portion. They contact and connect, continuously, without any interruption. In right revolutions or left revolutions *[clockwise or counter-clockwise turns]*, Shady and Sunny revolve, mutually entering and supporting.

> *Notes: This describes the alternating action of rotator muscle pairs, notably iliopsoas in the hips.*

8. Shady and Sunny oblique-partial,
cross-sign entry and support explained
陰陽斜偏十字入扶說 **Yinyáng xiépian shí-zì rùfú shuo**

> *Notes: "Cross-sign" (shízì 十字) indicates that hands cross to opposite legs, e.g. left hand over right leg. It can also indicate crossed arms. [20; 69:3, 7, 12a-b, 19b, 24; 72:17, 22]*

These are oblique-partial lateral-body, prone and supine dynamics.

a) In left oblique prone dynamics, Sunny Energy from spine lower-right is raised to spine upper-left, and obliquely enters the left-anterior Shady portion. In right oblique prone dynamics, Sunny Energy from spine lower-left is raised to spine upper-right, and obliquely enters the right-anterior Shady portion. Oblique Chopping and Oblique Parry hands use these.

b) In left oblique supine dynamics, Shady Energy from abdomen lower-right is raised to abdomen upper-left, and obliquely enters the left-posterior Sunny portion. In right oblique supine dynamics, Shady Energy from abdomen lower-left is raised to abdomen upper-right, and obliquely enters the right-posterior Sunny portion. Oblique Push and Raising hands use these.

> Notes: I take it that in a) prone dynamics, right hand turns backward and up overhead to chop left in front; while in b) supine dynamics, right hand scoops left in front and up to push left behind.

9. Shady entry, Shady support;
Sunny entry, Sunny support explained
陰入陰扶陽入陽扶說 Yinrù yinfú, Yángrù yángfú shuo

These are straight (direct) rising, straight advancing, "not partial nor leaning"[123] dynamics. In straight body, face-on dynamics, Sunny Energy does not get to enter the Shady portion. Shady Energy does not get to enter the Sunny portion. Each goes home to its original position. Above, reaching Hundred Assembly acupoint [crown of the head], they interchange. Below, reaching Bubbling Spring acupoint [behind balls of the feet], they concentrate. Shady and Sunny entry and support are only at the two terminals [head and feet].

> Notes: This describes vertically erect, fixated muscle actions in spine and legs, directed by erector spinae and sartorius. Upper body stretches against lower body: arm flexors pull up against leg flexors; arm extensors push down against leg extensors. This coordinates with reverse abdominal breathing.

10. Shady and Sunny,
Random Point entry and support explained
陰陽亂點入扶 **Yīnyáng luàndiân rùfú shuo**

These are Drunken Form dynamics. Drunken Form is suddenly ahead, suddenly behind; suddenly supine, suddenly prone; suddenly advancing, suddenly retiring; suddenly oblique, suddenly face-on. Their dynamics have no fixed forms. Energy likewise follows them to contrive entry and support. Nevertheless, in chaos' midst, they follow timing to deploy. Shady and Sunny do not mutually interfere. They are chaotic, and yet not chaotic.

> *Notes: Tàijíquán Theory has: "Suddenly hidden, suddenly revealed." The Drunken style is commonly associated with Monkey Boxing. [69: 5] The principle of antagonist pairs of muscles, once mastered, may be freely employed in multitudinous combinations. Tàijíquán Theory has: "suddenly conceal, suddenly reveal, left is weighted, then left is vacuous...." I take the principle of unimpeded mobility and surprise here in "random points" as akin to the skip step in boxing. [13; 29; 64]*

The Body's Twelve Channels

Notes: This title, and following sub-titles, are added by the translator.

The above is a general theory of one body's major Shady and Sunny *[meridians]*.[124] *[Cf.* The Yellow Emperor's Classic of Medicine.*]* Their entry and their support are like this:

i) Upper Limb Extensor Muscles

Hand-back is Sunny (yáng) and arm-exterior is Sunny. Three Sunny channels run along hands and arms' exterior side:

a) Hand Major Sunny channels start from little finger back *[small intestine]*.

b) Hand Sunny Bright channels start from index finger back *[great intestine]*.

c) Hand Minor Sunny channels start from ring finger back *[triple heater]*.

All three ascend, along arms' exterior-side running.

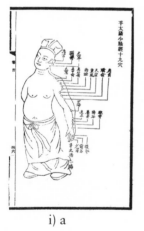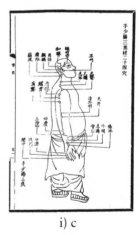

i) a	i) b	i) c

FIGURE 10: SUNNY CHANNELS OUTSIDE THE ARMS *(Chén Xīn 1919: 109, 101, 119)*

Notes: from left to right: a) Major, b) Bright, c) Minor Sunny yáng channels are on the outside of the arms. The Sunny channels correspond in position to extensor muscles such as triceps and brachioradialis.

ii) Upper Limb Flexor Muscles

Hand-heart (palm) is Shady and arm interior side Shady. Three Shady channels run along hands and arms' interior side:

a) Hand Major Shady channels stop at thumb inside *[lungs]*.

b) Hand Intermediate Shady channels stop at middle finger inside *[pericardium]*.

c) Hand Minor Shady channels stop at little finger inside *[heart]*. All three descend, along arms' interior-side running.

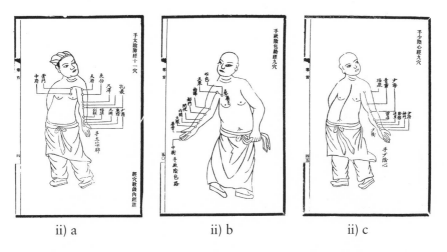

| ii) a | ii) b | ii) c |

FIGURE **11:** SHADY CHANNELS INSIDE THE ARMS *(Chén Xīn 1919: 99, 117, 107)*

Notes: from left to right: a) Major, b) Intermediate, c) Minor Shady yin channels are on the outside of the arms. The Shady channels correspond in position to flexor muscles such as biceps and brachialis.

iii) Lower Limb Extensor Muscles

Foot-back is Sunny and leg exterior side Sunny. Three Sunny channels run along feet and legs' exterior side:

a) Foot Major Sunny channels stop at little toe back [*bladder*].

b) Foot Sunny Bright channels stop at fourth toe back [*stomach*].

c) Foot Minor Sunny channels stop at second toe back [*gall bladder*].

The three channels all go along legs' exterior side, stopping at toe back.

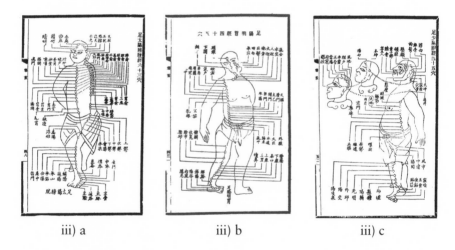

iii) a	iii) b	iii) c

FIGURE 12: SUNNY CHANNELS OUTSIDE THE LEGS (*Chén Xin 1919: 113, 103, 121*)

Notes: from left to right: a) Major, b) Bright, c) Minor Sunny yáng channels are on the exterior of the legs. The Sunny channels correspond in position to extensor muscles such as gluteus and quadriceps femoris.

iv) Lower Limb Flexor Muscles

Foot-heart (instep) is Shady, leg interior side is Shady. Three Shady channels run along feet and legs' interior side.

a) Foot Major Shady channels start from big toes' interior bottom *[spleen]*.

b) Foot Intermediate Shady channels start from big toes' interior top *[liver]*.

c) Foot Minor Shady channels start from little toe, passing foot-heart's Bubbling Spring *[kidneys]*.

The three channels all go along leg interior side, starting from toes.

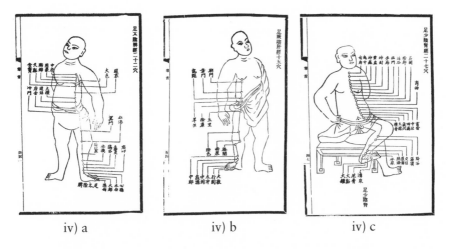

iv) a   iv) b   iv) c

FIGURE 13: SHADY CHANNELS INSIDE THE LEGS *(Chén Xin 1919: 105, 125, 111)*

Notes: from left to right: a) Major, b) Intermediate, c) Minor Shady channels are on the interior of the legs. The Shady channels correspond in position to flexor muscles such as the psoas and biceps femoris. Bubbling Spring (yôngquán) acupoint is the first acupoint on the foot, reading the bottom row from right to left, in c).

Foot-tips, extended and arched, point and tread. Knees and hips extend and flex, rise and drop. *Although application laws are unlimited, Shady and Sunny entry are spontaneously in oneness fixed.* When Form is coordinated, then Energy is not tugged or dragged. If Form is uncoordinated, then Energy is necessarily clogged and obstructed. In every place physically test, without overlooking the slightest detail, to contrive marvels.

> Notes: Tàijíquán Theory has: "Although its transformations have myriad ends, yet its logic is in one chain..." and "If double-weighted, then it is obstructed." Thirteen Dynamics Exercise has: "The entire body's idea is at essential spirit; if at Energy, it is obstructed."

II

11. Theory of the Head
論頭 Lùn tóu

The Head is round in the image of Heaven. It is the various Sunnies' assembly, contriving Essence and Marrow's sea (the brain). It is the interaction of Governor and Deputy meridians. It governs one body's Energy. Shady and Sunny entry and support altogether look to this. If this place is coordinated, then one body's Energy entirely enters. If this place is uncoordinated, then one body's Energy is entirely lost. Its Energy concentration's dropping point has one fixed place. You may not be unaware.

In Face-on Prone dynamics, to enter Sunny Energy, the Head must be prone and planted. Energy drops to brow and forehead interval *[gap or space]*. In Face-on Supine dynamics, to enter Shady Energy, the Head must be supine and lifted. Energy drops to brain posterior and occiput interval.

In Face-on Lateral dynamics, Shady and Sunny Energy both enter. The Head must be laterally planted. Energy drops to temples and ears' top. In Oblique Lateral Prone dynamics, for Shady and Sunny Energy obliquely to enter, the Head must be prone and aslant. Energy drops to temples and "sun and moon" (eyes) interval.

In straight rising dynamics, *"not partial nor leaning,"* neither prone nor supine, for Shady and Sunny Energy straight entry, the nose must be face-on and straight. Energy drops to the *Hundred Assembly* at the face-on crown-heart.

Again, you must know urging Energy laws, so as not to tug and drag. Thus, in Supine dynamics, to enter Shady Energy, chin lifts, chest must thrust up, abdomen must bulge out, hands must rise, feet must arch. Then the Triple Tips *[head-hand-foot]* being one Energy, Shady Energy naturally enters! In Prone dynamics, enter Sunny Energy, chin hooks in, back must bow, hands must drop, heels lift. Then the Triple Tips being one Energy, Sunny Energy naturally enters!

In lateral dynamics, Shady and Sunny together enter. Cheeks must lift, ribs must rise; one foot points, one foot drops; one arm rises, one arm thrusts. The Triple Tips being one Energy, Shady and Sunny together enter!

In straight rising dynamics, Shady and Sunny upward burst. Head must butt, shoulders relax. To arise and spring, you must arch feet and raise knees; then point toes and extend knees.[125] The Triple Tips being one Energy, Shady and Sunny both enter!

Lateral, oblique, prone, and supine may be deduced from these.

12. Theory of Hands
論手 Lùn shôu

Mr. Wú Chéng [1249–1333, leading neo-Confucian scholar from Jiangxi, who served under the Mongol Yuán dynasty] says:

> The hand has five fingers, fingers have three joints. Thumb's first-joint is hidden at the Thumb's interior: it is the image of Grand Polarity (Tàijí). Altogether there are fifteen joints. Both hands together add up to thirty joints in the image of a month's thirty days. The days in Winter are short, in Summer long. Spring and Autumn are equal.

> So Middle finger, belonging to the Heart-mind, rules Summer, being longest: it is Fire. Small finger, belonging to Kidneys, rules Winter, being shortest: it is Water. Index finger, belonging to Liver, rules Spring: it is Wood. Ring finger, belonging to Lungs, rules Autumn: it is Metal. These two fingers, being equal in length, are Spring and Autumn equinoxes.

> Thumb, belonging to Spleen, rules Earth. It flourishes through the four seasons, coordinating Four Virtues. It alone makes up one side. Therefore, if the four fingers are missing one or two, they can still hold objects. Without

the Thumb, they are of no use! It does not borrow, nor is compelled, it has heavenly cunning.[126] *[See Notes, below.]*

1) In finger laws, Inkslab Hand Energy drops to Little-finger outer edge; Vibration (dàng) Hand Energy drops to the rear of the palm. In these two hands, Five Fingers coordinate together as one piece, fingertips arching up. *[Chopping hands]*

 In all other hands, it is apt for five fingers' finger-joints to spread in a ring, arranged round in a circle, hooked and grasping like a bow. Energy then is raised up and concentrated, without dispersal. *[Claw hands]*

2) In vertical Opposing Hand and back Hook Hand, Thumb and Little finger mutually face to lead Energy. Water must join Earth: Heavenly One generates Water, getting Earth's Five to make Six. *[Beak hands]*

3) In level Shady Hand and level Sunny Hand, Thumb and Middle finger mutually oppose to lead Energy. Fire must join Earth: Earthly Two generates Fire, getting Earth's Five to make Seven. *[Thrusting hands]*

4) In supine Parry Hands, Thumb and Index finger mutually pair to lead Energy. Wood must join Earth: Heavenly Three generates Wood, getting Earth's Five to make Eight. *[Grabbing hands]*

5) In Shady Ward-off (pêng) Hand, Thumb, and Ring finger mutually pair to lead Energy. Metal must join Earth: Earthly Four generates Metal, getting Earth's Five to make Nine. *[Back handers]*

Thus of Metal, Wood, Water, and Fire, one without Earth may not be. If you know this, then fingers' mutual joining has a fixed, unalterable logic. If there is the slightest error, Energy does not enter!

As for applications, there are Nine Laws:

> *[cf. the Center in the* Tàijíquán Classic:*]*

1. Straight (direct) out, straight return.

> *[cf. the Four Sides in the* Tàijíquán Classic:*]*

2. Supine-up push and flick.
3. Prone-down sink and plant.
4. Outer-hook, outward deflect.

5. Inner-hook embrace and hold.

[cf. the Four Corners in the Tàijíquán Classic:*]*

6. Oblique push to right-above.
7. Oblique chop to left-below.
8. Oblique lead to left-above.
9. Oblique throw to right-below.

The Four Sides and Four Corners all straightly exit from the Middle road, and combine as the Nine Palaces.

Notes: **Five-Element Numerology and the Nine Palaces:**

This arrangement of hand techniques basically corresponds to the Four Sides in Pushing Hands, and to the Four Corners in Dàlyû of Tàijíquán. Most of the techniques and names above occur also in Tàijíquán, as does the use of the Five Actions for cardinal directions and center, below. "Uprooting" or "ward-off" (pêng), with joined thumb and ring finger, above, is noteworthy since it may be considered the fundamental dynamic in Tàijíquán. Aside from their metaphysics, Cháng's hand positions are grounded in practicality. The Nine Palaces are used in many boxing schools, e.g. Baguàzhâng, to map patterns of stakes or bricks to tread or interweave.

Magic squares were first revealed, according to legend, by a divine tortoise and horse, which emerged from rivers in central China. The Change Classic refers to the Luó River Writing and Yellow River Diagram.[127] *Odd numbers are Heavenly, even numbers Earthly. Each number from 1 to 5 is equated to one of the Five Actions: 1. Water, 2. Wood, 3. Fire, 4. Metal, 5. Earth, and so to the cardinal directions with Earth as center, and fingers with Thumb as center.*

Earthly (dì), as in "Heavenly and Earthly," is distinct from central Earth as soil (tû) of the Five Actions. Change's numerology uses Heavenly and Earthly to represent odd and even numbers, respectively. I amend Cháng's text where it confuses Earth's Five with Earthly even, or Heavenly odd Five.

The two diagrams below illustrate the Nine Palaces, from the Change Classic, *which I here interpret to illustrate Cháng's exposition of the five fingers, starting with the number 5 as central Grand Pole.*

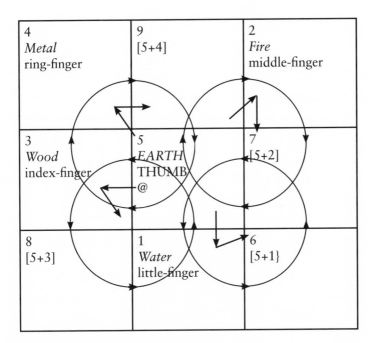

4 *Metal* ring-finger	9 [5+4]	2 *Fire* middle-finger
3 *Wood* index-finger	5 *EARTH* *THUMB* @	7 [5+2]
8 [5+3]	1 *Water* little-finger	6 [5+1}

DIAGRAM I: LUÒ RIVER WRITING'S DIAGRAM

All columns and rows of this square of numbers 1 to 9, with 5 in the Center, total 15. Numbers of the elements 1 to 4, added to 5, equal the next number: clockwise for even (Shady) 4 and 2; counter-clockwise for odd (Sunny) 3 and 1. These are the Nine Palaces.

This then forms a yinyáng double helix of clockwise and counter-clockwise spirals, like the "two-fish" Tàijí yinyáng circle, on opposing diagonals: (5+4=) 9 + (5+1=) 6 = 15; (5+2=) 7 + (5+3=) 8 = 15.

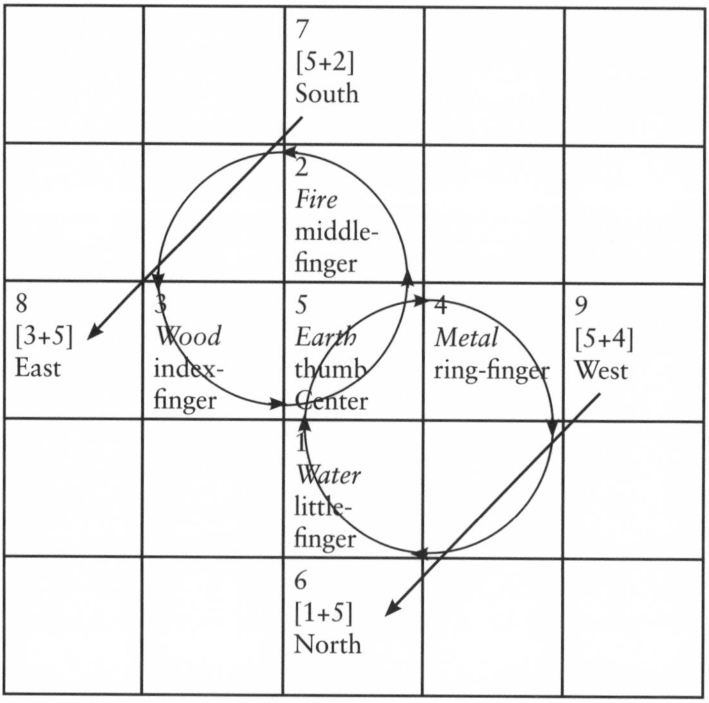

		7 [5+2] South		
		2 *Fire* middle- finger		
8 [3+5] East	3 *Wood* index- finger	5 *Earth* thumb Center	4 *Metal* ring-finger	9 [5+4] West
		1 *Water* little- finger		
		6 [1+5] North		

DIAGRAM II: YELLOW RIVER DIAGRAM

The inner numbers 1 to 4, on the cardinal sides, each added in turn to 5 in the center, give their corresponding outer number 6 to 9. Inner numbers plus Center total 1+2+3+4+5 = 15; outer numbers total 6+7+8+9 = 30. Grand total 15+30 = 45. This can produce a reversible "double fish" spiral or Shady-Sunny on opposing cardinals (South-East-West-North): counter-clockwise (5+2=) 7+8 = 15; clockwise (5+4 =) 9+6 = 15.

13. Theory of Feet
論足 Lùn zú

The ancients said: The head is round in the image of Heaven. Feet are square in the image of Earth. Again they said: Hands both cover and overturn in the image of Heaven. Feet cover, but do not overturn, in the image of Earth. They can support one body's weight, *"still as the mountain ranges."* They have boulder steadiness, moving like a boat's oars, without overtoppling's worries. Like Earth, they are pressed down still and immoveable; level, steady, and unswayable.

Their application has Vacuity and Substance. There is, of the two legs: one vacuous, one substantial. There is, of the two legs: forward vacuous and rear substantial; rear vacuous and front substantial. There is left vacuous and right substantial; right vacuous and left substantial. There is one foot's tip and heel, edge and instep, which should be vacuous and should be substantial. In general, if you are not substantial, you are not steady. If you are entirely substantial, then motion and shifting are inconvenient, so there will be over-toppling's disaster. If not vacuous, then you are insensitive. If entirely vacuous, then you are light, floating, and unsteady, so there is shaking and swaying's worry. Vacuity and substance mutually complement, only then can you get spontaneity's marvels. *[18; 30; 41; 57; 70:I-iii, II-i]*

> *Notes: Thirteen Dynamics Exercise has: "still as the mountain ranges" and "vacuity and substance need to be divided clearly...." Tàijíquán Theory has: "left is weighted, then left is vacuous; right is weighted, then right is ethereal... Sunny and Shady mutually complement...." Cháng analyzes weight distribution between the legs in greater detail than Tàijíquán Theory's "single-" and "double-weighting." The single foot itself is sub-divided into vacuous and substantial oppositions. Cháng's criticism of "entirely substantial" is echoed in the Tàijíquán stricture against double-weighting.*

Feet have extension and arching. When foot-tips extend, and downward enter, Energy downward descends, sinks and plants. When foot-tips arch and upward hook, Energy upward ascends and floats away.

They have sideways and straight-ahead. They have both feet parallel sideways; they have both feet parallel straight-ahead. They have T-sign (dīngzì 丁字) steps: one foot sideways, one foot straight-ahead. They have V-sign (bāzì 八字) steps: both feet slightly outward open, like the character for "eight." They have Goose-file steps, both feet half sideways, half straight-ahead, arranged the same in goose-file regularity.

There is wheeling and swinging. Wheels have half-spin wheels; laterally planted cartwheels; prone and supine, bottomless somersault wheels. Swings have outward swings and inward swings. There are stomp-kick and stamp-kick. Stamp-kick backward extends, stamp-kick forward exerts. There are toe-kick and side-kick. Toe-kick foot forward arches; side-kick foot sideways cuts. There are Twisting and Pounding: Twisting foot-tip rotation; Pounding foot heel vibration. They can urge and pack together one body's Energy.

> Notes: In Chén Tàijíquán feet-stamping against the ground—"vibrating feet" (zhènjiâo)—is employed to generate "shooting Power" (fajìng).

If body goes, but foot does not go, then it is tugged and dragged, and Energy is dispersed. How is it to support front-hand force? Front-hand force is at rear-foot. If rear-foot does not follow, body Energy does not enter. At most, it is only half-exerted. Energy does not fill up. The foot is a hundred bones' rudder, one leg's leader. If *slightly disconnected,* one body's Energy altogether does not enter! Stepping Laws' applications *may not but be carefully distinguished.*

> Notes: Thirteen Dynamics Exercise: "In the whole body every joint is inter-connected: don't allow the slightest interruption." Tàijíquán Theory concludes: "Students may not but meticulously discriminate."

In oblique dynamics, Forward Grab, use Goose-file steps, half-oblique, half-ahead. T-sign step, Forward Reach is T-step: front-step slightly lateral, rear-step completely straight-ahead. Backward Pull and Drag body is also T-sign step: front-step lateral, rear-step pointing straight ahead.

In small Four-Level dropping down, V-shape step feet-tips outward open. Straight body upward pressing, both tip-toe feet, together evenly extend. Feet back-tips go straight up vertically. Rising Spring step, one foot rises, one foot drops. Advancing step, rear-step first moves. Retiring step, front-foot first moves. Rising, you necessarily arch foot-tips. Dropping, you must extend foot-tips.

In Squeeze step lateral-body advance both feet side-step. In Squeeze step oblique-body advance, front-foot is lateral, rear-foot straight-ahead. In both, rear-step first moves. In Squeeze step advance, rear urges front. In Stealing step lateral-body advance, both feet side-step. In Stealing step oblique-body advance, front-step is lateral, rear-step straight-ahead. In both, front-step first moves. In Stealing advance, to bring up rear, front-step leads rear to pull the body. In Lateral-body retreat, two feet, both lateral, pull steps. In Oblique-body retreat, front-step is lateral, rear-step straight-ahead. They are both rear-step-led retreats, making front-foot pull backward.[128]

Rising Spring, Sideways Scissors: in left scissor, first move right-step; in right scissor, first move left-step. In Rising, arch foot-tip. In Dropping, extend foot-tips. Random Skipping has no fixed steps. Both foot-tips lift up and skip at will. *[10, 29, 64]* Twist step and Wheel Spin step are both on foot-tip; at the Dropping point, to foot outer-edges apply force. If you push me backward to retreat, both foot-tip points lift me up: you push me, but I do not topple. In Outward Embrace, front-foot plants. In Flexed Back Kowtow, both feet parallel are on tips, rigid knees. In Retreating Scissors, Chariot Wheel, feet extend tips, straight legs. You may not hook feet in retreat. In Energy Level, Open Stepping, both feet fiercely kick, level body, straight thrusts.

I roughly adduce the general to illumine variations. In conclusion: to follow dynamics is marvellous. Do not distort their Energy, do not oppose their Energy. Step law applications are thus obtained.

14. Theory of Fists
論拳 Lùnquán

Fists flex and do not extend. Grip the fingers firmly into a ball, concentrating their Energy. Their clenching law is with thumb-tip to pinch the opposite index finger third-joint's horizontal pattern. Four fingers roll tight and grip firm, all together applying force. You must cause them to be so they cannot be separated, and in striking cannot be dispersed. Only then do you coordinate orifices.

This is Earth connecting the Four Virtues: Five dynamics in a ball is concentration law. Its applications likewise have Four Cardinals and Four Corners, joined to the Central Palace: Nine Laws. *[12]* Its Energy does not spread over a whole body; its dropping point has a definite place. Follow dynamics physically to test. It may not be indiscriminately applied.

Thus, in:

Level-fist **down-plants:** middle finger second-joint leads Energy.
Level Sunny-fist **up-bursts:** middle finger root-joint leads Energy.
Lateral-fist **up-flicks:** thumb second-joint leads Energy.
Lateral-fist **down-chops:** little finger root-joint leads Energy.

No matter lateral or level, in straight bursts, little finger between root-joint and second-joint level-face leads Energy. When you understand this, the rest may be deduced.

15. Shady and Sunny, Rotation and Resolution theory
陰陽轉結論 Yīnyángzhuânjié lùn

Heaven and Earth's Way is not outside of Shady and Sunny. Shady and Sunny resolution issues from the Heavenly. So: "Stillness at its Pole becomes motion": Sunny continues from Shady. "Motion at its Pole becomes stillness": Shady succeeds to Sunny. Extrapolating to the Four Seasons: Autumn and Winter's passing connects to Spring and Summer; at harvest and storage's Pole, sprouting and generation follow. Spring and Summer's passing contacts Autumn and Winter; at sprouting and generation's Pole, harvest and storage follow. Shady necessarily rotates to Sunny. Then Creation's generation is complete. So it can generate generation (reproduce) inexhaustibly without any stops or rests.

> Notes: This is the Sòng dynasty neo-Confucian theory of "Grand Polarity" which Zhou Dunyí (1012–1073) and others extrapolated from Appendix I-5 to the Change Classic. According to Zhou Dunyí: "Without poles, yet it is the Grand Pole. The Grand Pole moves and generates Sunny. Motion at its pole becomes stillness. Stillness yet generates Shady. Stillness at its pole again becomes motion."[129]

Man is endowed with Heaven and Earth's Energy to be born, so he is a little Heaven and Earth. His dynamics are one Shady, one Sunny: rotation and resolution in successive contact. It is indisputable! So, high is Sunny, low Shady; supine is Sunny, prone Shady; extension is Sunny, flexion Shady; motion is Sunny, stillness Shady; face-on is Sunny, lateral Shady.

> Notes: Chén Xin writes on Tàijíquán's opening move Tucking in the Robe (lânjiayi; Yáng Grasp Bird's Tail): "Flexion is Shady, extension is Sunny."[130]

Dynamics if high necessarily drop to low: Sunny rotates to Shady. If you go high and higher, till you can go no higher, dynamics necessarily will not link, Energy necessarily will not be continuous. Dynamics if low necessarily rise to high: Shady rotates to Sunny. If you go low and lower till you can go no lower, dynamics will necessarily not link, Energy will necessarily not be continuous. Prone and supine, flexion and extension, motion and stillness, lateral and face-on are without exception all thus.

Among them are Shady again rotated to Shady; Sunny again rotated to Sunny. This one Energy being not Finished, again urge one Energy to supply it. It is not when Shady is Finished that you rotate to Shady; nor when Sunny is Finished that you rotate to Sunny.

Be enlightened to this: rotational pivots have fixed dynamics; contact and dropping have fixed Energies. There is nothing perverse or unreasonable, no tugging or dragging! Generally, dynamics slide rapidly and Energy flows smoothly at midpoints without intervening breaks. Once there is interruption, then you must start another furnace fire. In fact, if you seek speed, you conversely become slow; if you seek keenly, you conversely become dulled.

> Notes: "Finishing" (jìn) refers to the total discharge of Energy. [15; 17; 18; 22; 50; 54; 57; 69:15, et passim; 70:I-iii]

> Tàijíquán Theory has: "Supine ('look-up'), it is still higher; prone ('look-down'), it is still deeper." Thirteen Dynamics Exercise has: "one Energy ... are all thus." "Don't let there be broken continuity places ... be without the slightest intervening break."

16. Triple Tips Contrive Energy's Guiding Rope theory
三尖爲氣之綱領論 San-jian wéi qì-zhi ganglîng lùn

> Notes: The Triple Tips are head, hands, and feet. Sub-titles here are supplied by the present translator.

a) The Head
All affairs, if concentrated at one, are governed, because they have a ruler. Although there be a thousand or myriad threads quantity, in summary all go home by one track. As in marching an army there are the commander's plans; in governing the household there are the householder's rules. Only then, with unified Mind and co-operative Force, can affairs be achieved. To refine Form (body), refine Energy. Movement is the key to human-nature's fate: its Energy's leader, Energy's home resort: may it be unresearched?

> Notes: Thirteen Dynamics Exercise has: "It is ruled in the waist." Tàijíquán Theory has: "Though its metamorphoses are myriad, "One principle pervades them.'"

The Head is all limbs' junction, it leads one body's Energy. If Head does not coordinate, then one body's Energy does not enter! In prone dynamics, if Head is supine, then Sunny Energy does not enter! In supine dynamics, if Head is prone, then Shady Energy does not enter! In left-side prone dynamics, if Head is conversely twisted right, then right-half Shady and Sunny does not enter. In right-side prone dynamics, if Head is conversely twisted left, then left-half Shady and Sunny does not enter. Horizontal and vertical dynamics are likewise.

In straight rising dynamics, if the head conversely retracts, then lower Energy cannot ascend. In straight dropping dynamics, if the head conversely butts-up, then upper Energy cannot descend. In spinning right, if the head conversely looks left, then Energy does not enter right. In spinning left, if the head conversely looks right, then Energy does not enter left.

b) Hands [10]

Three Shady channels end at hands' interior, three Sunny channels start from hands' back. They open arm blood-Energy's paths; finger-law flexion and extension, concentrating and dispersing; hand and wrist prone and supine, extension and flexion. If once uncoordinated, then arm Energy does not enter!

When level Sunny-hands straight issue, yet conversely palms hook-hands, Energy does not enter. When level Shady-hands straight issue, yet conversely palms hook-hands, Energy also does not enter. When Shady-hands downward plant, with palms flexed, then Sunny Energy does not enter. When Sunny-hands upward burst, with palms flexed, then Shady Energy also does not enter.

When level Shady-hands forward press, with wrists hooked, then Shady Energy does not enter. When level Sunny-hands plant, with wrists hooked, then Shady Energy also does not enter. When lateral-hands straight hit, with crooked hands, then Energy does not enter. When lateral-hands sink to enter, with arched hands, then Energy also does not enter. The rest may be similarly deduced.

c) Feet [10]

Three Sunny channels end at the feet's back. Three Shady channels start at feet's underside. They contrive legs and hips, going to-and-fro on blood-Energy's path. If foot-tips, heels, outer edges, and insteps; ankles' extension or arching, inside and outside, once have any uncoordination, then body-Energy does not enter!

In supine dynamics, if kicking foot-tips extend, then Sunny Energy does not enter. In prone dynamics, if planting foot-tips arch, Shady Energy does not enter.

In rising dynamics' straight thrust, if foot-tips extend, then Energy cannot ascend.

In dropping dynamics' downward fall, if foot-tips arch-up, then Energy cannot descend.

17. Passing Energy theory
過氣論 **Guòqì lùn**

Dropping to a point, hard and rigid, fierce and courageous, invincibly, relies on whole body Energy. It entirely *Finishes in one place.* Yet some use it and Energy does not go, or Energy goes but is tugged and dragged. It is not smooth, because they still do not know passing Energy laws.

Generally, man's body Energy is shot from Fate's Gate (kidneys), Energy's source, and manifests at the four extremities. Energy's pouring and flowing channels throughout must have no obstructions. When there is no tugging or dragging, only then can it come and go smoothly and efficiently, nimbly and undetected.

Therefore, Upper Energy is at the lower: to enter low, do not drag it down. Lower Energy is at the upper: to enter up, do not obstruct it above. Front Energy is at the rear: it complies with the rear, so the front of itself enters. Rear Energy is at the front: it conforms to the front, so the rear of itself goes. Left Energy is at the right, so retain the idea at right. Right Energy is at the left, so retain the idea at left.

> *Notes: This explains the application of mutually antagonist muscle energies. As in Newton's law of motion, action and reaction are equal and opposite. Indeed, they support each other and when concentrated create a spring-like force. Thirteen Dynamics Exercise has: "If there is upper, then there is lower. If there is front, then there is rear. If there is left, then there is right. If the idea wishes to go up, first lodge a down idea."*

Thus:

> In Straight Smashing Hand, entering Energy forward, if you do not rein-in the rear-hand, projecting rear-elbow, Energy does not get to enter from the rear.
>
> In Up-Thrusting Hand, if lower hand does not thrust down and shoulders do not drop, Energy does not get to ascend from the ribs.
>
> In Divided Swing, if the chest does not close, [31] Energy does not get to enter backward.
>
> In Combined Embrace, if the chest does not open, Energy does not get wrapped forward.
>
> In Straight Rise, you must arch your feet.
>
> In Straight Drop, you must retract your crown.
>
> Left-hand Energy is at the right foot; right-hand Energy at the left foot.
>
> In Prone dynamics, Planting dynamics, and Forward Reaching dynamics, lift rear-foot heel.
>
> In Falling and Dropping, "sit" (bend) your arms.
>
> In Lifting dynamics, point your feet.
>
> In Planting and Knocking, do not arch the foot, fearing to be upward butted.
>
> In Kicking and Sweeping, do not extend your foot, out of concern for being downward dragged.

Extend and fill them, dynamic by dynamic, so they are all thus. Overall Energy drops home firm to one place. Energy comes not from one place. Just diffuse its sources, communicate its flow, then its road is smooth and efficient. Naturally, you will not get "at every step to make camp," or to tug and drag with no advance's problems.

> *Notes: "At every step to make camp" is a cautious strategy of consolidated advance, setting up fortified camps every few miles, described in the* Three Kingdoms Romance.[132] *It is the "blockhouse strategy" used by Chiang Kaishek in 1934 to uproot communist guerillas from their mountain base in Jiangxi, mocked in Máo Zédong's poem, causing Máo to lead the survivors on the Long March, westward and northward. Here it has the negative sense of clumsiness, and failure to advance smoothly due to excessive caution.*

18. Hard and Soft Mutually Complement theory
剛柔相濟論 **Gangróu xiangjì lùn**

Dynamics, without the Triple Tips, do not Drop. Energy, without Triple Exertions, does not Finish. This is what is meant by "Shady revolves around Shady midst one Sunny *[Abyss: ☵]*; Sunny revolves around Sunny midst one Shady *[Brilliance: ☲]*." Surely the Dropping place and Finishing place are Energy-concentration and blood-coalescence's stopping and homing locale.

When appropriate to use hard laws, intermix Sunny with Shady, so Energy and blood flow smoothly. When appropriate to use soft laws, do not deviate from this. If you purely use hard laws, Energy spreads over the whole body, tugged and dragged inefficiently. In dropping to a point, it will certainly not be valiant and furious. If you purely use soft laws, Energy is dispersed and unconcentrated, and does not go home firmly. In dropping to a point, it will certainly not be hard and rigid.

When you should be hard but are soft, Energy does not concentrate. When you should be soft but are hard, Energy does not diffuse. Neither gets "mutually complementary" marvels. So to be good at hard and soft is like "a dragonfly skimming water": one touch and it rises. Pass Energy like a wind-wheel (windmill), spinning and revolving, running endlessly. Hard and soft mutually complement, then you will be without shortness of breath's insubstantiality, clumsiness, and inefficiency's troubles. *[13; 30; 41; 57; 70:I-iii, II-i]*

> Notes: "Hard and soft mutually complementary" is a key concept in martial arts. (See Introduction: ii.) The penultimate hexagram of the Change Classic—hexagram 63, Completion (Jìjì: ䷾)—has alternating hard and soft lines of "fire" (☲) under "water" (☵). Thus, hard encloses soft in "fire," while soft encloses hard in "water," which are combined to restore the pure hard of primal Sunny "Heaven" (☰) in mystic alchemy.[133] Tàijíquán Theory has: "Shady and Sunny mutually complement." Thirteen Dynamics Exercise has: "Energy is like a carriage wheel."

19. Twelve-Joint flexion and extension to and fro:
Dropping Energy inside-outside, top-bottom, front-rear theory
十二節屈伸往來落氣內外上下前後論
Shí'èr-jié qushen wânglái, luòqì nèiwài shàngxià qiánhòu lùn

The Triple Tips are Energy's leaders. They are Energy's home resort places. Men merely know these three places should be hard and full, fierce and valiant. They do not know that the dropping point requires the whole body to be "hard and rigid as stone," so I can be unfearful of the enemy's bursting rush, and not worry whether I can resist it. *[Change Sinews Classic]*[134]

The means of its hardness and rigidity is from each bone's joints. Bone joints are empty cracks. They are the human body's streams and valleys. They are where Spirit's illumination flows and pours. These places, with Essential Spirit filled, are then *like iron or steel.* When you flex them, they cannot be extended; when you extend them, they cannot be flexed. Energy and force are then complete.

Arms have shoulders, elbows, and wrists: three joints. Legs have hips, knees, and ankles: three joints. Left and right combined they make twelve joints altogether. These are the body's major joints. The hand's capacity to grasp and the foot's capacity to step entirely depend on these. *Like a sandbag, gradually filled,* even a soft object may become hard and rigid. However, Energy drops following dynamics. It has: front or rear, inside or outside, top or bottom portions.

> Notes: *The* Change Sinews Classic, *attributed to Bodhidharma (c. 530), but only attested from c. 1700, quoted here, also prescribes sandbags as a tool for strengthening the body to make it like iron. [1; 24; 34; 50] Thirteen Dynamics Exercise has: "Extremely soft and supple, only then extremely hard and steely."*

Thus in:

a) Lateral-body, straight dynamics, double-hand **Forward Push:** elbow-heart (center) Energy fills up above; hand-wrist Energy arches up; shoulders both detach. Knees bend, backward protruding, Energy fills up behind; ankles extend, Energy filling up in front; hips both inward retract, Energy butts inside.

b) Lateral-body, double-handed **Down Chop:** elbow-hearts' Energy fills up ahead, wrists' Energy *Finishes* below; front-shoulder detaches down, rear-shoulder rising up. Front-knee flexes, butting kneecap; front-foot instep pointing to ankle, front-hip bending. Rear-knee extends; rear-foot ankle outer-edge stamps and rises up, rear-hip extending.

c) Face-on body forward pouncing, double-hand lateral, **Vertical Forward Hit:** elbow-hearts' Energy fills up to the center; wrists' Energy consolidates on the outside; shoulders both detach. Kneecaps forward butt, Energy consolidating in front; ankles flex and grip, Energy butting behind; hips flex and grip.

d) Low Four-level, double-hand **Level Lift:** elbow-hearts' Energy fills above, wrists' Energy fills up inside, shoulders both detach; knees separate to swing, Energy consolidates outside; ankle and insteps apply force, hips swing open.

The rest may be accordingly deduced.

20. Triple Tip Alignment theory
三尖照論 San-jian zhào lùn

Refining Form does not exceed motion and stillness. In motion, Energy is lifted up and undispersed; *"still as the mountain ranges,"* unshakeable: then you can go and come without hindrance. *Every time I see a vulgar student, in motion and stillness both unsteady,* it is surely because he has not researched whether his Triple Tips are aligned or not. If the Triple Tips align, you will have no east crooked and west aslant calamities. If the Triple Tips are not aligned, tugging here and dragging there, you will necessarily have swaying and shaking's faults.

Notes: "Triple Tip non-alignment" (san-jian bú-zhào) of nose, spear, and foot is listed in Qi Jiguang's Spear Manual (c. 1562) as one of three faults, together with incorrect stance of body-law and failure to thrust at the right moment.[135] *Triple Tip Alignment, a concept shared with Xíngyìquán, is fundamental to Cháng boxing and spear. Thirteen Dynamics Exercise has: "still as the mountain ranges." Tàijíquán Theory has remarkably similar sentence construction: "Every time I see someone of several years" pure practice who cannot maneuver and adapt, invariably letting himself be controlled by men, it is because "double-weighting's fault" has not been realized."*

[Stances:]

a. Like a Cross-sign, left foot in front, right hand exactly aligns with left-foot tip, head aligns with right hand. Then top and bottom being in one line, neither twisted nor slanting, are necessarily steady. *[8; 69:3, 7, 12a-b, 19b, 24; 72:17, 22]*

b. Lateral-body: right foot in front, right hand in front follows its dynamic. Head aligns with right hand, right hand aligns with right foot.

The rest are modeled on these.

21. Triple Tip Arrival theory
三尖到論 **San-jian dào lùn**

Triple Tip reach means Motion or Stillness together arrive. It is not: this first, that later; nor this fast, that slow. Mutually tugged and dragged, they will not arrive. Generally, when Energy takes men, its dropping point is just one tip. Yet just one tip's Energy is at the whole body. If one tip does not arrive, there is tugging and dragging: body-Energy does not enter! Self-refinement will naturally not be efficacious and speedy. In destroying (cuî) men, not to be hard and steely is all from this fault. All refining form requires you minute by minute to pay attention to these three places, so as to contrive coordination of orifices.

Notes: Thirteen Dynamics Exercise has: "Deploy power as if a hundred times tempering steel, so nothing hard is undestroyed... Minute by minute bear in mind...." [70:II-i]

22. Face Flesh Varied Colors theory
面[咽]肉變色論 Miàn[yan]ròu biànsè lùn[136]

Where this refined Energy is refined to completion's place, *True Prime,* filled sufficiently, from inside penetrates outside. Energy concentrates and blood coalesces to solidify in a block of symptoms.

True Prime is evidently the central acupoint in the lower abdomen, identical to Primal Sunny and True Unity Energy. *[—]*

Men's natal endowments, though one, yet receive Energies differently. From the Five Actions, they have Five Form, Five Nature, Five Color identities:[137]

a) So he who receives Wood Energy at birth, [38] his Form is lean and long, his Nature angry, his Color grey-green.

b) He who receives Fire Energy at birth, his Form is pointed and sharp, his Nature joyful, his Color red.

c) He who receives Earth Energy at birth, his Form is short and thick, his Nature melancholy, his Color yellow.

d) He who receives Metal Energy at birth, his Form is lithe and beautiful, his Nature sad, his Color white.

e) He who receives Water Energy at birth, his Form is fat and glossy, his Nature timorous, his Color black.

Where refined Energy is refined to the ultimate place, and *Finishing* place, there being nothing more to add, then exercise is complete, rounded, and full. True Energy is sufficiently filled. Energy at once retracts and coalesces. Energy stops, blood concentrates. Blood flowers in color. Energy and blood do not flow. Flesh and skin, following Energy, retract close to bones.

> *Notes: Blood flowering in color is a sign of health. Thirteen Dynamics Exercise has: "Energy adheres to the back, and is absorbed into the spine bones."*

Five Forms' True Energy is all manifested externally. Each, following endowment, is displayed. So there are green, black, red, white, and yellow: five types of Color. If there is one man in whom all five in combination are manifest, these Five Energies were in combination received, and Colors therefore are mixed in manifestation.

If one body is cold as ice, this is because the True Sunny is entirely retracted into the Central Palace and does not penetrate externally. If you understand this, then you know that flesh of the face follows Energy's coming. Color variation follows Energy variation, issued from the Heavenly (nature). It is no illusionist technique.

Notes: This section's psycho-physiology, derived from (Jìn) Huáng Fûmì (215–282), resembles Galen's theory of the four humors of cold, hot, wet, and dry, based on the elements of earth, fire, water, and air that came to dominate the medicine of Rome and medieval Europe.

23. Activating Energy theory
行氣論 **Xíngqì lùn**

These, in Crossing Hands, are knowing the road's laws. When hands once attack, Energy takes one side. It cannot on four sides both together take. If force straight attacks, lacking lateral force, I intercept it laterally. If it attacks laterally, lacking straight force, I intercept it straight. Upward attacks, lacking downward force, I flick them up from beneath. Downward chopping, lacking upward force, I hit them from above. Oblique and face-on, flexed and extended, without exception are thus. This is the "pound vacuity" law.[139] "Attack where he is undefended." *[Sun Zî]*[140]

Notes: Here is the art of combat, "crossing hands," drawing on the ancient military classics, chiefly Sun Zî (c. 500 B.C.). They correspond closely to the concept of dynamic "single-weighting" in Tàijíquán. They utilize nature's inherent imbalance of forces: "Energy takes one side."

If I attack and he uses these laws, I do not return hands; I just rotate hands to urge the Second Energy to hit him. If he again converts, I again rotate hands to urge the Third Energy to hit him. This is ambush law, "issue where he does not expect." *[Sun Zî]*[141] You just must control his active Energy, so you can enter the target.

Generally, when his Energy comes, before his Energy ceases, I ride and destroy it. It may be east or west, no matter left or right, I meet its source. Its Moment is just at one movement. If he moves, I instantly move. *[44]* He has no leisure to contrive force. If I wait for him not to move, and then move, he on the contrary will ride my activated Energy! In this there is no room for a hair's breadth. Students should pay attention.

> *Notes: Thirteen Dynamics Exercise has: "If he slightly moves, I myself first move." Tàijíquán Theory has: "...what is called "out by a hair's fraction, wrong by a thousand lî." Students may not but carefully distinguish."*

Let him be furious and valiant, Energy is always partial:
For This to have, and That to lack, is Heaven's nature.
Straight intercepts cross-wise oh! Cross-wise intercepts
     straight.
First Energy urges Second, Second urges Third.

Let him, with slippery speed, go back by the far road:
Protected myself, in ease and safety, I naturally "stick and
     link."
If you ask: whence comes this marvellous maxim?
It is just at activated Energy's one move's interval.

> *Notes: Chén and Yáng Tàijíquán's Hitting Hands Song urges: "Let him with great force come to hit me ... Touch, stick, link and follow, don't let slip or butt." [26]*

24. Face Section, Five Action theory
面部五行論 **Miànbù wû-xíng lùn**

Anger moves Liver oh! Sound moves the Heart-mind,
     [blood]
Nostrils flare, breath urgently shoots Lungs' Metal.
     [oxygen]
Lips open and purse to stimulate Spleen Energy. *[saliva]*
Brows frown, a pure oblation from Kidneys pursuing.
     [adrenaline]

Notes: Saliva is swallowed, moistening the throat and aiding digestion. The eyebrows frown in concentration to release adrenaline from the kidneys.

The Five Action Energies internally correspond to the Five Organs:

Liver corresponds to Wood,
Heart-mind corresponds to Fire,
Spleen corresponds to Earth,
Lungs correspond to Metal,
Kidneys correspond to Water.

Externally they communicate by Seven Orifices. Eyes are Liver's orifice; ears are Kidneys' orifice; mouth is Spleen's orifice; nostrils are Lungs' orifice; tongue is Heart-mind's orifice. Their Essential flower pours to the eyes. Five Colors divide as the Five Mountain Ranges. Forehead is the Southern Range, colored red; occiput is the Northern Range, colored black; left cheek is the Eastern Range, colored green; right cheek is the Western Range, colored white; nose bridge is the Central Range, colored yellow.

Notes: The Five Ranges are China's ancient holy mountains, representing gods of the five directions.

Again, eyebrows, assisting life, belong to Liver's Wood. Nostrils, communicating breath, belong to Lungs' Metal. Eyes, concentrating Essence flower, belong to Kidney's Water. Tongue, governing sound and note, shot out from the Elixir Field (dantián) *[50; 52]*, belongs to Heart-mind's Fire; Lips, governing intake, belong to Spleen's Earth.

Altogether, one movement interval's dynamics do not exceed flexion and extension; Energies do not exceed retraction and release.

In the Face, the Five Actions form images. Likewise necessarily follow their mutual correspondences, then you will get Energies' mutual combination marvels.

[Energy Vocalizations:]

So, in retractive compression dynamics, Energy from limb joints is retracted and collected into the Central Palace. At the Face, eyebrows must frown, eye pouches must retract, nostrils must flare, lips must purse, Energy must inhale, the sound must go *"yi."* This is internal Energy's retraction and form's image's concentration.

In expansive detached dynamics, Energy from the Central Palace shoots out to limb joints. At the Face, eyebrows must relax, eyes must protrude, nostrils must distend, lips must open, Energy must exhale, the sound must go *"ha."* This is internal Energy's release: its external image is open.

> *Notes: These vocalized yi and ha sounds may be compared with sounds prescribed in Tàijíquán, such as the eight sounds of Lî Yìyú's "Hitting Hands, Discharge and Release, and the Yáng transmission's "Hold firm the Elixir Field to refine internal exercise: Heng and ha, two Energy, marvels are inexhaustible."*[142]

Pay attention to thorough refining. Internal Energy follows the external, external form corresponds to the internal. When internal and external are as one, hard and rigid as stone, then use induction laws. First with hands slap it, next with fists hit it, last with stones bag and wooden club strike it. From light to heavy, gradually inducing, gradually substantiating *[cf. Change Sinews Classic]*. Naturally you will not worry about the Face being without Energy!

Vulgar students do not realize. They say you make a god's head and face, a weird appearance to scare men. How could they contrive to become "penetrating the Primal, attaining the Principle" knights!

> *Notes:* Change Sinews Classic *similarly advocates use of massage, "stones bag" and "wooden club" to toughen the body, starting from the abdomen, by progressively intense pounding over two hundred days, yet, in contrast with the above, never mentions the face. [1; 19; 34; 50]*

25. Concentrate essence to assemble spirit, Energy and Force Source theory
聚精會神氣力淵源論 **Jùjīng huìshén qìlì yuānyuán lùn**

> *Notes: The generative sequence is "**Essence**" jing > "**Spirit**" shén > "**Energy**" qì > "**Force**" lì. The first three, Essence-Spirit-Energy, are the triad of Daoist meditation and medicine.*

Spirit is Energy's soul brilliance: this means Spirit transforms into Energy. Energy without Essence is not transformed: this means Energy again tranforms into Essence! In general, man at birth receives pre-Heavenly Spirit to transform into Energy. He accumulates Energy to transform into Essence and complete this Form body. After birth, he relies on post-Heavenly water and grain liquids to transform into Energy. He accumulates Energy to transform into Spirit. It coalesces in the Elixir Cauldron, meets in the Yellow Court [Spleen]. [1; 34; 62; 69:7]

If the magic ["soul" líng] brilliance does not leak, its adamantine courage is invincible. It is Internal Elixir's ultimate treasure, Energy and Force's root and origin. Therefore, Energy is formless, belonging to Sunny and transformed by Spirit. Blood has matter, belonging to Shady and transformed by Essence. Spirit is void; therefore, if its magic brilliance is unleaked, it transmutes inexhaustibly. Essence is substance, therefore it fills up and solidifies, hard and rigid, invincibly. Spirit necessarily borrows Essence, Essence necessarily adheres to Spirit. When Essence and Spirit join as one, Energy and Force are then generated.

So it is known that Energy and Force means Essence and Spirit's ability to overcome things. *Without Essential Spirit, there is no Energy and Force!* Martial defense knowing this just strives to concentrate Essence to meet Spirit, so as to strengthen Energy and Force. Yet they do not know how Essence is concentrated, how Spirit is met. They expend their whole life Heart-mind and Force but find nowhere to start from. They do not know that Spirit by Energy is met; Essence by Spirit is concentrated.

> Notes: Thirteen Dynamics Exercise: *"The whole body is concentrated at essential Spirit, not at Energy. If at Energy, it is impeded. He who has Energy lacks force; he who nurtures ["lacks"] Energy is pure adamant."*

If you wish to seek Essence concentration and Spirit assembly, if you do not concentrate Energy you will be unable. Concentration's law is just for the Grain Way [anus] to contract, and Jade Stalk [penis yùjīng] to retract, causing lower Energy entirely to be raised up, and not run down. Pluck Heaven and Earth's Energy and with full force inhale, causing upper Energy entirely to return below and not upwardly disperse. Down and up congeal together, completely concentrated in the Central Palace. Then Energy concentrates and Essence congeals. When Essence congeals, Spirit assembles. Naturally from inside to outside, there is nowhere that is not hard and rigid! This is what the South Forest Virgin meant by: "Inwardly consolidate the Essential Spirit." *[45]*[143]

> Notes: *This exact line, from the South Forest Virgin in the Hàn dynasty historical romance* Wú and Yuè Spring-Autumns, *is used by Tàijíquán's Thirteen Dynamics Exercise.*

You must just refine every day, and soon contrive a root. Only then can you use it to go forward, so nowhere is not hard and rigid. Otherwise, you will be like a gun without gunpowder, or a bow without string and arrows: barrel empty, with nothing to shoot. Then, if you wish to seek valiant ferocity and fast speed, sea-flipping and mountain-toppling, dynamics that are irresistible, you will necessarily be unable. This, in refining Form and refining Energy, is most necessary: be careful of it and secrete it. On no account recklessly divulge it, or you will incur Heaven's banishment.

26. Get the Gate to Enter theory
得門而入論 Démén -ér rù lùn

There is a saying: "The Buddha has outer gates. If you do not enter the outer gates, you are then a gate outsider (layman)."[144] Generally, in boxing to destroy an opponent one must approach his body so as to be able to topple him. Just as things are stored in a room, so one must find the gate to gain access to them. Otherwise, even though one has divine ability, it is no use.

Hands have three gates. Wrists are first—this is the great gate. Elbows are second—this is the half-way gate. Upper-arm roots (shoulders) are third—this is the inner gate. Then you approach the inner courtyard and can "ascend the hall" to "enter the chamber"! *[Confucius:* Analects*]*[145]

So, if you cross hands only at the Wrist, the opponent can draw back or extend, moving at will and without limit. Then hands nimble will win, and hands slow will lose. You will never be able to destroy an opponent and knock him down with a touch.

> Notes: *Tàijíquán Theory* states: *"Have force hitting lack force, hands slow yielding to hands fast: is entirely pre-natal, natural force, and is unrelated to study's force."* The distinctive phrase *"hands slow ... hands fast"* echoes Cháng's *"hands nimble ... hands slow."* The idea of each writer is parallel: skill can overcome speed.

He who pays attention to the Elbow has advanced a further stage, but the opponent can still move. You cannot control the power of certain victory unless your eyes are fixed on his upper-arm root (shoulder). No matter whether he attacks first or I attack first, just at this point focus attention. I meet firm his arm, sticking and linking inseparably. Following my transmutations, as I wish deploying, there is naught but as I wish. He naturally cannot escape out of my range.

> Notes: The three gates are wrists, elbows, and shoulders as in *Tàijíquán* pushing hands and *dàlyû*. *Tàijíquán Theory* has: *"This in general does not go beyond hands slow yielding to hands fast...."* [38] *Tàijíquán's Hitting Hands Song*: *"Let him with great force come to hit me ... Touch, stick, link and follow, don't let slip or butt."*[146] [23]

27. Lead hand and second hand, front- and rear-hands theory
頭手二手前後手論 **Tóu-shôu, èr-shôu, qiánhòu shôu lùn**

Outsiders ("outside the gate"), on entering hands mutually to compete (xiangjiao), make many false moves. Through having ten faults, they cannot get victory:

1. Before crossing hands, to be unable to concentrate Energy for the future, empty chested without anything. Energy is shot neither fast nor furiously. This is the first fault.

2. Not knowing to place hands under the chest, so as to watch for sudden attacks above and below. This is the second fault.

3. Before crossing hands, setting up a dynamic first, with empty gaps clearly visible. This is the third fault.

4. Using dodging dynamics to advance, not daring directly to advance, "*to discard the near to go afar*, to be labored and not at ease." [*Huáng Shígong*]¹⁴⁷ This is the fourth fault.

5. When advancing, necessarily to step up crossing body to change dynamics, wide and not honed. This is the fifth fault.

6. To cross hands only at the wrists, not knowing to advance the body. This is the sixth fault.

7. To let pass the lead ("head") hand without hitting. This is the seventh fault.

8. The second hand, having been caught firm, still not to hit. This is the eighth fault.

9. Only after third or fourth hands, to burst and hit. This is the ninth fault.

10. To duck and dodge out of contact, without *sticking* and *linking* (nián, lián). This is the tenth fault.

> Notes: These hints define the art of close combat. They explain the importance of getting in, adhering to the opponent, and not wasting an opportunity to strike directly. [31; 69:15; 70:I-ii] Tàijíquán Theory similarly has "Many wrongly "discard the near to seek the far.'" Hitting Hands Song urges: "Touch, stick, link and follow...."

If you have these ten faults, when crossing hands, how can you not be defeated? Before you cross hands, concentrate Energy and collect spirits, setting your hands crossed below your chest. See which of his feet is in front, then stick close to that side of his body. Focus your attention on the root of his upper arm, and control the root of his upper arm. This is the law of dodging behind the gate, to await his activity.

If I issue the first hand, I extend it towards his upper-arm root. Having won the first hand, I do not wait for the second hand. If he issues the first hand, I likewise get to his upper-arm root. There is no need to look to his other hand. Then if he bursts to hit, he will be late and transmuted! This law is the art of *deflecting an inch to make him miss by a foot.* Aim for his upper-arm root. If at this point you deflect by an inch, his hand will be over a foot.

> Notes: *Tàijíquán Theory borrows a similar line from Hàn dynasty Change Classic apocrypha: "Out by a hair's breadth, wrong by a thousand lǐ."*[148]

The wonders of: "pounding the empty gap";[149] "issuing where he does not expect, attacking where he is undefended" *[Sun Zǐ]*;[150] "swift thunder allowing no time to cover the ears" *[Tàigong; Qi Jìguang]*[151] are all at these.

Sometimes you meet nimble hands retiring in a flurry of blows. I don't exchange hands nor bend upper arm, but urge on second Energy to hit him. If I strike his left, he retires his left and advances his right. I do not pull back my hand but shift to strike his right *[text: has "left"]* upper-arm root. I am at the circle interior, he at the circle exterior. *[Shàolín Staff]*[152] I am "at ease; he labors." *[Sun Zǐ]*[153] Though slippery and quick, he will not escape the trap. This is the secret of lead hand striking lead hand. At times you also bring up the back hand. This is using what it is fit to use, not what you are compelled to use. When what is unfit to use is still used, then movement invariably brings the body across. Every time I see one use this and get hit, it is invariably because he has not seen this fault.

> Notes: *Chéng Chongdôu's 1616* Shàolín Staff *pioneered this terminology of the circle's interior and exterior in relation to the span of an opponent's weapon.*
>
> *Tàijíquán Theory has: "Every time I see ... one of himself by others controlled, it is because double-weighting's error has not been realized."*

28. Ignition Energy theory
點氣論 Diânqì lùn

> As if from dreamland in a jolt startled,
> As if realizing the Way by sudden awakening;
> Like skin accidentally burnt by a fiery spark;
> As cold invading pores makes one shiver,
> Is Thought's actual scenario.
>
> Exceedingly fast and furious.
> Original True Energy flows out thick:
> Vibration's Thunder rapidly shoots,
> *Brilliance*'s Fire smokes and blazes.

Notes: Sudden awakening is characteristic of Chán Buddhism enlighten-
ment. [70:I-iib] Vibration (☰) and Brilliance (☲) are trigrams that
together form hexagram 21, Chewing (Shìhé: ䷔), of the Change
Classic. *Combining images of thunder and lightning, it is a metaphor*
for law enforcement and the harsh penal system.

Vulgar students, not having realized the Prime Central Orifice
[dantián], cast it aside to search elsewhere. How will they get
awakened? This takes men's flesh: it is hard and rigid, irresistible.
Its Form deeply enters the bone marrow, severing blood plasma
(róngwèi). Whatever Energy takes always hurts. When it hurts, it
does not communicate. Its logic is such. It can sever Energy and
blood's way, causing it not to connect. Obstruction of Energy
and blood's circulation causes it not to flow through. It may part
bones and cut sinews, bringing about death in an instant. Energy's
applications are great!

You just need to understand its accumulation, know its shooting,
and apply soul in its use. Only then can it enter the bow span, as
if shooting a bull's-eye. Correct your bodily form, "not partial nor
leaning" *[1; 4; 9; 11; 36]*, like an arrow straight, flight feathers
evenly balanced. Concentrate Central Energy—spirit coalesced,
Energy filled. Like opening a bow, loosing and drawing, square
and circular. Pull full, so aiming with spiritual valor that you may
transfix a willow leaf and "penetrate seven layers of armor."[154] That
is at Discharge and Release (safàng).

Notes: Champion archers Panwâng Dâng and Yâng Yóuji in Chû, in 575 B.C., are reported to have shot through seven sets of armor. Thirteen Dynamics Exercise: "Store Energy like opening a bow, shoot power as if releasing an arrow." Yáng Family "Discharge and Release: Secret Maxims" has four key-words: "Raise-up, Draw-in, Relax, Release."[155]

So Energy is shot like a gun ignition, like a "cross-bolt leaving the string." *[Sun Zî]*[156] It abruptly reaches. If you familiarize yourself with these words, naturally you can get mind-responsive hands' marvels. On no account take this as idle talk and pass it over.

"I call this *['zealous wife's']* Essence and Spirit's ultimate *[Jî Yún has: 'Sincerity's ultimate']*. I by no means consider it strange. Surely, where Spirit pours, Energy immediately concentrates there. Where Energy concentrates, Spirit also coalesces. Spirit Energy having coalesced and concentrated, Image is immediately generated there. Where Images radiate, traces immediately appear there. The living's Spirit Energy moves Here; the dead's Spirit Energy responds There. The two, mutually combined, thereupon resolve into this Form. So it is said: 'From the Mind are generated Images.' Again it is said: 'If there is utmost sincerity, then metal and stone for it will break *[Jî Yún has: 'open']*'"[157]

Notes: The above concluding paragraph is taken verbatim, unacknowledged, from a collection of supernatural tales on ghosts and female fox-spirits by Jî Yún, published in 1800. It was identified by my friend Dr. Ulrike Middendorf. The story in question tells how, after the death of her husband, a woman hanged herself in their bedroom. The living image of her late husband was then found imprinted on the wall. Yet neither of the two could paint, nor had others entered the room.

Jî Yún explains such "miracles" by the pseudo-science of Energy-response. The importance given to "utmost sincerity" in Mèng Zî and Great Learning made it a corner-stone of Confucianism.[158] *Hán Ying of early Hàn writes: "At a valiant knight's one shout, three armies all giving way is the knight's sincerity." He relates how Xióngqú of Chû, travelling at midnight, saw a tiger and shot it. On inspection, the "tiger" turned out to be a recumbent rock, which his arrow had penetrated right up to its flight. "The stone for it opened up."*[159] *Amazed, he shot another arrow at the rock only to see it bounce off. This was because he no longer had the sincerity.*[160]

A century or so earlier, rationalist philosopher Xún Zî (c. 315–235 B.C.) simply listed a recumbent rock taken for a tiger as a case of mistaken identity, due to faulty sense-perception. If Xún Zî knew the whole story, he evidently did not consider its spiritualist aspect worthy of comment.[161]

Du Mù (1459–1525), who visited Shàolín in the 11th month of 1513, is the first writer to note the Shàolín martial arts tradition. He remarks of a curious stone there, which appeared to reflect Bodhidharma's image: "So they say, Essential Sincerity may penetrate metal and stone."[162]

PART B
MARTIAL DEFENSE
武備參考 *Wûbèi Cankâo*

III

29. Boxing Laws' Source: Introduction
拳法淵源序 Quánfâ yuanyuán xù

Now boxing is surely not "gods appearing, demons vanishing dynamics." *[c.f. Chéng Chongdôu: Shàolín Staff]*[163] All men from birth onward, before three weeks pass in play time, can move laterally and face-on, prone and supine, high and low. They extend and flex, level stride and random point *[10; 13; 64]*, advance and retire, stamp and kick. Each kind of dynamic is invariably brought out. Regrettably, they cannot interconnect to fill them out.

I myself followed teachers over forty years, constantly making timely experiment, somewhat opening up obstructions, remotely thinking on latent mutual combinations. Only then did I understand what the Book *[of Mencius]* says:

> *[The Way is like a high road. How is it hard to know? Men's problem is in not seeking it.]* Sir, go home and seek it. You will have a surplus of teachers.[164]

Truly, this is no deception!

Now, among my comrades are many men who from me study and practice. Therefore I plainly speak, writing it down, so they may easily enter. Now I take *Hitting Laws*, setting them out as follows. This forms my introduction.

Notes: Cháng, in stating his aim to demystify martial arts, appears to cite—and take a passing swipe at—Chéng Chongdôu's (1616) Shàolín

Staff *for religious supernaturalism. Cháng here emphasizes the role of the individual student, in experimenting and thinking, to seek his own instruction.*

30. Coordinated Refinement of Central Twenty-four Dynamics
合煉中二十四勢 Héliàn zhong Èrshísì-shì

Coordinated Refinement Laws are refined form's fifth-level training (gongfu).[165] They are Form and Energy coordinated in one practical law. They include rising and dropping, high and low, lateral and straight-on, prone and supine, oblique slant and twist. Each has a fixed law. Summarizing their dynamics, there are 72 to match the *[five]* 72-day seasons. Extrapolating their dynamics, there are 360 to match the 360 degrees *[5 × 72 = 360]*. 360 are excessive and difficult to practice. I merely select their essentials to make 72. I further separate them into three, as high, mid, and low, each with 24 to match the 24-day Energy periods *[3 × 24 = 72 of the Chinese agricultural calendar]*.

> *Notes: Five basic elements of Cháng's system that I can enumerate are: Essence, Spirit, Energy, Form, and Coordination. Chén Zengzhì and Chén Wànlî cite ten levels of Cháng Boxing. Within this, the mid-range Twenty-four Fists "Central Dynamics" correspond to fifth-level gongfu; high-range "Floating Dynamics" are sixth level; and low-range "Sinking Dynamics" are seventh level. As for the higher levels, these must await future revelations.*

High Twenty-four Dynamics have rising, springing, flying, and wheeling. Low Twenty-four Dynamics have ground-level rolling and ducking. Central Twenty-four Dynamics have neither rising and springing, nor ground-level rolling and ducking. The Central Twenty-four are surely man's endowment from Heaven and Earth's Shady and Sunny Energy at birth. Their ascents and descents from Low to High, High and again Low, are the Triple Talents' *[Heaven-Man-Earth's]* arrangement by natural logic.

While rising springs and groundwork, beginners cannot precipitately practice, yet just these Middle Twenty-four Dynamics, though unable to exhaust the Central Dynamics' variations, yet from these entry of hands may be contrived the beginner's first step. To practice them feels remarkably easy. According to the postures refine them completely, then take the High and Low's Forty-eight Dynamics to refine thoroughly. Thus, Extraordinary and Regular transmutations naturally reproduce without end. Then, why must you memorize more set routines, to make months' and years' burdens?

Before this, refine legs, refine arms; refine hands, refine feet; refine head, refine shoulders; refine elbows, refine body. Refine Internal Energy, refine induction of Energy, refine primal Energy. These various explanations all have separate refinement laws. As for head, hands, and feet—what are their coordination laws? When dynamics already rotate and contact—what are their linking laws? When should they be hard, when should they be soft—what are their applications' laws?

Without experiencing this stage of discussion and research, and this stage of experimental refinement, the Triple Tips will not align, and will not drop firm and steady. If the Triple Tips do not reach, This is ahead, That behind. Shady and Sunny conflict; Energy is discontinuous. Hard and soft are upside down: tugged up and dragged down. To be "steady as Grand Mountain, nimble as a wily hare" is impossible.

Overall, the Form (body) is to lodge Energy. Energy is to urge Form. When Form is coordinated, Energy is naturally effective. When Energy is effective, Form is naturally nimble. They are not two affairs: they do not borrow and lend. As refinement's laws, dynamic by dynamic, are exhausted, so the Triple Tips are coordinated. In motion and rest check that the Triple Tips completely align. Shady rotates to Sunny; Sunny rotates to Shady. Do not disconnectedly place, separately start furnaces.

Be soft passing Energy; hard dropping to a point. Each must mutually complement, and thus never lose sequence. *[13; 18; 41; 57; 70:I-iii, II-i]* If upper Energy is below, lower Energy above, analyze their tugging and dragging. If front Energy is behind, rear Energy in front, resolve their obstructions. Dynamics, without the

Triple Tips, do not drop. (*[original commentary:]* Head, Hand, Foot) You must make the Triple Tips drop to a point. Energy without Triple Urgings does not reach. If it does not reach Triple Urgings, do not issue hands. (*[original commentary:]* Heart-mind, Spirit, Energy) In killing dynamics *[attack]*, discern their variations. In rescue dynamics *[defense]*, check out their comprehensivity. Like this, refine onward.

"When familiarity peaks, skill is born."[166] Do not lose the rules. By Spirit illuminate them, and keep them in person. Yet worldly refiners of Form are not illuminated to this, the final achievement of refinement laws and entry hands' applications. Further, they do not fathom these central details, so reverse and oppose them. They apply force in plenty, but achieve little. How could they know that this research is the Internal Elixir's root foundation? It is Heaven and Earth's precious secret. To the wrong man, do not transmit; at the wrong time, do not transmit; at the wrong place, do not transmit.

Of those who obtain my Way, the great may use it to "return to their root source, and transcendentally ascend." The small may use it to strengthen sinews and bones, repelling disease and extending years. You do not merely "chop the hard and break the sharp"[167] to complete this art, and nothing more. All my comrades should be diligent and careful, treasuring and secreting it. Do not divulge it to the wrong men, so as not to incur guilt and Heavenly retribution, or be ungrateful for your teacher's painstaking mind.

> *Notes: Here the author, in a personal note, explains that spiritual enlightenment, then health, is the highest goal of martial arts. "Transcendentally ascend" refers to the Daoist ideal of physical ascension to Heaven. The phrase "chop the hard and break the sharp" derives from an ancient expression for soldiering: "wearing the hard (armor) and grasping the sharp (weapon)," as used in the poem of Chén Wángtíng (seventeenth century), founder of the Chén martial lineage.*[168]

> [INDENTED COMMENTARY]

To refine Form, coordinate Energy. To refine Energy, return to Spirit. To refine Spirit, go home to Void. Form is hands and feet, the organs and skeleton. Energy is Shady and Sunny in circulation. Spirit is Mind's magic marvel. Touched off, it immediately shoots. Resonating, it subsequently communicates. Void is No Pole (Infinity, Wújí). Shady and Sunny are rooted in the Grand Pole (Tàijí). "Grand Pole is rooted in No Pole."[169] Ultimate Non-being encloses Heaven and Earth's ultimate Being. Ultimate Void encloses Heaven and Earth's ultimate Substance. It is not associated with "color or image" [rûpa];[170] It is not caught by "net or noose."[171] If in traces you seek it, you lose it! Do not apply force, then you can induce out natural (spontaneous) force. Moreover, you may conveniently rotate and exchange, and not reach shooting difficulties.

Notes: "Grand Pole (Tàijí) is rooted in No Pole" derives from Sòng Confucian Zhou Dunyí's "Without Pole, yet the Grand Pole." Tàijíquán Theory begins: "The Grand Pole Without Pole is born." The above elevation of Void is close to Chén Xin (1919), who goes on to quote the Buddhist Heart-mind Sûtra: "Color (form, rûpa) is void; void is color...."[172] Whereas Tàijíquán Theory dismisses "natural" (zìrán) force as simply innate ability, in favor of learned skill, the above commentator seeks to tap it spontaneously, by not using conscious force. This is the paradox of studying to be spontaneous. Ultimately the two opposites meet.

[INDENTED COMMENTARY]

This explains the Twenty-four Words' starting dynamic. [69:1. Shady] These Twenty-four Words are just one Energy. Every dynamic must have Energy. It concerns all these Twenty-four Words. However, in application, following in response to transformations, there are differences. The Twenty-four Dynamics are all intake Energy laws. Intake of Energy by head and face will be described. All intake of Energy from the head and face makes its start. Its essential is in rotation in four circles: left to right rotates one circle; right to left rotates one circle; front to rear rotates one circle; rear to front rotates one circle.

In general, furrow the brow and dilate the nostrils, upper lip retracted back, lower lip pointing forward, like an elephant arching its trunk. *[48]* The saying: "Intake Energy as if swallowing a stream" *[35; 52]* applies to this. Overall, it is like the mouth swallowing an object. With full force once inhale, then Energy intake is sufficiently solid to fill up front and rear, left and right in four circles, adapting to dynamics spontaneously. Each dynamic only has one circle. It is not every dynamic having four circles.

31. Theory of Beginners' Entering Hand Law
論初學入手法 **Lùn chuxué rùshôufâ**

All beginners, at entering hands time, should have both shoulders loose and lively: they must not be stiff and hard. Both elbows should be inwardly linked and downward: they should not circle outward. Foot-tips should grip the ground: they must definitely not be flat set. Flat setting makes rising feet inefficient. Front-foot must smoothly forward step, solidly, with foot-tip point on the ground. Back-foot must be obliquely set, but not too solid as to cause the whole foot to tread the ground.

As for the head, it follows dynamics. If they rotate to Sunny, it is also Sunny. If the dynamic is Shady, it is also Shady. If the dynamic is neither Shady nor Sunny, the head likewise is neither Shady nor Sunny. If the dynamic obliquely twists, the head likewise obliquely twists.

> *Notes: Cháng favors a light step, weighted on the toes or ball of the foot, not spread evenly over the whole foot as taught in much contemporary Tàijíquán. The head turns according to the dynamic of each individual technique.*

Hands, left and right, flexed or extended, adapt to men's dynamic, whether far or near, in deployment. There is really no fixed rule. In general, adapting to men's hands, far or near, high or low, my hands follow, high or low, flexed or extended. Only legs' flexion and extension have a fixed rule. The front leg definitely may not be too flexed. If too flexed, it deviates into kneeling knee. Again, it may not be too straight. If too straight, it may be faulted as straight and hard.

Notes: Cháng warns against over-extension and under-extension of the legs, as in Tàijíquán Theory; but not of the arms. This may be considered inconsistent.

Rear-leg straightness or flexion looks to step-law, big or small. In big step-law, rear leg freely unfolds: only then can force be applied outward. In small step-law, rear-leg flexion or straightness with front-leg flexion or straightness makes little difference.

The body being prone or supine also entirely looks to step-law, being big or small. In big step-law, the body must be slightly obliquely forward, in half-lateral dynamics. In small step-law, the body should be set at the two legs' center. It must also be in a half-lateral dynamic.

Triple Tip Alignment is nose-tip, hand-tip, and foot-tip, above and below, all aligned. Triple Tip Arrival is eyes, fists, and feet, none first nor last, all together arriving. Triple Coordination is feet, hands, and eyes mutually coordinated.

In all issuing hands, no matter adopting which dynamic, or hitting men in what place: my eyes and spirit's focus, hands hitting, and foot-tips advancing, should altogether advance, and altogether arrive. All hitting dynamics, no matter which dynamic, should hit men forcefully and steadily. Front-foot, whether at men's feet inside or outside, should with foot-tip struggle to advance to his body's rear. Only when Triple Tips into alignment drop are they good.

As for the theory of Opening the Gate, without distinction of left or right dynamics, my wrists' hard bony place thrusts onto men's elbow front soft flesh, and forcibly chops it, in "axe chopping wood" manner. If I take men's upper arm and chop down, my fists follow its contact. Only then will I get the dynamic, and men will be unable to slide out of it.

Notes: "Axe chopping wood" also describes Xíngyìquan's Chopping Fist (piquán). [69:12]

Dropping to a point's actual appearance is:

Head like a dragonfly skimming the water,
Fists like a mountain goat butting its head,
Feet are purple swallows entering a forest.
[49; 69:11b]

Dropping to a point's logic is exactly like:
Cloud-center struck thunder and lightning.

Shooting's dynamic Moment is like:
A crossbow-bolt leaving the string. *[Sun Zî]*[173]

Only if students immerse their Minds to apply force will they enter expert subtlety's realm.

> *[INDENTED COMMENTARY]*

> Beginners should not speak of refining Energy. First make body-laws, steps, and eyes coordinate. Also, you may not employ Force. You should adapt to dynamics naturally, slowly wheeling and dancing. Strive to let the outer form be comfortably set as one family. Next make it light and mobile, rounded and fluent. Rotate joints, balanced and steady, one by one according to posture. Dynamic by dynamic, unfold and loosen. Let joint by joint, bones and frame, place by place relax and open. Only then do you get to the marvellous. *Every day altogether do one hundred repetitions.*

[I re-position the above paragraph's last sentence here from Nourish Energy, where the rest of this paragraph was repeated and where I now delete it.]

> Notes: *The emphasis on natural relaxation and flow, the ban on attempting to refine Energy in initial stages of practice, not employing force and having a daily routine, strike chords with Tàijíquán.*

[I further re-position the following paragraph from the end of 33, Twenty-four Fist, where it does not fit.]

Intercept and blocking laws do not go beyond four words: Open (kai), Close (hé), Flick-up (tiâo), and Crush (ya). After deflecting and blocking, directly enter. Outward deflection (bo) is to Open. Inward deflection is to Close. Upward deflection is to Flick-up. Downward deflection is to Compress. Forward advance is Direct Entry. These "Open" and "Close" are not refinement of Energy's open and close. Don't mistake them.

Notes: The four deflections are: inward, outward, upward, downward. Tàijíquán Theory lists Five Actions as left, right, forward, backward, and fixed. Energy's opening and closing, from the breathing, is here distinguished from the limbs' opening and closing. Direct entry, defined here, is a key concept. [27; 69:15; 70:I-ii]

32. Theory of "Correct Energy"
論正氣 **Lùn zhèngqì**

Notes: Unattributed paraphrases and quotations comprise this section.

[Mencius:]

The Will unified shakes into motion Correct Energy. Energy ultimately moves the Will. Rub and polish, holding to the Will. "Be good at nourishing Expansive Energy. Extremely hard, extremely great, it fills Heaven and Earth's interval." Human nature receives from it.[174]

[Poetry Classic:]

"Twisting, turning,
Waking and sleeping,
I think on her."[175]

[Zhuang Zî:]

"Great it is with nothing outside,
Small it is with nothing inside."[176]

[Central Norm:]

It is "pervasive yet hidden" oh! hidden yet pervasive.[177]

Notes: Mèng Zî, "Mencius," c. 300 B.C. of (Shandong) Zou, preached that human nature is good, and described a psycho-physical Energy and valor springing from "Righteousness," yì. He further says: "What you do not get in Mind, not to seek it in Energy is permissible ... Hold your will, do not violate your Energy ... The Will unified moves Energy; Energy unified moves the Will...."[178] Change Sinews Classic: "Internal Strength Theory" quotes, with explicit attribution to Mèng Zî, the very lines used above.[179]

Southern Sòng patriot Wén Tiānxiáng (1236–1283), refusing to submit to Mongol conquest, wrote a famous Correct Energy Song in prison, where he died. Yú Dàyóu (1503–1579), general and martial artist who defeated Japanese pirates, entitled his writings "Correct Energy" Hall Collection.

[*Yú Dàyóu:* Sword Classic:]¹⁸⁰

a) "A thousand words, myriad sayings" conclusion is: Entice his old force to pass by, while new force is not yet shot out, and ride it."

b) "Resonate (xiâng) and then advance; advance and then resonate. If this is discriminated clearly, then one may speak of skill."

c) "Make your staff head penetrate his staff head underside, either from left side once rising and shaving, or from right side once rising and shaving. You need to have resonance as gauge. Overall, it is one logic."

d) "[*On commencing hands,*] always recognize the staff, do not recognize the man. This saying is most apt. [*As for "recognize the man, don't recognize the staff,' theory, this is when his staff is already defeated, just recognize the man to subdue him.*]"

e) "On no account be greedy to hurt him. To await his move, for me to move again is permissible. [*Either on contact, or flicking up, advance and go to hurt him.*]"

f) "If I enter and am by him hit, [*feeling defeated,*] then rapidly to jump into retreat is strictly taboo."

*Notes: Qi Jìguāng reproduces Yú's whole Sword Classic, with attribution. The above six maxims are selected from its final section.*¹⁸¹ *"Resonance" (xiâng) denotes the sound of a "beat" in fencing against an opponent's weapon to exploit their resistance.*

33. Twenty-four Fist tablature—introduction
二十四拳譜序 Èrshísì quánpǔ: xù

At Hûláo [*Pass, on the mountain road south to Shàolín*], Zhang Ba, by the age of thirty, had studied the arts of spear, saber, sword, and halberd. There was none in which he was not expert. His Divine Fists' Twenty-nine Dynamics (shénquán: èrshíjiû-shì), no one in the world knows. Alas![182]

Notes: Zhang Ba's biography (Introduction: xii) identifies him as active in late Míng (c. 1630). He has some resemblances to the mysterious Jiâng Fa of Chén Tàijíquán tradition.

If a man knows them, he is not necessarily in practice high; and the high do not seek for men to know. Rather they just fear lest men should know. Should someone know, it is indeed no different from not knowing.

When young, I had a strong craving for the martial. In my schooling's leisure, I had no time for other tasks but exclusively in "whirling and dancing" (wûdâo) made my recreation. Though my elder-brother frequently admonished, private lessons were ultimately impossible to give up. Yet, to transmitted teachings having no gate, obstructed on east and west [*"leaving the near to scheme for the far"*], I labored without result[183] and was deeply ashamed of having no accomplishments.

Ten years later I met, in the Hénán prefecture of Luòyang, Yán Shèngdào, who pointed out one or two things, and I rather felt I had made progress. After another ten years, I got Word Boxing's Forty Laws (Zìquán sìshí-fâ). From my own ideas I added thirty items to make a total of seventy examples. Nevertheless, it was too many to remember. So I reduced them to twenty-four, giving them names and indicating their vital points. This allows the student conveniently to practice them. Afraid of "gluing down the tuning-frets to play zither," and dissatisfied with their inflexibility, I used clear winter leisure to take the twenty-four and expand each one, dividing into eight, in a combined total of one hundred and ninety-two. Vertical and horizontal, extraordinary variations are therein all provided. If the world has one who knows, he may not necessarily be pleased. Should they sink and disappear, to the end of my life I will have no regrets.

Notes: I re-position the final paragraph here in Xú Zhèn's edition to the end of 31, above.

34. Nourish Energy theory
養氣論 Yângqì lùn

Now Energy above communicates with the Nine
    Heavens,
Below communicates with the Nine Pools,
In the middle it spreads across Nine Continents.
There is nowhere it is not, nowhere is it unconnected.

Secrete it in one Heart-mind,
Fill it to circulate one Body.
To shoot it has a Way.
For the essentials, one must get its secrets.

Though Six Faculties govern Energy, Energy is all shot from Five
Organs. Though Five Organs secrete Energy, Energy in return all
exits from Six Faculties. Six Faculties—where are they? They are
above. The Five Organs—where are they? They are below. Between
above and below what thing is there? One calls it: *Yellow Bedroom*.
Another calls it: *Prime Pass*. A third calls it: *Grand Polarity
Chamber*. A fourth calls it: the *Way Trunk Pivot*.

> *Notes: Yellow Bedroom (huángfáng) here is distinct from Yellow
> Compartment. A mystic work on internal spirits of the body, attrib-
> uted to Lady Wèi (c. 300), is entitled* Yellow Court Classic, Huángtíng
> Jing. *Chén Wángtíng (seventeenth century), in his celebrated poem on
> creating boxing sets for his offspring, names this volume as his con-
> stant reading.*[184] *[1; 25; 62; 69:7] "Prime Pass" is a taboo substitute
> for "Mystery Pass" (xuánguan).*

Filling above, it contrives Heaven's Pass. (Masculine Qián, as
South, contrives the Head.) Its extremity below contrives Earth's
Axle. (Feminine Kun, as North, *[contrives the Abdomen.]*) Heaven's
Pass issues from Lunar Cave *[west]*. Earth's Axle shoots from
Heaven's Root *[east]*. Within the Lunar Cave and Heavenly Root's
gap, it *[the sun]* comes and goes, and the Thirty-Six Palaces have
springtime.
    Energy shooting is like water flowing. One exhalation is a thousand
lî, one inhalation a thousand lî. Its marvels reside in exhausting the

Heart-mind. Energy collects, entering into the Spirit Chamber (the Yellow Bedroom), hard as adamantine, round as a rolling pearl, square as a set-square. It is shot from the Head, having Five Actions' portions. It centers in the body, having Shady and Sunny distinctions. Five Actions need to follow Shady and Sunny (Shady and Sunny interact). Shady and Sunny, revolving from one Energy, complete "utmost greatness and utmost hardness" *[Mencius]*.[185] Heaven and Earth cannot contain it. This is what is meant by *[(Sòng) Chéng Hào's]*:

> The Way, communicated from Heaven to Earth,
>   has something at Form's exterior.

> *Notes: Chéng Hào (1032–1085), of neighboring Luòyáng, was a pioneer of neo-Confucianism, which drew on Buddhist and Daoist metaphysics to develop the holistic theory of Tàijí, "Grand Polarity." Here is Chéng's whole stanza:*[186]

> *...Myriad things, in tranquility contemplated, all self-fulfill;*
> *The Four seasons, in excellence arising, with Man identify.*
> *The Way communicates from Heaven to Earth something at Form's exterior:*
> *My thoughts enter windy clouds' transmogrified shapes midst....*

What this Book says of refining Energy is all "External Strength" laws. As for "Internal Strength," it is in the *Change Sinews Classic*. *[1; 19; 24; 50]*

[I omit here the paragraph for beginners, which was repeated from the end of 31, above, q.v.]

> *Notes: This is the sole mention of the* Change Sinews Classic, *Yìjîn Jing, by name. "External Strength" and "Internal Strength" are its chapter titles. Cháng in his opening chapter maintains that his Central Energy combines both external and internal. [1] It may be that the* Change Sinews Classic *here refers to Cháng's own Part A on cultivating Energy, above, while "this Book" simply refers to the present Part B on martial defense. If this comment is by the author himself, it is odd that he should use a different title.*

[INDENTED COMMENTARY]

Above it is at "Brilliant" (Lí Trigram) *[☲]*,
Below at "Abyss" (Kân Trigram) *[☵]*.
Brilliant's center void *[_ _]*, at Crown's Limit *[head]*, is
    Shady;
Again, Abyss' center filled *[__]*, at Fate's Gate *[kidneys]*,
    is Sunny.
The Central Palace, below the navel, is the Yellow
    Bedroom:
Shady and Sunny's interchange and meeting place.

Heart-mind is Ruler Fire; Fate's Gate Deputy Fire.
When Ruler Fire moves, Deputy Fire follows it.
Ruler Fire is master, Deputy Fire assists it.
Fire's liver Energy is Sunny:

Abyss Palace's [☵] Sunny Energy [__]
from the back, passes to the front;
from below, it ascends above.
Brilliant Palace's [☲] Shady Energy [_ _]
from above descends below.
Two Energies interact in the *Central Palace,*
so Energy concentrates!
When Energy concentrates, Force is generated!

Notes: *This refinement of Energy theory relates to breathing, explained
in 37, below.*

35. Refined Energy's secrets
煉氣訣 Liànqì jué

Energy by the Heart-mind contrives the Body.
(Energy must follow the Mind)
Heart-mind by Energy contrives applications.
(Mind can deploy Energy)
Five Actions root in one Heart-mind.
Shady and Sunny have no partial weighting.

Above and below they circulate one body.
Sectional positions are each different:
Forward is Sunny, and backward Shady;
Supine is light, and prone weighted.

Notes: Tàijíquán Theory has: "Be lively as a carriage wheel: Partially sunk, it follows; double-weighted, it is obstructed." Thirteen Dynamics Exercise has "Energy like a carriage wheel." Cháng uses "partial weighting" in the negative sense of unbalanced, whereas Tàijíquán employs it to mean able to pivot round a point.

Shady returns to the Shady place to resolve.
Sunny returns to the Sunny place to move.
Above originally is Shady's beginning. (That is *Brilliant
    Palace*: ☲)
Below is Sunny's fulfillment. (That is *Abyss Palace*: ☵)

Above and below solidify in the Center.
Central Energy is extremely hard and rigid.
Circulating above, it surges to Heaven.
Circulating below, its dynamic is like a mountain.

Notes: Thirteen Dynamics Exercise has "extremely soft and supple, only then extremely hard and rigid (jianyìng)."

Left destination requires right resolution.
Right destination requires left pull.
Forward advance is like flowing water,
Above hitting is like lifting a mountain.

Dropping to a point is like a flying rock:
Moment in shooting is like "crossbow bolt leaving the
    string." [Sun Zî][187]
Energy is shot like wind's sound;
Energy's "intake is like swallowing a stream." [30; 52]

Advance like stars pursuing the moon;
Retreat like a tumble-weed's rotation.
Fingers should hook in connected application.
Both shoulders move like scissors.

Above and below, one Energy coalesces:
People are enriched, the nation naturally secure.
If you understand these secrets,
To refine them is naturally not difficult.

All one body's advance and retreat, motion and stillness,
from Heart-mind contrives mastery. Heart-mind is ruler, issuing
commands. Heart-mind has no form. Just because it has no form,
so it can form, and not be formed by form. By ideation it is known.
From Fate's Gate, it contrives support. Fate's Gate is where Energy
is generated. It is one body's trunk pivot. It is the prime minister,
transmitting the ruler's orders. With the head, it leads hands and
feet. The Head is the multitude ministers' manager, governor, and
field-marshal. It commands great ministers' category. Hands and
Feet are the ministers who handle a hundred affairs. Therefore, in
every dynamic's restraint and relaxation, retraction and shooting,
Heart-mind is first. Fate's Gate is next; the Head is again next;
Hands and Feet are yet again next.

> Notes: Fate's Gate, the mìngmén acupoint between the kidneys, is
> equivalent to Central Energy and Grand Pole here. Thirteen Dynamics
> Exercise has: "Heart-mind contrives the command-pennant...."; "The
> chief-minister is at the waist."

[INDENTED COMMENTARY]
Spirit moves, Heaven follows:
Purely empowering the self-so [natural].
(If you once twist and fabricate, it is gouging!)

Restraint and relaxation are at the hands,
Transmutations from the Heart-mind.
Follow the Moment to move;
Human force does not participate.

36. Receive, Balance, Uplift
承停擎 **Chéng, tíng, qíng**

Heaven and Earth having intercourse,
A myriad things are born.
(Shady and Sunny exchange. They exchange, and force is
   born.)
"Not partial nor leaning," *[1; 4; 9; 11; 28]*
Energy is evenly balanced.
(Therefore dynamics are not voided.)

For a thousand autumns, a myriad years,
Constantly lift and concentrate:
Having just harmonious coordination,
One Energy communicates.

37. Liver Rises, Lungs Drop
肝起肺落 **Ganqî fèiluò**

Ending and beginning Myriad Things are Spring and
   Autumn:
Shady and Sunny ascend and descend as one Energy's
   circulation.
If you wish to understand liver rising, lungs dropping:
Just at exhalation and inhalation midst seek.
(Liver is Wood, Lungs Metal. One Energy is the Two's
   interaction, meeting at the Central Palace.)

Surely Liver belongs to Wood, so it can generate Fire. Liver's Fire
moves, so Energy from below ascends above. It is Sunny (*Abyss* ☵
trigram's Sunny —). Energy from which force is born. So Energy and
force's root source is at Fate's Gate Central Pole. Therefore it is said:
Sunny Energy resides below.

Lungs belong to Metal. Metal overcomes Wood. Therefore it can
squeeze Liver Energy and cause it to descend below. Descending is
Shady (*Brilliance* ☲ trigram's Shady _ _). Therefore it is said: Shady
Energy resides above.

Resident below, Energy is shot in motion unstoppably: thus Sunny Energy *ascends* above. Resident above, Energy is confined and not allowed to escape: thus Shady Energy *descends* below. The Two Energies interact in the Central Palace. Therefore they are called Central Energy.

> Notes: *I understand this to be an alchemic explanation of reverse abdominal breathing, whereby abdominals contract on inhalation, and relax on exhalation. Thus, Sunny Energy of inhalation ascends the back from Fate's Gate (mìngmén) between the kidneys, and from the liver. Shady Energy of exhalation descends to the abdomen's Central Palace (dantián) below the navel. In terms of the* Change Classic, *the two final hexagrams 63 Completion ䷾, fire under water, and 64 Incompletion ䷿, water under fire, alternate as exhalation and inhalation respectively.*

38. Old and Young Mutually Follow
老少相隨 Lâoshào xiangsuí

(Between hits, one Energy, not even slightly delaying, is called "Following.")
Young follows old, oh! Old follows young:
Old and young, mutually following, are naturally
    marvellous.
Unified heart-mind, coordinated idea, once together shoot:
(Speed, speed, speed: Hands fast hit hands slow.) *[26]*
What fear of other men's many cunning tricks?
(Speed is being "last to shoot, first to reach." *[Sun Zî]*[188] Ride his gap to move: borrow his Energy already activated, and his dynamic not yet stopped. Meet the Moment to shoot: the more speed, the more marvellous.)

> Notes: *"Old" and "young" refer to forces spent or latent, in a cycle of striking. "Following" is a key component also of Tàijíquán's art of sticking hands. "Borrow his energy … meet the Moment to shoot" is echoed in* Thirteen Dynamics Exercise: *"Moment from the self shoots; Force is from men borrowed"; and Yáng "Discharge and Release: Secret Maxims": "Lift clear his body, borrow his force."*[189] *[38; 53; 70:I-ii, II-ii] "Speed" here is desirable not in striking per se, but in reactively utilizing an opponent's force to return it to him. [26]*

39. Theory of Hands and Feet
論手足 Lùn shôuzú

Issue hands, as if detaching shoulders, inside joining
  elbows;
Left and right support and aid, like flowing waters.
Strike, moving head and tail, as one thread arising:
In Hitting Laws, what need is there for Uproot, Pull, and
  Hook? (pêng, pan, gou) *[41]*

40. Shady and Sunny Rotate and Resolve
陰陽轉結 Yinyáng zhuânjié

Shady revolves to Sunny, oh! Sunny revolves to Shady:
Shady and Sunny's resolution mutually share a root.
If you wish to know Shady and Sunny resolution's cause:
Still for Shady and Sunny's resolution place search.

41. Theory of Hitting
論打 Lùn dâ

I straight issue, he Uproots, Pulls, and Sends (pêng, pan,
  sòng); *[39]*
Against Uproot, thrust; against Send, kick; against Pull,
  use Lift.
"Hard and soft mutually complement," like a wheel
  rotating,
Just as, unintentionally, a blazing fire sparks.
[13; 18; 30; 57; 70:I-iii, II-i]

*Notes: Attack and defense, hard and soft mutually complement, as in
Tàijíquán pushing hands. Tàijíquán Theory has: "lively as a carriage
wheel...."*

42. Theory of Deflection
論攔 Lùn lán

If he strikes left, oh! I strike right,
What need in one place bitterly to seek?
If vertical comes, horizontally deflect, bold as lightning:
I receive, he sinks, then just use throw.

43. Agility and Speed Application Laws
捷快用法 Jiékuài yòngfâ

(Eyes do not get to blink before a gun's ignition moves.)
    Lazy and more lazy, relaxed and more relaxed:
    My Energy, still unmoving, is like a sick dotard.
    Suddenly, one sound of spring thunder moves:
    A thousand chariots, ten thousand horses into battle burst.

44. Hitting Laws: General Secret
打法總訣 Dâfâ zôngjué

If he does not move, oh! I do not move:
If he is about to move, oh! I first move. *[23]*

*Notes: This Secret recurs almost verbatim in Tàijíquán's Thirteen
Dynamics Exercise. [47]*

45. Discussion of Issuing Hands
講出手 Jiâng chushôu

"Inwardly consolidate essence and spirit,
Outwardly show peace and calm.
Appear like a virgin,
Attack like a ravenous tiger.
He who gets my Way
With one can stop a hundred."

*Notes: This is a quotation from the South Forest Virgin, who allegedly
taught this handfighting method to King Goujiàn (c. 500 B.C.) of Yuè
(Zhèjiang) to prepare him for the battle to reclaim his kingdom.*[190]
[25] The opening couplet recurs in Thirteen Dynamics Exercise.

46. Discussion of Hitting Laws
講打法 **Jiâng dâfâ**

a) In all lateral and face-on dynamics, one should put the body at the two legs' center. The Triple Tips must into alignment drop. One may not let this be before, that behind.

b) Both legs may not be too wide. Both hands may not reach too far. If too wide, then rotation of the body is not efficient, and you can hardly avoid toppling and tripping's disaster. If you reach too far, then rotation of joints is not efficacious, and lower dynamics are not generated.

c) The word "hitting" is like Chángshan's snake dynamic: [Sun Zî][191]

"Hit its head, and the tail responds.
Hit its tail, and the head responds.
Hit its center. then head and tail both respond."

Notes: Hengshan, "Constant Mountain," was also named Chángshan to avoid imperial taboos. It was traditionally venerated as the Northern Range, Bêiyuè, home of the god of war and water, symbolized by a snake, perhaps the one described above by Sun Zî, entwined round a tortoise. The shrine was officially sited in Quyáng (Hébêi), until the Qing dynasty, which relocated it to a mountain near Dàtóng, Shanxi.

47. Discussion of Igniting Energy
講點氣 **Jiâng diânqì**

Before Energy moves, oh! Mind first moves:
After mind moves, oh! Energy then bursts.
The Mind's movement is like a cannon's fire;
Energy's arrival is like a bolt from a crossbow.
If students comprehend primal whole Energy,
What need to fear that others have perfect skill?

Notes: The opening couplet is a corollary of Hitting Laws: General Secret. It anticipates Tàijíquán Theory. [44]

48. Intake Energy
納氣 **Nàqì**

Head and face upward raise, so the throat's Energy easily enters. The mouth's upper lip upward slightly retracts, the lower lip forward pouts, like an elephant arching its trunk. *[30]* Both small eye-corner channels downward embrace up to the corners of the mouth.

The back spinal channel from the waist goes up, past the crown of the head, to the mouth's lips. In front center, it goes from below straight up to the mouth's lips.

> Intake of Energy's form is just four circles:
> From left to right, revolve one circuit.
> Right to left, revolve one circuit.
> From below to above, revolve one circuit.
> From above to below, revolve one circuit.

Head and face's form is like this. Overall, adapt to the punch's dynamics in applying them.

49. Theory of External Form
論外形 **Lùn wàixíng**

The head is the body's leader. The body commands the arms, the arms command the fingers, and Fate's Gate is the body's trunk-pivot: *[cf. 31]*

> Head is like a dragonfly, skimming the water
> Fists like a mountain goat, butting its head.
> Waist is like a cock crowing, tucking-in its tail.
> (If tucked-in, Energy from rear to front is collected and not
>   dispersed.)
> Feet are like purple swallows, entering a forest. *[31; 69:11]*
>
> Groin (dâng) is open in front, closed behind, and in the
>   middle rounded.
> The head's Hundred Assembly Acupoint is at the crown;
> Bubbling Spring Acupoint is at the foot-heart; *[behind
>   ball of foot]*
> Assembled Shady Acupoint *[perineum]* is between the
>   two excretions.

Hundred Assembly Energy downward concentrates;
Bubbling Spring Energy upward raises;
Assembled Shady Energy supports one body.
Ascending and descending Energy all collects in the
    Central Palace. *[dantián]*

This is coordination.

> *Notes: Fate's Gate is behind the Elixir Field (dantián) near the body's center of gravity. I take "roll-up" juân of the cock's tail to mean "tucking-in." I treat the comment that follows as an interpolated note, though it is not signalled as such in the received text.*

50. Three Energies coordinated as One Energy
三氣合爲一氣 **San-qì héwéi yi-qì**

The initial dynamic, before crossing hands, first concentrates Energy. To concentrate Energy, ruler fire moves, deputy fire assists. From behind the waist, it collects in front: Sunny Energy from below upward bursts into the chest diaphragm. The mouth intakes Energy, from the lungs dropping: Shady Energy descends, entering into the Elixir Field (dantián). *[24; 52]* Shady and Sunny interact in what is called Liver rising, Lungs dropping. This is called: "as one coordinated, two dynamics."

> *Notes: This describes generation of Energy by "reverse abdominal breathing." The intake of breath starts by lifting the diaphragm, "rising from the liver" to inhale from the mouth, then "dropping from the lungs" to exhale, as if pushing air down to the lower abdomen. The first Energy is inhaled and exhaled, the second just inhaled, and the third is just a total exhalation. "Sunny" fresh air is pictured rising and "Shady" stale air falling within the body. Tàijíquán Theory describes it: "Energy sinks to the Elixir Field."*

The whole body together forward advances. Lower Energy again upward surges. Mouth again once takes in Energy, taking it in to above the navel and below the heart. Upper body downward once collects. The whole body's bone joints, joint by joint, are packed firm. Strive to make them hard and solid. The body, though furiously and valiantly advancing forward, upper arms and hands are both backward squeezed. It is named "Turn-Around." Turn-Around is half-coordination. Like this, then, dynamics advance and Energy is still more concentrated! Generally, when the whole body forward pounces, hands again Turn-Around, so bone joints naturally can squeeze tight, "hard as iron or stone."[192] [Change Sinews Classic] This is Second Energy.

Approaching the dropping-point time, if you feel force is insufficient but have no chance to Turn-Around, again making bones and flesh to one place compress is named "to Finish." This is called Third Energy. Like a gun, the tighter it is loaded, the more resonant and forceful it is.

On beginning practice, first study Concentration; then study Turn-Around; last study Finish. When trained force is ripe, the Three Energies coordinate as One. Only then do they have applications. When coordinated, there is no place uncoordinated. When opened, there is no place unopened.

Notes: Late Míng dynasty Chéng Chongdôu's Shàolín Staff, which is combined with spear technique, has "Finish" Head spear thrust: "Back-hand pushes spear-butt, straight to chest-front." There is also a "Finish" take-down to the ground as prelude to a flanking maneuver.[193] [15; 17; 18; 22; 54; 57; 69:15, pass.; 70:I-iii]

Triple Urging power is characteristic of Xíngyìquán. Here the hard metaphor of the Change Sinews Classic applied, not statically, but in the compression phase, prior to release, as with gunpowder. [1; 19; 24; 34] Thirteen Dynamics Exercise has a similar structure: "Once moving, nothing is unmoved. Once stilled, nothing is not still."

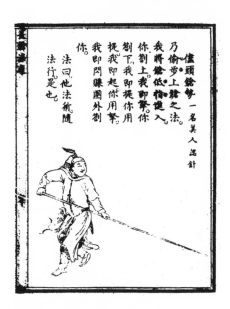

他起槍頭滾勢一名美人認針

FIGURE 14: FINISH ENERGY IN SPEAR FIGHTING

Finish Head Spear dynamic from Chéng Chongdôu's (1616): *Shàolín Staff.*

Finish (jìn) in spear action refers to decisively grounding an opponent's spear or staff, stealing a step to circle round and take him in the rear. It is also known as "Beautiful Lady Discerns Needle" (Mêirén Rènzhen), a pun on "every man in earnest." The first version depicting a monk is from a reputedly secret copy; the second shows a Míng spearman in dress uniform, with leopard cummerbund. (Xú Hèlíng 1930: 96, Matsuda 1975: Chángqiangfâ xuân: Líhua Liùhéqiang: 39 (8); (Míng) Máo Yuányí (1594–c. 1641) 1621: Wûbèi Zhì 89: Shàolín Gùnfâ Chánzong: 47 (41). [cf. FIGURE 23; 69:9]

Upward is Sunny, downward Shady;
Stillness is Shady, motion Sunny;
Retreat is Shady, advance Sunny;

Energy upsurge is Sunny, downward intake Shady.
Back is Sunny, abdomen Shady;
Issuing hand is Sunny, return hand Shady:

You may not cling to one in theory.
Supine is Sunny, prone Shady.
Be soft in passing Energy,
Hard in dropping to a point.

51. Big and Small dynamics explained
大小勢說 Dàxiâoshì shuo

Close dynamics, do not mind their being too small. They require Energy coordinated sufficiently. Open dynamics, do not mind their being too big. They require force to shoot out. They do not simply extend the body to be big, or flex the body to be small.

Force is spontaneous force. So, for beginners, necessarily not to apply force is correct.

> Notes: Like Tàijíquán, Cháng advocates cultivation of spontaneous, natural (zìrán) force. [30; 35; 36]

52. Central Energy
中氣 Zhongqì

Energy from kidneys, shot from rear to front, from groin-center passing, from below straight upsurges. You must below close the anus, so that Energy does not downward leak. When Energy surges up to the chest and is almost about to issue! you must use the mouth with full force to inhale.

Above close the throat. Energy from above directly descends to the Elixir Field (dantián). [24; 50] Both shoulders once collapse, both elbows once sink, both ribs once concentrate. Energy of itself is lifted to the Central Palace. Don't let your chest center have nothing!

Inhalation of Energy is what is called: "Intake Energy as if swallowing a stream." [30; 35]

Energy must at the body's center, directly ascend, directly descend. You may only with idea know it, with spirit apprehend it. If you must grasp and seek for what is its appearance, what is its form or traces, then you gouge! you speculate! Not only will you get no achievement, you will get a sickness that is not slight.

53. Borrow Active Energy
借行氣 **Jiè xíngqì**

Borrowing active Energy is borrowing a man's Energy in action to hit him. Generally, when his dynamic shoots out, already nearing my body, before contact, I then take this moment to shoot my dynamic. He desires to retreat but cannot, desires to deflect but is too late. Thenceforth there are no untowards possibilities. If slightly too soon, then he can still retreat back. If slightly too late, then I have already suffered loss. This is what is meant by: "Be last to shoot, first to reach" (hòufa, xianzhì). *[Sun Zî]*[194]

In this way, meet the Moment on the beat. Follow timing to find the appropriate. Then there is no worry about skill not being high! Various schools call it: "according to his plans, make plans." Borrowing force to employ force is no more than these maxims. What is meant by "surprise battle neutralizes the regular" (jingzhàn jìnzhèng) at this time is used.

"Borrowing energy" is "borrowing force" in Yáng Family's "Discharge and Release Secret Maxims."[195] *[38; 70:I-ii, II-ii]* "Surprise" is one of the Twenty-four Dynamics *[69:20]* and "Surprise Battles" is one of the "Twenty-four Spear" techniques. *[70:I-ii; II-ii]*

54. Seize Energy
奪氣 **Duóqì**

I have heard: before crossing hands with men, first seize men's Energy. *[Sun Zî]*[196] Now crossing hands to deflect his hands is called First Gate. Deflecting his elbow is called Second Gate. Controlling his shoulder root is called Third Gate. So, when he attacks with his hand, first control his shoulder-root. This means: Ascend the Hall to Enter the Chamber. Reach out and take it, then he naturally cannot rotate his hand, so vertical and horizontal are controlled by me!

The Record *[Sun Zî]* says: "Attack where he is undefended ('unprepared'), exceed his expectations." Again: "His dynamic is dangerous, his timing is short." Again, value divine speed: "Be at ease to lie in wait for the labored."[197] These ideas should be well understood. Mobile and lively laws have no other way. Deceptive skill is surely from familiarity born, from stillness won.

"Finishing" is when, about to make contact, concerned that force is insufficient, that Energy is not full, again to take bones and flesh in one place, and forcibly once Finish. Just like with a musket, after gunpowder is packed in, fill it up with iron pellets. If the gunpowder is solid, one sees that its ignition has force. So it is said: Turn-Around. Other books say: like flying lightning. It must be after Finish that shooting of dynamic is like this. If not for the word "Finish," it is incomprehensible. *[15; 17; 18; 22; 50; 57; 69: 15, pass.; 70:I-iii]*

Notes: Here is a rare but explicit reference to firearms.

IV

55. Rising and Springing explained
起縱說 **Qîzong shuo**

Training (gongfu) overall is at Exhalation:
Purity overthrowing impurity.
In particular, it is at cultivating Stillness.
Total exhalation in the "Finish" phase is the key point.

56. Five Action Faculties
五行能司 **Wû-xíng néngsi**

Liver presides, seated in Vibration's East; *[Wood: ☵, ☰]*
Spleen's faculty's overall management is at the Central
  Palace. *[Earth: ☶, ☷]*
Heart-mind rules *Brilliant* fire's divine transmutations:
  [Fire: ☲]
If Kidneys can fill up, Energy and force abound. *[Water:*
  ☵]

Do you wish to know of Lungs' House, what does it
  manage? *[Metal: ☱, ☰]*
Divisive distribution, rhythmic control are its faculties.
The Five Actions' marvellous applications are truly like
  this:
If you know how to exhale and inhale, spontaneous
  essence communicates.

Notes: Vibration (☳) and Brilliant (☲) are names from the eight
trigrams of The Change Classic. *Lungs represent Metal (gold) and*
Heaven. This reflects the Hàn dynasty correlation of the Five Actions
("elements") with the eight trigrams. [37]

123

57. Theory of Applied Exercise
論用功 Lùn yònggong

At commencing dynamics time, Energy should be relaxed and lively. Energy should be raised but not rigid. At the dropping-point, only then altogether Finishing, employ to the finish your whole life Energy force. Then you begin to get "hard and soft mutually complementary" marvels.[198] *[13; 18; 30; 41; 70:I-iii, II-i]*

(N.B. Finish, after Turn-Around, again takes bones and muscles to one place, in one Finish to finish inward. This then appears to Finish outward.)

Throughout the body, everything should by Energy be raised. The crown-heart upward leads. Only then shoot forth dynamics. In general, the body should be set at both feet's center, straight rising and straight dropping. Only then will it be without slanting crookedness or imbalance faults.

Feet may not be flat set, entire foot treading the ground, or you will make force's application dead, leading you to commit rotational dynamic lack of agility faults. Just use the foot-tip to touch the ground; drop to a point and Finish. Only then will you be without unsteadiness and inefficacy's disasters.

> *Notes: Thirteen Dynamics Exercise has: "being slow and heavy's concerns...."*

First, Triple Tips must be aligned. Triple Tips are head, hands, and feet. Next, Energy must urge a Triple Finish. Finish is power: head, hands, and feet's Triple Powers.

(N.B. This discussion of "Finish" is indeed Finish outward. With "Bones and Muscles to one place, in one Finish," it seems at odds. Further check.)

> *Notes: The writer of these "N.B. (àn)" comments appears to confuse the concentration turn-around (huízhuân) phase of Finish with its final discharge. [15; 17; 18; 22; 50; 54; 69:15; 70:I-iii] Energy > Bones > Muscles is the internal triplet; head > hands > feet is the external triplet. This essay is the only one to use the word "power," jìng, in place of Energy. Two graphs are used, one non-standard, both with the "horn" classifier, which I take as equivalent.*

At first applying exercise time, both upper arms should be soft and lively. On no account may you employ force. Fists must be rolled up tight, to forearms level and straight-facing. They may not face upward nor be hooked downward or slant out. Forearms come and go soft and lively. Only then can you refine to extreme speed and ferocity's position, without dropping into forced rigidity and dead power's pitfall.

Fists are rolled tight, straight-facing forearms. Only then can you refine power law outward. When you touch men's skin, your whole body is as if hit by lightning in appearance. Exerting force as one power, Triple Tips into alignment drop: only then can you hit solidly with power, and men can hardly block or parry!

If fists are supine as if in a cocked head attitude; hook-down in a raise hook form; or outward slant in a twisted crown manner, then not only is force not useable outward, hitting men is not heavily weighted. Dropping onto men's bodies necessarily causes injury to your own wrists, and you can hardly apply exercise!

To concentrate (zân) bone joints: front bone joints backward concentrate, rear bone joints forward concentrate. Upper bones downward concentrate, lower bone joints upward concentrate. "Concentration" means coordinating, so nowhere uncoordinated.

Turn-Around is coordination's half. Finish is a small Turn-Around. All boxing dynamics have straight (direct) entry: this is the shooting dynamic. There is drawing circles. There is making hands once twist. These are all Turn-Around's idea. Simply: from retreat to make advance—this sums it up. Just unite before joining hands. First make one's own Energy and force once to vibrate, once to concentrate and Turn-Around.

Then at the time of crossing hands, employ dynamics, adapt my body, start to advance. Before touching his body, you need not let force be shot out and dissipated. So, you must Turn-Around to lift his Energy. When you then near his body, so it is convenient to shoot dynamics; fearing it is still insufficient, then you need again to add one Finish. Only then are Energy and force valiant, so that men can hardly resist.

So to study this Way, first draw a big circle, gradually drawing smaller and smaller, until at completion, there are circles, yet no visible circles. They are purely as ideas known, naturally leaving no trace.

58. Valiant Energy's root source
勇氣根源 **Yôngqì genyuán**

Heaven and Earth's Correct Energy collects in my center:
Capacity great, flowing dynamic, the whole body fills.
Mèng Zî called it: Flood-like Energy (Hàorán-zhi qì).[199]
What other Energy can compare with its ability?

59. Head
頭 **Tóu**

Head symbolizes Heaven, oh!
    Its trigram is *Strength.* [☰]
Sideways or face-on, prone or supine,
    It is naturally Heaven-like.
Major, Minor, Shady and Sunny channels all derive from
    this.
In Shady and Sunny's entry and support; it is not idle.

Notes: The text has "Minor Shady, Minor Sunny channels." I amend as above in the interests of sense.

60. Level Shoulders
平肩 **Píngjian**

Both shoulders lift up, as if moving a carrying-pole:
Lifting Energy is entirely at shoulder-bone tips.
Front opening, rear shutting, are Heaven-like marvels:
Paired peaks in opposition tower, naturally impressive.
    [69:20]

61. Slanting Shoulders
仄肩 **Zéjian**

One shoulder high, oh! One shoulder low.
High high, low low, not equally level.
Lower, rise in succession, variously transforming:
Seven deflections, ten dynamics indeed produce wonders.

62. Central Energy Song
中氣歌 **Zhongqì ge**

Don't say baby boy *[lead]* and girl *[mercury]* the two
    apart are split:
Between them Yellow Hag *[earth]* makes a strange
    marriage.
Topsy-turvy, they copulate in the Yellow Compartment's
    [spleen] interior,
Clasping, embracing, and tenderly kissing.[200]

Notes: The alchemist's elixir is cinnabar (dan), red mercuric sulphide. Their chemical reaction is described by (Hàn) Wèi Bóyáng in mystic sexual terms using trigrams from the Change Classic. *This also represents the meditational fusion of conscious mind (mercury/fire) with the autonomous nervous center (lead/water) of the lower abdomen (elixir field). The imperial coach had a Yellow Compartment (huángwu),* [01] *yellow being the color of emperor, center, earth, and spleen. Cf. Yellow Bedroom/Court. [25; 34; 69:7]*

63. Hips
胯 **Kua**

One hip lifts up, oh! One hip drops,
Rising and dropping, high and low, applications are
    many.
The lower body's trunk-pivot is entirely here:
Don't let this ground be vainly idled upon.

64. Feet
足 **Zú**

Feet tread the ground, oh! Dynamics like a mountain.
Pointing tip-toe and level treading are naturally Heaven-
  like:
They just have following skip with random points. *[10;
  13; 29]*
Lifting Energy's many techniques are at the foot-tips.

*Notes: Unlike most modern Tàijíquán teachers, Cháng repeatedly
emphasizes the importance of being on your toes.*

65. Hands
手 **Shôu**

Both shoulders droop, oh! ten fingers link:
Their generation and conquest control Five Actions
  entirely.
The enemy eats a horizontal push, seeing a Triple
  Arrival:
To his face directly enters the Triple Transmission.

*Notes: This refers to the interaction of fingers and thumb according to
the Five Actions [12; 14], as well as to the Triple Tip Arrival theory.
[21]*

66. Elbows
肘 **Zhôu**

Both hands hang down, oh!
  both elbows bend,
Thrice invited Zhugé Liàng,
  men cannot resist.
Flexion may extend, oh!
  extension may flex,
After all, use of short overcomes use of long.

Notes: Zhugé Liàng (181–234 A.D.), master strategist of the Three Kingdoms wars, was thrice invited in his thatched cottage to take office by ruler of Shû, Liú Bèi, who aspired to restore the Hàn dynasty. Traditional "inviting hands" folds hands and bends elbows. Elbows are a devastating short-range weapon.

67. Knees
膝 **Xi**

Elbows have tips, oh! Knees have caps,
Knee caps still more than elbows are effective.
Left and right hook and link, once kneel down:
To Gold Cock on One Leg law there is no answer.

FIGURE 15: *GOLD COCK ON ONE LEG*

This technique, later incorporated into Tàijíquán, is shown here from General Qi Jìguang's (c. 1562) boxing manual and in application from popular encyclopedia.

Gold Cock on One Leg features in both Qi Jìguang's *Boxing Classic* and Tàijíquán. It also figures in Chéng Chongdôu's *Shàolín Staff Law*. A pictorial encyclopedia *Wànbâo Quánshu* (seventeenth-century edition) shows its self-defense application as a knee strike.[202]

68. Beginners' Items
初學條目 **Chuxué tiáomù**

The study of boxing's requirements:

1) You need a quiet place to practice. Don't show off your spirit in front of people or boast of your skills. Only thus can you make progress. The *Analects [of Confucius]* say:
   "A hundred artisans in workshops perfect their work;
   Gentlemen through study attain to the Way."[203]
   It is really so!

2) You should have a serious attitude. It cannot be treated as child's play. Thus you can prevent the faults of carelessness and lack of mental concentration.

3) You should understand the principles, transmit its spirit, consider its terminology, and think on its forms. Then you can become expert in its marvels and enter the fine detail.

4) No matter whether regular or irregular, sideways or reversed, the various dynamics require the body be placed between the legs as "steady as Grand Mountain" *[Tàishan, Shandong]*. If it is in the slightest twisted or off-balance, then you will stumble and become ridiculous!

5) If front leg horizontally stands, big-toe Energy needs to turn inward, with back-leg vertically standing, heel twisted outward, so the knees face each other. Then there will be no instability. The groin will also be securely protected.

6) Steps must not be too long, or you may in haste lose balance and topple over. As long as you can jump high there is no need to worry about distance. The high-word comes above the far-word; the far-word comes below the high-word. Then you will surely have the means.

   Notes: Chinese has an expression for excellence "high and far" (gaoyuân).

7) *A left movement must have a right response*; a right attack must have a left support. Left and right must be mutually generative. Then one gets marvels of Shady-Sunny (yinyáng) circulation.

Notes: Thirteen Dynamics Exercise has: "When there is left, there is right...."

8) Use your "whole life force, then you can become powerful. Just as:
> A lion seizing an elephant uses its full force, and in seizing a rabbit likewise uses its full force. Its full spirit is deployed. Naturally there is nothing rigid unbroken. If you say: I fundamentally have no force, is it not all over?

Notes: In Chán Buddhism's Pointing to the Moon Record, a monk asks about the parable of the lion using full force whether seizing a rabbit or an elephant. A Senior replies that it describes "the force of not cheating."[204] In Tàijíquán, Chén Xin speaks both of "a cat catching a mouse" and "a lion seizing an elephant."[205] Thirteen Dynamics Exercise has: "spirit like ... a catching-rat cat ... Like hundred-times tempered steel, leaving nothing rigid unbroken."

9) At pausing places you should sink your force; at pivoting points you should be lively and adaptable.

10) Force must be expressed; energy must be retained. If you can issue, every place has fight; if you can retain, every step has a spring. In spring there is fight, in fight there is spring. Appearing and disappearing, they are transformed. You may not go by things' images: to go by things' images is wrong.

11) Feet and hands coordinate, hands and eyes coordinate, eyes and mind coordinate; mind and spirit coordinate, spirit and Energy coordinate, Energy and body coordinate. There is nothing more marvellous than this.

Notes: These are the "Six Coordinates," Liù-Hé, characteristic of Xíngyìquán. The first three are the external coordinates; the second three the internal coordinates.

12) First apply exercise, so that the whole body's blood and Energy circulate. Then there can be primal unity of Energy.

13) First practice virtuous conduct. In all things be respectful and reverent, modest and humble. Don't quarrel with people. This is the true gentleman.

14) To make one dynamic efficacious and lively, it must be done approximately a thousand times before it is well practiced. If it is not well practiced, do it another thousand times.

15) Make receptivity your root. In every undertaking be calm and patient. Greet people with friendliness, then you can escape disaster.

16) Do not let corrupt scholiasts (fûrú) know. If they once know they will quote scripture and ancient precedents and speak a lot of misleading and irrelevant maxims that annoy people. Be careful to avoid this. You may keep it secret.

Notes: The scholiasts or scholar gentry ruled China's civil service, recruited by means of public examinations in the ancient Confucian classics, which promoted social conformity above practical skills.

17) Do not lightly with violent men engage in contests (bîshì). At best they may think your skill is not high; at worst you will provoke their rage. When you meet, flatter them. Do not belittle them. Then they will be pleased and gladly praise you.

18) Do not lightly disclose it to people; still less do not randomly pass it on to others. If you lightly disclose to people, they will indulge in hearsay and gossip and not put your mind to it. If you randomly pass it on to others, then the wrong kind will cause trouble and you will certainly not escape.

Notes: This call for discretions reflects the climate of Qing dynasty to political and social repression.

19) Start by coordinating posture, study eyes and steps. Do not say you will first memorize the overall schema, and once familiar with it then correct the details. If you later try to correct them, they will never be correct. The *Changes* say:[206]

> Ignorance is to be nurtured to correctness.
> It is the Sages' task.

20) Work at a proper business. Do not use your skill to do evil or immoral activities. *Shady Tally [attr. Yellow Emperor]* says:[207]
> "Gentlemen get it to firm themselves in adversity.
> Small men get it to lose their lives."

["Gentlemen get it to firm their bodies. Small men get it to make light of their lives."]
Can one not be cautious?

21) Be upright and of few words. Make it your mission to be a hero by the laws of the Sages. Then you can be wise and protect yourself.

22) Understand with mind and spirit, broaden your knowledge and experience. You must know what ordinary people do not know; be able in what ordinary people are unable. Investigate principles then the result is certain. Go deep, then your mind will penetrate. Then you will become a teacher to others.

23) Concentrate your mind to direct your will, devote your mind to exhaust your force. Then you will progress from day to day, like lightning engulfing a form. If you are complacent, thinking you are already perfect, you will not realize that you have been rejected by the Great Elegance. The Master (Confucius) said:[208]

> I am a man who from enthusiam forgets to eat, joyful and forgetful of sorrow, unaware of old age about to come!

Is this not profound?

24) First look at the Twenty-four Main Dynamics, then look at the set of Subsidiary Dynamics. The main is to establish the body-work; the subsidiary is to perform their applications. When main and subsidiary complement each other; when body-work and applications are both complete: don't worry about martial skills not being higher than men!

25) No matter old or young, wise or foolish, you should devote your mind and dedicate your force, and, until it is complete, do not stop. The Master (Confucius) said:[209]

> If a man in one time can do it, I will in a hundred times. If a man in ten times can do it, I will in a thousand times. Ultimately, I will be able to master this Way! Though stupid, I will be enlightened; though weak, I will become strong.

In stillness think on it. Verily, verily.

26) There are always braggarts who think themselves clever. They say of other persons' boxing that at one glance they know it. They don't realize that, while at one glance they knew it, if again they glance, they won't know it!

This boxing's principles are deep and cannot be compared with the superficial. Its dynamics have many extraordinary features and cannot be compared with the ordinary. There are fellow students who, after studying many months, cannot reproduce its dynamics, and, after many years, cannot understand its principles. So to say that with one stamp it is attainable, isn't it hard?

V

69. Twenty-four Word Theory
二十四字論 Èrshísì-zì lùn

Shady and **Sunny** are the Words' Ancestors, and should be considered Energy's Progenitors:

1) **Shady** creeps down, like clouds covering a mountain.
2) **Sunny** soars up: Its dynamic cannot be climbed.

Do not consider these *[Shady and Sunny]* as exhalation and inhalation theory. They just to *ascent* and *descent* refer.

3) **Receive** receives the above.

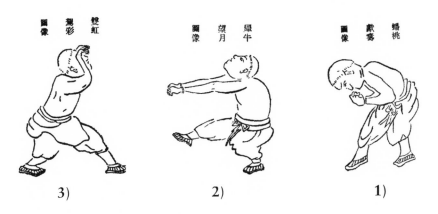

3)   2)   1)

<small>DYNAMICS **1–3**, FROM RIGHT TO LEFT</small>

4) **Balance (stop)** Energy is not partial.
5) **Raise** is immovable. Raise is like lifting water.
6) **Sink** Energy underneath collects.

6)   5)   4)

DYNAMICS 4–6, FROM RIGHT TO LEFT

7) **Open** is joyful like rocking a boat.
8) **Enter** is like water pouring in.
9) **Finish** power is much the same as turn-about/revolving. *This Finish power is like lightning.*

9)   8)   7)

DYNAMICS 7–9, FROM RIGHT TO LEFT

10) **Bounce** (explode) dynamic is a gun's flying smoke.
11) **Charge** dynamic is fierce and brave.
12) **Chop** dynamic is like a knife slashing.

12)   11)   10)

DYNAMICS **10–12,** FROM RIGHT TO LEFT

13) **Tug** dynamic is like tugging a rope.
14) **Push** dynamic is like pushing a mountain.
15) **Oppose** is straight and unbendable.

15)   14)   13)

DYNAMICS **13-15,** FROM RIGHT TO LEFT

16) **Devour** dynamic is like working scissors.

17) **Sticking** does not separate.

18) **Follow** as if star chasing.

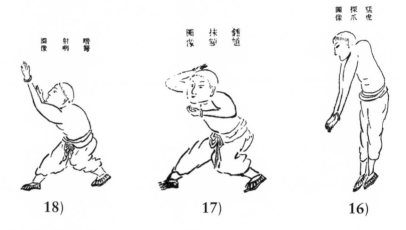

DYNAMICS 16–18, FROM RIGHT TO LEFT

19) **Dodge** dynamic mostly to the side drops.

20) **Surprise** is like cross-bow bolt leaving the string.

21) **Hook** dynamic is mostly bent.

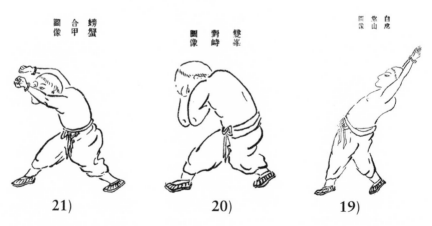

DYNAMICS 19–21, FROM RIGHT TO LEFT

22) **Connect** like lotus-root threads tugs.
23) **Advance** is unstoppable.
24) **Retire** like a dragon coils.

DYNAMICS 22–24, FROM RIGHT TO LEFT

This sequence may not be confused.

Its great dynamics must be discriminated.

Advice to latterday students: these maxims must not be carelessly
transmitted.

Main and Subsidiary Dynamics: a) and b)

Notes: Here I consolidate a summary of the twenty-four a) Main dynamics with their b) Subsidiary dynamics, in groups of three, as per received lay-out. Each of the Twenty-four Dynamics illustrates the Energy of one Word, as follows.

These, though Subsidiary, dynamics may not be neglected. Generally, for *substance* (tî) first seek out the Main. At time of *application* (yòng), mostly take the Subsidiary. This is because the Main are mostly dead (fixed), while the Subsidiary are mostly alive (adaptive). The Main are mostly face-on. The Subsidiary, being mostly oblique, are advantageous for advancing and retiring, apt for rotation and interchange. So I append them at the end to provide alternatives.

1. **SHADY (Yin 陰):**   a) **Coiled-peach birthday present.**

 b) **Liú Hâi plays with toad.**

2. **SUNNY (Yáng 陽):**   a) **Rhinoceros gazes at the moon.**

 b) **Compliant hands push boat.**

3. **RECEIVE (Chéng 承):**   a) **Twin-Rainbow chariot colors.**

 b) **Soft hands raise gun.**

4. **BALANCE (Tíng 停):**   a) **Fairy proffers tray.**

 b) **Old Farmer turns sieve.**

5. **LIFT (Qíng 擎):**   a) **Monkey presents cup.**

 b) **Snake enters sparrows' nest.**

6. **SINK (Chén 沉):**   a) **Paired flying swallows.**

 b) **In muddy water, seek pearl.**

7. OPEN (Kai 開):
   a) White swan spreads wings.
   b) Second Aunt holds silkworms.

8. ENTER (Rù 入):
   a) A beauty drills into grotto.
   b) In tiger's cave, reach for pups.

9. FINISH (Jìn 儘):
   a) A pair of dragons enter the sea.
   b) Two dragons herd horses.

10. BLAST (Pèng/beng 硼/崩):
   a) Hegemon King raises tripod.
   b) Stone splits, Heaven is startled.

11. CHARGE (Chuàng 創=闖):
   a) Flying geese swoop onto lake.
   b) Purple swallows enter forest.

12. CHOP (Pi 披=劈):
   a) Treasure swords double chop.
   b) Draw sword to bisect snake.

13. TUG (Qian 牽):
   a) Monkey tugs rope.
   b) Fierce tiger backed into a corner.

14. PUSH (Tui 推):
   a) Both hands push mountain.
   b) "Iron Fan" shuts gate.

15. OPPOSE (Dí 敵):
   a) Directly tallied and delivered letter.
   b) On galloping horse, push sabre.

16. DEVOUR (Chi 吃):
   a) Fierce tiger's reaching claws.
   b) White snake entwines creeper.

17. STICK (Nián 黏):
   a) Zhongkuí rubs his brow.
   b) Vajrapâni twists lock.

18. FOLLOW (Suí 隨):
   a) Hidden crossbow shoots eagle.
   b) "Crimson Cloak" nods head.

19. DODGE (Shân 閃):
    a) White Tiger barges mountain.

    b) Avalokiteshvara presents palms.

20. SURPRISE (Jing 驚):
    a) Twin peaks tower up.

    b) Golden hooks hang jade.

21. HOOK (Gou 勾):
    a) Crab closes its claws.

    b) Tug ox across hall.

22. CONNECT (Lián 連):
    a) Boy bows to Buddha.

    b) Zhang Fei's trick horsemanship.

23. ADVANCE (Jìn 進):
    a) Butterflies in pairs fly.

    b) Secretly ford at Chéncang.

24. RETIRE (Tuì 退):
    a) Gold cat catches rat.

    b) On Flower Mountain look at fruits.

No. 1: Coiled-peach Birthday Present

Shady hands issue. Sunny hands retract to mouth-underside. Energy drops to elbow-tips. Right foot in front, left foot behind.

Two knights enter an orchard,
Coiled-peaches to pick they come.
Supine hands are proffered firmly,
Head offered at Jasper Terrace.

Notes: *This dynamic exemplifies a flexed, down-facing, and prone "Shady" position. The flexor muscles correspond generally to inner faces of torso and limbs, and Shady channels of acupuncture. Prone torso is balanced by supine fists. The actions resemble the "ducking and weaving" and crouch of international boxing. There are upper cuts to the head, but also "foul" strikes below the belt, and "downward-planted" head butts. Seven Stars figures in Tàijíquán.*

This image sets the tone for the whole subject. Martial arts are founded on courtesy and respect, and their aim is to promote health and longevity. There are also implications here of loyalty and filialty. Two knights and peaches here are metaphors for fists. Three reckless swashbucklers, who showed disrespect to Duke Jîng of Qí (547–509 B.C.), were offered two peaches in order to provoke a dispute, which ended in the death of all three.[210]

Jasper Terrace and Pool (see next stanzas) belong to the palace of Great Goddess, Queen Mother of the West, on Mt. Kunlún in the Himâlayas, said to have a paradise in which peaches of longevity grow. Dongfang Shuò (160–? B.C.), rumored to have stolen magic peaches, was "court jester" under Hàn "Martial Emperor" Wûdì (r. 140–87

B.C.), an aspiring seeker of the elixir.[211] *The legend of Queen Mother's party incorporates the Eight Immortals from the Yuán dynasty, as well as Monkey who, like Dongfang Shuò, purloins the peaches to gain immortality in* Westward Travelogue.[212]

SHADY: 8 dynamics

Beyond the seas, coiled-peaches grow several thousand spring-times:
(Shady hands both extend: use light force.)
At sunrise plucked, they bear dew fresh.
(Sunny hands retract to mouth-underside: use heavy force.)
Air is warm in the orchard, blossoms brush the face:
(Left hand grabs. Right hand supine strikes the face.)
Wind blows branches and trunks, leaves attach to men.
(Left hand compresses; right hand chops: close to groin-center.)

Who can steal them? Dongfang Shuò!
(Inverted Elbow dynamic: right hand strikes genitals.)
How could he be a gluttonous, treacherous subject?
(Seven Stars dynamic: from below, upward rotating, hit mouth.)
In reverence and respect, he proffers them at Jasper Pool top:
(Rotate to the right, step. Sunny fists butt up to brow-top.)
Joyfully wishing the Queen Mother happy birthday and long life.
(One fling. Both fists join together, compress below the chin.)

a) Shady—Main Dynamic

Right in front, left behind. Both hands, Sunny and flexed, issue from chest-front. Both elbow-tips' Energy inward retracts, with heart Energy mutually spreading as one. Head downward once plants, Energy dropping to *Crown-gate* (dîngmén). Hit *Pit-of-stomach* (guànzhong) and chin.

b) Shady—Subsidiary Dynamic: Liú Hâi plays with a Toad

Both fists mutually facing, flex and adhere below ears. Elbow-tip Energy drops to lower abdomen's left and right. Head is downward prone. Whether inside or outside, together block with forearms.

Notes: Liú Hâi is a popular immortal and symbol of wealth from the Yuán period (c. 1300), depicted as an overgrown child playing with a string of cash and a giant toad. He is the hero of a Húnán Flower Drum play, as a filial young woodcutter who marries a mountain fox-spirit.

No. 2: Rhinoceros Gazes at the Moon

Rotate to Shady hands, one push. Head backward is supine. Energy drops to occiput *Pillow-bone*-tip. Right foot in front, left foot behind.

The rhinoceros can divide waters:
Straight extending two hooves.
It raises its head in one gaze:
A jade wheel hangs in the west.

Notes: This dynamic exemplifies an extended, up-facing, and supine or "Sunny" position. The extensor muscles correspond generally to outer faces of body and limbs, and Sunny channels of acupuncture. Supine torso is balanced by prone fists. This is a mid-section attack with fists.

The rhinoceros became extinct in central China about two thousand years ago. In the verses that follow, it is conflated with the Kuí ox, ridden by Lâo Zî who dozed on its back on his way west. The rhino's impenetrable hide was used for armor. Its formidable horn is credited with medicinal potency, and here with ability to burn underwater. The horn shape embodies the crescent that grows to full moon, the "jade" or "icy wheel."[213]

Bîng Jí (d. 55 B.C.) was a judge who defied the order of Hàn Emperor Wûdì to execute the infant and future Emperor Xuan (r. 73–49 B.C.). After his succession, Bîng Jí became premier and earned a reputation for great wisdom.[214] *One day, ignoring rioters, he showed great concern for a panting ox. When asked the reason, Bîng Jí replied that offenders would be handled by the proper authorities, but an ox panting in spring indicated unseasonal heat, imbalance of "Shady and Sunny," which could have dire consequences for the nation's agriculture.*[215]

Lâojun, "Old Lord," is Lâo Zî, said by legend to have migrated west, riding an ox, via Hán'gû Pass to Qín in Shânxi, where he composed his Way Virtue Classic, Dàodé Jing, at Lóuguantái.[216]

Huá Yuán, general of (Anhui) Sòng, in 607 B.C. was betrayed by his charioteer and captured in battle by (Hénán) Zhèng. He escaped before his ransom was paid but was mocked by construction workers on Sòng city wall for abandoning his armor. Huá retorted: "An ox has skin, a rhinoceros still more. I shed my armor, so what?" but they sang in reply: "Since you have skin, red lacquer it. How about it?" In 594 B.C. Chû besieged Sòng to enforce a treaty against it building city walls. Food was exhausted. Huá Yuán by night visited the Chû commander and told him frankly: "We are exchanging sons to eat, and carve up the carcasses to cook. Though the city-wall treaty ruins the nation, we will not obey it." Chû, shocked by his honesty, withdrew.[217]

General Wen Jiào (288–329) of the Jìn dynasty (265–419), returning from a victorious campaign to (Jiangxi) Wûchang, heard that the depths of Niúdûji had water monsters, which he illuminated with a rhinoceros torch. That night a spirit visited him in a dream to ask why he had trespassed on their realm.[218]

SUNNY: 8 dynamics

The rhinoceros from birth communicates with Heaven:
(Birthday Present dynamic: Both hands Sunny retract—No. 1, preceding.)
Supine, gazing at the bright moon, in one Energy joined.
(Both Shady hands once push: head backward once supine.)
When it pants, don't trouble Bîng Jí to ask:
(One retracts Sunny, one shoots Shady. Rapidly exhale and inhale.)
Ridden away, it once accompanied Lâojun's slumbers.
(Devour [No. 16] left hand, right leg riding on forearm-top.)

Huá Yuán led soldiers, clad in its hard armor:
(Both hands rein-in firmly, adhering to left-ribs' gap. Supine chest.)
Wen Jiào lighted its horn, to shine on depths of the abyss.
(Right-foot stance, left-foot curling; body forward prone: Sunny front-fist, Shady back-fist.)
Rays shoot into a cold lagoon, the icy wheel is stilled:
(Recumbent Ox Sways Head dynamic.)
To part the watery regions, its sharpness has no superior.
(Both hands downward grip, both fists directly enter.)

a) Sunny—Main Dynamic

Step-law as before. Both hands, rotated to Shady, forward straight extend. Head forward, one toss, Energy drops to occiput. Hit navel.

b) Sunny—Subsidiary Dynamic:
Compliant Hands Push the Boat

Both hands rotate to Shady. Straight burst, upward one thrust. Head backward, one toss. Energy drops to occiput-top. Hit thigh-root (groin).

No. 3: Twin Rainbow Chariot Colors

Both hands hook, backs resting at eye-corner tops. Energy butts hand-backs. Left foot in front, right foot behind.

> **Lucky lights abruptly arise:**
> **Auspiciously filling a long rainbow.**
> **Five-Color chariots fix**
> **A double bridge across space.**

雙虹
鴛彩
圖像

Notes: Hooked hands menace head and face. Cross-sign figures in the cross-hands of Tàijíquán and is a key grappling technique. It is explained [20] as hands aligning with opposite feet. Know-sign (知字 zhīzì) is unexplained.

The Seven Stars of Northern Dipper (Plough) and Pole Star are revered as the palace of the Supreme Deity. The apparent rotation of the Dipper about the Pole served as a seasonal clock.[219]

Su Qín (d. 317 B.C.) [No. 12; 71:9, 26], a "knight errant" diplomat of the Warring States period, strove to broker an alliance of six kingdoms against Qín, which threatened to overwhelm them. "Dividing cocks from hens" means separating the men from the boys.

"Gate's interior" indicates between the opponent's arms; "pushing the moon" refers to punching the face; and "letting drop a colored rainbow" describes the flow of blood.

RECEIVE: 8 dynamics

Lâo Zî rides an ox from Hán'gû's east:
(Gazing at Moon dynamic: both hands straight push—No. 2, preceding.)
Purple vapors surge and sparkle, filling long space.
(This body dynamic: Shady-hands adhere to temples.)
"A fairy points to the road," clouds return to ravine: *[71:37; 72:16. Qi Jiguang: Rattan Shield and Broadsword no. 3]*
(Know-word [Nos. 13, 18] hands, Cross-sign dynamic.) [20; Nos. 7, 12a–b, 19b, 24; 72:17, 22]
Crane chariots burst into the sky, birds escape their cage.
(A Piece of Glue in Hemp. Eagle dynamic.)

Daoist Priest, observing stars, checks the Dipper Ladle:
(Left hand is high raised, right hand back butts under chin.)
Su Qín, sword on back, divides hens from cocks.
(Rotate step, prone body: right hand in front, left hand behind.)
Supple hands lift a gun, smoke and fire rise.
(Hook hand-backs: lift and hit under chin.)
At gate's interior, push the moon, letting drop a colored rainbow.
(Both hands fiercely push: trip out. As before fists at chest-front hook firm.)

a) Receive—Main Dynamic

Two feet in parallel stance, two elbows flex. Both hands hook, adhere to temple-undersides. Energy is raised. Hand-backs touch upper arms.

b) Receive—Subsidiary Dynamic: Soft Hands Raise a Gun

Both hands' fingers hook, adhering to eyes' left and right corners. Energy is raised to hand-backs. Hit chin bone.

No. 4: Fairy Proffers Tray

Shady hands drop, Sunny elbows backward retract. Energy compresses two hand-backs. Left foot in front, right foot behind.

Lâozû attends the altar:
Light fills a jade tray;
Fairy hands proffer firmly:
Inside is a Golden Elixir.

Notes: *"Proffering" is a technique that first depresses, to break the opponent's root, then raises his center of gravity, to grapple and throw. Proffer (pêng) equates to Uproot (pêng) and also relates to explosive Blast (beng). [Nos. 5b; 10] Yú Dàyóu's (1503–1579) fourth move in his* Sword Classic *of stave-fencing has this dynamic's exact title. [70:I-iii, -v]*

"Fairy" (xian) may also be translated "immortal" or "saint." An important feature of Daoist religion, they are believed to reside deep inside secret mountain caves, or in a heavenly paradise. Lâozû ("Old Ancestor") is Lâo Zî in the role of magician alchemist who achieves immortality by means of a "Golden Elixir." We saw above how this conflates with the Buddhist concept of the indestructible vajra, adamantine body. [1]

"Two dragons play with a pearl" [72:7] here reflects the fabled encounter of Confucius with his teacher Lâo Zî. The similar expression "Two dragons fight for a pearl" is first recorded in the dialogues of Chán Buddhist master Zhàozhou Guanyin Cóngshên (778–897).[220]

A monk asked: Two dragons fight for a pearl. Who is the winner? Master said: This old monk is just busy watching.

It is a metaphor for the yinyáng struggle for truth. Yú Dàyóu applies it to fencing.[221]

Hán Xiang Zî, psychic, one of the Eight Immortals, carries a flower basket.[222] *Lyû Dòngbin, scholar-knight errant and poet, wears a sword over his back.*[223] *These two minor historical characters of late Táng (ninth–tenth centuries) were, during the Yuán dynasty, numbered among the Eight Immortals of Daoism. Here they depict two kinds of throw: one over a leg, and one over the back.*

Bestride Tiger figures in Tàijíquán.

BALANCE: 8 dynamics

Fairy chariot from afar approaches, descending colored clouds:
(Chariot Colors dynamic: Shady hands flex hooks, adhering to eye-corners—No. 3, preceding.)
The mutual meeting is hardly accidental.
(Bow body, Join Hands dynamic.) [No. 22]
The Master (Confucius) thrice bows to detain the honored guest:
(Both hands in front fold, make a "deferring to guest" attitude.)
Playing with a pearl, the two dragons brush off dusty dirt.
(Both hands horizontally brush, make a "cleaning table" attitude.)

Single leg astride flower basket, Hán Xiang Zî; *(Left hand holds firm,*[224] *right hand plucks elbow. His body-center lengthens and rises.)*
Obliquely over back treasure sword, Lyû Dòngbin.
(Bestride Tiger dynamic is also possible, but back-throw arm is more wonderful.)
On gold tray, flavors fixed, the elixir drug is proffered:
(Supine hands to chest, one thrust.)
One pill into the abdomen: Energy for eternal spring-time.
(Two hands once cover: to navel-top, once lightly slap.)

a) Balance—Main Dynamic

Left foot in front. Both hands rotate to Sunny. Downward jerk. Energy drops to the ten-fingers' back.

b) Balance—Subsidiary Dynamic: Old Farmer Turns Sieve

Both hands rotate to Sunny. One hand long, one hand short. Thumbs outward revolve. Compress forearms.

FIGURE 16: YÚ DÀYÓU'S *FAIRY PROFFERS TRAY*

Míng general Yú Dàyóu took two Shàolín monks to train on campaign in 1561 against the Japanese pirates, and later sponsored a martial training center at the monastery. This is his *Sword Classic's* stick-fencing technique no. 4.

No. 5: Monkey Presents Cup

Two hands cup like a wine cup, vertically below the nose. Energy circles thumbs and index-fingers. Right foot in front, left foot behind.

Drink this jade nectar,
Served you in golden cup.
I urge you, sir, again to finish:
Till you are like mud in one heap.

圖　獻　猿
像　杯　猴

Notes: This dynamic has punches to nose and head and is combined with uprooting, as in the previous example. Compare it with Baguàzhâng's White Monkey Presents Fruits or Monkey Presents Cup.[225] This dynamic alludes to Monkey, Sun Wùkong, in Westward Travelogue, *where he crashes the gods' party and becomes drunk on fairy wine.[226] [10; Nos. 13, 24] Imagery of "Drunken Monkey," itself a style of Chinese boxing, is evident here. Jasper Lake and Jasper Terrace [No. 1] is the abode of fairy immortals who serve the wine of longevity to Western Queen Mother.*

LIFT: 8 dynamics

Holding a tray, I bring the wine in:
*(Proffer Tray dynamic: both elbows, backward tensing, extend
palms—No. 5, preceding.)*
Left and right, line on line, the banquet opens.
*(Two hands once separate. Shady Energy outward opens to
Finish.)*
To honor you, I've already raised two cups:
(Both hands bursting up, hit nose.)
I urge you again yourself to Finish a third cup.
(Rotate body, again bursting, hit mouth.)

Once by Jasper Lake, I swallowed jade nectar:
(Supine face, towards mouth midst, one gulp. [No. 1])
"Climb that high rock," fill the golden chalice.
(Both hands lift to head-top.)
On wall top, a cloudy brew, shall we pass by or not?
(Covering hands, hit head.)
'Smelling fragrance, to dismount horse' is delight indeed!
(Pull Sleeve dynamic: make a "tying-up horse" attitude. Hit face.)

*Notes: Wáng Wéi's (701–761) drinking song "Sunny Pass" is sung in
three reprises:*

> *I urge you, sir, again to finish one cup of wine,*
> *Westward, beyond Sunny Pass, are no old friends.*

*There is a play between draining three cups and the triple Finish
exerted until the opponent is unconscious, or "punch drunk.'*

*"Climbing that Rock, I gaze towards my elder brother oh!" is from the song
of a corvée laborer thinking of home, in the archaic* Poetry Classic.[227]

*"Smell fragrance, dismount horse" (wénxiang xiàmâ) is a famous inn
sign slogan. Critic Jin Shèngtàn (c. 1610–1661) wrote a famous essay
on happy moments, entitled "Thirty-three: Is it not delight indeed?"[228]
Thirty-three is the number of heavens in Indian myth.*

a) Lift—Main Dynamic

Rotate body, right foot in front. Two hand-edges cup, in plucking wine-cup manner. Index-fingers upward flick, little-fingers Energy urges hard upward vertically. Ride upper arms.

b) Lift—Subsidiary Dynamic: Snake Enters Sparrows' Nest [Nos. 6, 11]

Two hands, rotating to Shady, upward once uproot (pêng). Little-finger once supine, rear-hand rotating to Sunny, upward once bursts. Energy drops to middle-finger first-joint. Hit chest cavity.

> Notes: Uproot, with Barge (kào), is a spear technique, in Míng dynasty manuals.[229] They are two of the basic eight dynamics of Tàijíquán.

FIGURE 17: BAGUÀZHÂNG'S WHITE MONKEY PRESENTS FRUITS
Wáng Shùjin's Baguàzhâng No. 7 (Wáng Shùjin 1978: 91).[231]

No. 6: Pair of Flying Swallows

Body ducks, hands droop, fingers cup, head dips. Energy points to foot-tips. Rotate body, two feet parallel.

Swallows unfold wings,
Two wings low drooping:
They are not floating on water,
It's just as if they carry mud.

Notes: Swallow dynamics feature low evasion and surprise attacks to the lower body. This is comparable to Swallow form in Xíngyìquán.[230]

SINK: 8 dynamics

Swallows, exploiting Spring, pair by pair come:
(Presents Cup dynamic: both hands thrusting rise, hit face—
    No. 5, preceding.)
Their feathers, overlapping, in sequence open.
(This body dynamic.)
On mountain head's blue clouds, they first test their scissors;
    (Cross and fork hands, push chest: with supine face, he trips
    out.)
At sea-bottom, purple nimbi at will they take and cut.
(Down Thrust dynamic, hit groin.)

At Wáng and Xiè's hall fronts, to fix their nests they go:
(Snake Enters Sparrows' Nest dynamic [Nos. 5b, 11], obliquely hit throat.)
From river and lake bank tops, their beaks carry mud home.
(Carrying Mud dynamic: left-hand Shady, right-hand Sunny.)
Piercing flowers, dropping waters, in fluttering dance:
(Pair of Flying Swallows dynamic: two hands parallel stir. Drop, Sink, and Finish.)
In clear autumn flying about, jade swoops into bosom.
(Camel dynamic [No. 7]: supine hands, hit rib-pit.)

Notes: Wáng and Xiè were ruling clans in Nanking, capital of the Jin dynasty (A.D. 265–419). (Táng) poet Liú Yûxí, lamenting how the mighty are fallen, wrote:

> *Old time Wáng and Xiè mansion-front swallows*
> *Fly into ordinary, common people's houses.*

A memoir on the glorious reign of Táng Emperor Mínghuáng (r. 713–755) relates that the mother of premier Zhang Shuo, on conceiving him, dreamt that "a jade swallow swooped into her bosom."[231] *Swallows, harbingers of spring, are an ancient fertility symbol.*

a) Sink—Main Dynamic

Two hands once fling, two foot-tips hold the ground. Two hand-edges adhere together, hit perineum, *Devil's Eye* acupoint. Energy downward thrusting, directly enters earth's interior. Compress thumbs firmly.

b) Sink—Subsidiary Dynamic: In Muddy Water, Seek the Pearl

Both hand-edges compress firmly. Thumbs urge small-fingers. Feet in turn rise. Head downward ducks. Energy drops to forehead and temples. Compress hand-backs.

FIGURE 18: SWALLOW FORM IN XÍNGYÌQUÁN

Xíngyìquán's no. 8 Swallow Form, performed by Chén Pànlíng's disciple Léi Xìaotian at Táizhong. (Léi Xiàotian 1979: 235)

No. 7: *White Swan Displays Wings*

Two hands once separated, two fists are upward supine. Energy points the two foot-tips. Feet both tip-toe.

On sand top, a flock of swans
Shimmer like white clouds.
They fly rising on unfolding wings:
Love slays Right-Army General [*calligrapher swordsman Wáng Xizhi*].

圖 亮 白
像 翅 鵝

Notes: Dynamic tension between flexor and extensor muscles is employed, both in parallel hands and counter hand positions, in the manner of "reeling silk power," as explained in the Subsidiary Dynamic. White Swan/Crane Displays Wings and Cross-Sign figure in Tàijíquán. "Swan" (ngé), the Chén version, [32] *and "crane" (hè) sound somewhat alike. [Nos. 12, 20; 71:10, 36; 72:24]*

Wáng Xizhi (306–365) of Zhèjiang was Right-Army General under Jìn. Inspired by watching swans, he developed the flowing hand for which he is celebrated as prince of calligraphers. Wáng reputedly copied out the Yellow Court Classic *in exchange for swans.* [233] *"Yellow Court" represents the spleen and body center.* [234] *[1; 25; 34; 62]*

OPEN: 8 dynamics

Snow-white swans lie on sandy shore:
(Swallows dynamic: ducking body, two hands once separate—
No. 6, preceding.)
Unfolding wings, they wish to fly, bursting up to heaven.
(This body dynamic: burst out to hit nose and mouth.)
Both shoulders parallel open a spreading feather fan:
(Camel dynamic [No. 6]: two hands once separate.)
Twin feet skip and leap, dropping palms and fists.
(Spring up, both fists downward thrusting.)

"Cinnabar Phoenix, preening feathers, pays court to the dawn
sun," [No. 11].
(Cross-sign [20; Nos. 3, 12a-b, 19b, 24; 72:17, 22], Lift Gate
dynamic: right flicks up, left hits.)
Purple Swallows enter the window, evading side screens.
(Penetrate Forest dynamic [Nos. 8, 11]: left hand once parries,
right hand hits ribs.)
At leisure, he wrote out the Yellow Court and, immediately
(Chop Mt. Huá dynamic [Nos. 12, 20]: right hand downward,
one pull.)
From Right-Army General's cage departing, one flock returns.
(Use Shady-Sunny two hands: Rip Rabbit dynamic.)

a) Open—Main Dynamic

To the front, once leap. Two hands parallel separating, thumbs
outward, once flash. Elbows adhere to ribs. Hit forearms' inner flesh.

b) Open—Subsidiary Dynamic:
Second Aunt Holds Silk Cocoons

Two hands both Sunny is possible; one Shady, one Sunny is
also possible. Small-fingers urging thumbs outward, once wave.
Alternatively, Shady hand thumbs urge little-fingers outward, once
push; this is also possible. Twist wrists.

> *Notes: Second Aunt is goddess of silkworms. Spinning silk from silkworm*
> *cocoons provided the metaphor for "Reeling Silk Power," chánsījìng.*
> *This is a key concept of counter-spiralling forces in Chén Tàijíquán,* [35]
> *and in Thirteen Dynamics Exercise: "deploy power as if unreeling silk."*

No. 8: Beauty Drills Cave

Extend arms, down thrust. Dip head and duck. Energy slides to back-foot tip. Right foot in front, left foot behind.

The cavern gate has a stone:
"The more you drill, the harder it gets."
A beautiful maiden comes hither:
With folded hands, advancing.

圖　鑽　美
象　洞　女

Notes: By relaxing the shoulders you can penetrate a powerful opponent's defenses and attack his center. The beautiful maid, in her mountain cave, is doubtless Iron Fan Princess, the Râkshasa wife of the Ox-demon, who kidnapped Táng monk Tripitaka in Westward Travelogue. *[Nos. 14, 22]*

Single Whip is familiar from Tàijíquán. [No. 9; 70:III-i; 72:9, 13, 19, 30] Hawk Penetrates the Forest is a Xíngyìquán move.[236] *[Nos. 7, 11]*

In a valiant attempt to describe the teaching of his master, Confucius:[237]

Yàn Yuan gave a heartfelt sigh, saying:

Looking up, it is still higher. The more you drill, the harder it gets. Spying it ahead, suddenly it is behind.

Tàijíquán Theory gives this text a new twist in regard to pushing hands' power:

Look up (prone), it is still higher; look down (supine), it is still lower.

Spring-Autumns Annals in the first month of 644 B.C. record: "Six ospreys retreat in flight over the Sòng capital." There was a shower of five meteorites and strong wind. The next year Hegemon Duke Huán of Qí died amidst disorder.[238]

ENTER: 8 dynamics

> **Flip hands, prone gaze: a stone wall hangs.**
> *(Spread Wings dynamic, two fists separate upward—No. 7, preceding.)*
> **Its center has a tiny, tiny one-cave heaven.**
> *(Two hands cross-fork, extend two fingers, high pointing.)*
> **Great General, fierce and brave, you cannot see his neck:**
> *(One fling: two hands thrust to the groin; head downward looking.)*
> **Pure Maiden, delicate and slight, seems to have no shoulders.**
> *(Forward once push. Face should be supine.)*
>
> **"A hawk penetrates forest," its body wishing to advance;** *(Step up, thrust hands, hit throat.)*
> **"Six ospreys retreat in flight," frustrated they cannot go forward.**
> *(Backward oblique, foot stamps. Turning hands throw.)*
> **Raising head, suddenly you encounter a wide plot of ground:**
> *(Leap Stream dynamic. Rotate body, Single Whip.)*
> **A lovely girl saunters around, at will peacefully napping.**
> *(This body dynamic.)*

a) Enter—Main Dynamic

Body to feet-front. Head downward, once ducks. Two hands extend straight, hand-backs barging reach out. Hit lower abdomen.

b) Enter—Subsidiary Dynamic:
In the Tiger's Cave, Reach for Cubs

Both hands rotate to Shady. Energy drops to middle-finger first-joint. Head downward ducks. Energy drops to *Crown-gate*. Hit breast-sides.

Notes: Ban Chao, conqueror of the Western Regions of Central Asia under Hàn emperor Míngdì (58–75), used this metaphor: "If you do not enter the tiger's cave, how will you get tiger cubs?" It became a Chán Buddhist saying.[239] *It also recalls Aesop's fable of the mice: who will bell the cat? A radical plan's execution depends on individual courage. Chén Xin criticizes the concept as befitting only those super-endowed with courage, and unsuitable for ordinary folk. Chén warns against over-extension, beyond one's borders.*[240]

FIGURE 19: XÍNGYÌQUÁN'S HAWK PENETRATES FOREST
Chén Pànlîng's Xíngyìquán no. 7 Hawk Form. (Léi Xiàotian 1979: 211)

No. 9: A Pair of Dragons Enters the Sea

[Cf. No. 15]
Both hands fiercely turn back and once charge. Energy butts middle-finger tips. Right foot in front, left foot behind.

Sengyóu Finished painting dragons:
They broke the wall and flew away.
Two by two, they enter the sea:
Who can stop them?

*Notes: "Finish" (jìn) here means the total discharge of power. [*FIGURES *14, 23. 15; 17; 18; 22; 50; 54; 57; 69:pass.; 70:I-iii] This dynamic includes surging up from a sitting position on the ground and kicks, including turning "whirlwind legs." Single Whip, again, figures in Tàijíquán. [No. 8; 70:III-i; 72: 9, 13, 19, 30]*

The bottom line of Male (Sky), first hexagram (Qián: ☰) of the Change Classic, reads: "Submerged dragon. Do not act."

Zhang Sengyóu "Monk Yóu" (sixth century), a general and leading painter of the southern Liáng dynasty, at Jinlíng (Nanking) was famous for painting Buddhist iconography, especially dragons, which he imbued with life by dotting in the pupils of their eyes.

A Chinese Buddhist saying goes: "The bitter sea is without limits: turn your head, there is the shore." It refers to the sea of universal suffering in samsara, according to the Buddha's teaching. "Blue clouds" are a metaphor for promotion or social climbing. Yakshas (second verse) are demonic followers of Vaishrâvana, identified with Kubera, god of wealth, who fled from his evil brother Râvana in Sri Lanka, north

to the Himalâyas. There, like Shiva or Vishnu, Vaishrâvana reigns on
Mt. Meru or Kailâsha, by Lake Manasarovar and the source of the
four great rivers Indus, Sutlej, Brahmaputra, and Ganges. Yakshas also
patrol the ocean for the Dragon King, the Hindu Nâgarâja.

FINISH: 8 dynamics

Dragon virtue, sunny and hard, low submerging, hides in
(Drill Cave dynamic, head ducks, left foot back stamps—No.
  8, preceding.)
Bitter Sea's unlimited, watery vast expanse.
(Plumb Sea dynamic. Left palm Shady, right palm Sunny.)
When you dot its eyes, it flies off, and cannot be held back:
(To the right, once Finish. Eyes once glare.)
Its surging armor, leaping comes: none can resist.
(To the left, once Finish. Shoulders once sway, to face front.
  Once rotate, transmute and then Finish. Only then do you
  get the secret.)

Exerting claws straight ascend the blue cloud road:
(Hit with one slicing foot, hands once slap.)
Trailing tail still brings an azure wave wake.
(Coiled Scorpion Tail, foot-point once kicks.)
Yakshas backward sit, a thousand mountains move:
(Sit on the ground. Once crossed, two hands press the ground.)
Whirlwind one kick touches the upper gray.
(Whirlwind slicing feet lead Single Whip.)

a) Finish—Main Dynamic

Left foot in front, both hands Shady, extend straight. Steps advance with Energy forward. Hit two breasts underside.

b) Finish—Subsidiary Dynamic: Twin Dragons Herd Horses

Two hands are both Shady. Inch-steps advance, one halt by one halt. Energy has three issues and three entries. Hit short-ribs.

Notes: Great war-steeds, swords, and spears were likened to dragons.
Here the two dragons are the hands of a master that subdue lesser
mortals.

No. 10: Hegemon King Raises Tripod

Both hands once flick up. Toe-tip stance. Energy is led to middle fingertips.

A tripod towers a thousand autumns:
Heavy as mountains and rivers.
The Hegemon King lifts it:
Upward in one jerk.

Notes: A sharp pull-down on both wrists of the opponent propels the body upward in a leap or uproots him.

The tripod, symbolizing the divine right to rule the "rivers and mountains" of the world, is China's "Holy Grail" (the magic cauldron or chalice in Celtic myth). The legendary Yû, founder of Xià, cast nine to symbolize the nine provinces of his empire. Great bronze cooking tripods were buried with Shang kings. "Hegemon King," Bàwáng, is the title assumed by Xiàng Yû (233–202 B.C.) of Chû, "over eight 'feet' tall, with the force to lift up a tripod-cauldron." [Nos. 12, 14; 70:II-ii; 72:23] Xiàng Yû's "hissing roar" was terrifying. He overthrew Qín's empire in 208 B.C. and sacked their capital at (Shânxi) Xiányáng. Finally, he was encircled by rival Liú Bang (247–195 B.C.) of Hàn at (Anhui) Gaixià. Xiàng Yû broke out with his cavalry, and a local prefect urged him to cross the Yangtze to set up a smaller realm in the east in Jiangdong:[241]

> *Xiàng the King laughed and said: "Heaven has ruined me. What would I cross for? Again, I and Jiangdong's eight thousand sons and younger brothers crossed the Yangtze to go west. Now, not one man returns. Even if Jiangdong fathers and elder brothers were sympathetic to making me king, what face would I have to see them? Even if they should not say anything, would I not just be shamed in my heart? ... I hear Hàn will buy my head for a thousand pieces of gold and a city of myriad households. I will do you a favor." Then he slit his own throat and died.*

BLAST: 8 dynamics

Chû nation's Hegemon King, one generation's hero:
(Entering Sea dynamic—No. 9, preceding.)
With supine face, his hissing roar already generates wind.
(Both hands resting under chin, head upward looks.)
Over-turned hands pressing come: force enters the earth;
(Two hands downward press.)
Up-turned hands, parted go: the dynamic traverses space.
(Both hands lift up to head-top.)

Left rotate three rounds, as if picking mustard-seeds; [with ease]
(Left side, one jerk, lift up.)
Right retire two steps, like flying geese. [in line]
(Right side, one jerk, lift up.)
Black clouds cap the summits: through the middle run; [No. 10; 71:39; 72: 5, 13, 19, 24, 26, 31–34]
(Level rotation, spin around.)
Eight thousand sons and younger brothers, all to the end loyal.
(Upward once lift, eyes downward looking.)

a) Blast—Main Dynamic

Two feet in parallel stance, fists from groin-center jerk up, straight extending above the head. Energy drops to middle-fingers' first-joint top. Hit pulse-channels.

b) Blast—Subsidiary Dynamic: Stone Splits, Heaven Is Startled

Both-feet-together stance. One hand's lateral thumb Energy once leads. From inside the groin, jerk up. Rear-hand to front-forearm, Finish force slaps. Blast his pulse-channels.

Notes: Monkey King, born from a stone egg, emits a light ray that shocks the Jade Emperor (Indra) in his Thirty-third Heaven.[242]

No. 11: Flying Geese Swoop on Lake

Head is downward planted, hands behind back. Energy shoots to *Crown-gate*. Right foot in front, left foot behind.

Wild geese together fly,
In that voidy midst;
High to low, once ducking,
Plunge into Dòngtíng Lake.

圖 投 飛
像 湘 雁

Notes: These dynamics combine rapid evasory mid-section head butts and low groin attacks.

Dòngtíng Lake is a vast body of water, located between Húnán and Húbêi provinces, by the Yangtze River. The "Five Lakes" normally embrace the lakes of Póyáng in Jiangxi, Dòngtíng and Qingcâo in Húnán, Danyánghú and Tàihú in Jiangsu. Héngyáng is a city of Húnán on the Xiang River.

Mallard ducks are emblems of conjugal bliss.

At the battle of (Húbêi) Chángbân, in which Cáo Cao (155–220) defeated Liú Bèi (162–223), Zhang Fei held the bridge on horseback to cover the retreat of Zhào Zîlóng.[243] [Nos. 12, 22b; 70:II-i; 71:21; 72:8, 25]

CHARGE: 8 dynamics

In the darkness they unfurl wings, aligned in goose formation:
(Raise Tripod dynamic, like geese flying high—No. 10, preceding.)
At Five Lakes they leave tracks, by waters' gray expanse.
(Hands separate. Head downward plants, right foot in front.)
A hungry eagle, laterally winging, pursues common fowl:
(Left hand lifts up to hit groin. Use hand-back to Finish.)
Cinnabar Phoenix, preening feathers, pays court in the sunlight.
[No. 7]
(Right hand chops down. Snatching Nest dynamic [Nos. 5b, 6] bursts up.)

White egrets stretch claws, spotting young fish:
(Dodge-body Present Palms dynamic.) [Nos. 19b, 22]
Flowery mallards dip heads to peck rice grains.
(One scissors. Right hand downward presses, head downward ducks.)
Startled by cold, their sounds pierce Héngyáng Harbor:
(Scissors back. [Zhang Fei] Backward Climbing Bridge dynamic.)
They plunge towards Lake Dòngtíng, rejoicing in peaceful contentment.
(Plant head, Cannon dynamic [Nos. 17–19, 21, 24; 72:35]: front-hand is low, rear-hand high. Extend straight. Oblique Level body-dynamic.)

a) Charge—Main Dynamic

Both hands once sweep, then once separate. Right foot in front, enters to groin. Head forward-butts. Energy drops to forehead-top. Hit solar plexus.[244]

b) Charge—Subsidiary Dynamic:
Purple Swallows Enter Forest

Front-hand horizontal, adheres to two breasts. Rear-hand straight hooks, pointing to rear-hip side. Front-thumb and little-finger both flex, three fingers straight thrust. Rear-hand jerks up, hard and firm. Front-hand aimed at rear-hand pulse-top, once slaps, just like "Thunder out of Earth: exertion (fèn)." [Change Classic, *hexagram 16, Joy (Yú, Earth-Thunder:* ☷☳ *)]* Hit lower abdomen.

> *Notes: "Purple Swallows Enter Forest" is twice used specifically to describe adroit footwork. [31; 49] This low attack with hooked hands suggests Single Whip Low Posture in Tàijíquán; cf. Hawk Penetrates Forest [Nos. 7, 8].*

No. 12: Treasure Swords Double Chop

Left knee butts rising, two hands separately slap. Energy returns to one place. Left foot in front, right foot behind.

Sun Quán in shooting rage
Chops and breaks the letter desk.
Liú Master draws his sword:
Stone divides into two pieces.

Notes: This dynamic combines chops, butt, and knee attack, followed by body throws. "Chop" (pi) [8; 12; 14; 19; 23; 31; Nos. 1, 7, 11–13, 18, 20–21, 23–24; 71:10, 15, 36, 43; 72:8, 16, 20, 24] is one of the Five Fists of Xíngyìquán. Tàijíquán has Chopping Backfist (pishenchuí). Another "chop" (zhuó) was the preferred technique of Wáng Zhengnán (1617–1669), master of Internal Boxing, ascribed to Daoist saint Zhang Sanfeng of Wûdang.[245]

Tiger Hold Head [Qi Jìguang's Boxing Classic; Wáng Zhengnán's Internal Boxing] relates to Chén Hold Head, Push Mountain[246] and Yáng Hold Tiger, Return to Mountain. Cross-sign, a grappling position, likewise figures in Tàijíquán.

Su Qín [No. 3; 71:9, 26] in the early third century B.C. brokered alliances against Qín, which ultimately in 221 B.C. unified China. In 207 B.C. after sacking the Qín capital of Xiányáng (Xi'an), Xiàng Yû (233–202 B.C.) camps at Hóngmén, Bàshàng. Xiàng invites rival Liú Bang (247–195 B.C.) of (Anhui) Pèi. He asks his younger brother Zhuang to do a sword dance and thereby stab Liú Bang. Fán Kuài of Pèi, ex-dog-butcher and retainer of Liú, hearing of the danger, bursts in. Taking wine with a shoulder of pork, Fán Kuài draws his sword to carve it and so covers his master's retreat. Later, Liú Bang's sword bisects a white snake, an omen of becoming emperor (see accompanying verses). [Nos. 10, 14; 70:II-ii; 72:23]

Liú Bèi (162–223), "First Master" with blood-brothers Zhang Fei and Guan Yû, strove to continue Hàn in Shû (Sìchuan). At the battle of (Húbêi) Chángbân, Zhào Yún, alias Zîlóng, a gallant knight, spears the nephew of usurper Cáo Cao and captures the famous sword Qinghong, "Blue Mercury."[247]

Sun Quán, Zhòngmóu (181–252), future emperor of Wú, on receipt of a letter from Cáo Cao ordering him to fight Liú Bèi, hacks the desk.[248] *Liú, entering a marriage alliance with Sun, wields his sword and prays to Heaven that, if he can succeed in achieving royal hegemony, he will cut the stone into two pieces.*[249] *[Nos. 11, 22; 70:II-i; 71:21; 72:25]*

CHOP: 8 dynamics

Su Qín, roving ambassador, on his back bore it home:
(Swoop on Lake dynamic: two hands behind back, head ducks—No. 11, preceding.)
Treasure swords out of their scabbard, both chop open.
(This body dynamic. Two hands chop open. Hit down.)
Xiàng Zhuang toasts drinks, how could he have no purpose?
(Cloudy Summit dynamic.) [No. 10; 71:39; 72:8, 19, 24, 26, 31–34]
Fán Kuài, in carving meat, truly has talent.
(Chop Mountain dynamic.) [20; No. 7; 71:10, 15, 36; 72:24]

Zhòngmóu in a rage chops the Dragon Letter desk.
(Twice raise slicing feet. Trick Horsemanship dynamic.) [No. 22b; 72:8]
A lady joyfully reclines beside her make-up table, *(Tiger Hold Head [No. 17, 19], Cross-Sign dynamic.) [20; Nos. 3, 7, 12b, 19b, 24; 72:17, 22]*
Stone is divided into two pieces by Liú the First Master, *(Both hands at once slap. Slicing kick.)*
Blue Mercury also follows Zîlóng's coming.
(Sway Mountain, Ambush Sword dynamic.) [No. 17; 72:36]

a) Chop—Main Dynamic

Two hands both sideways. Kneecap upward once butts; two palms downward once hack. Thumbs' Energy urges little-fingers. Hit wrists.

b) Chop—Subsidiary Dynamic: Draw Sword to Bisect Snake [72:8]

Cross-sign foot-steps. [20; Nos. 3, 7, 12a, 19b, 24; 72:17, 22] Front-hand Sunny, from below lifts up. Rear-hand, straight vertical, at front-side laterally chops. Thumb urging little-finger, downward once hack. Front-hand Energy drops to middle-finger first-joint. Alternatively, it drops to little-fingertip top. Hit the forearm-back one acupoint.

No. 13: Monkey Tugs Rope

Two hands grab head, towards bosom once plant. Energy cups the fingertips. Left foot in front, right foot behind.

On his head a cord:
He pulls and wrenches.
Monkey tugs firm,
Topsy-turvy he is planted with one trip.

猴
兒
牽
繩
圖
像

Notes: *Powerful downward pulls and grabs bring an opponent to the ground.*

"The crimson zither-string in trembling motion" (see verses) is the central string of the twenty-five-string sè, which responds sympathetically to the other strings but is not to be played.

Velvet ribbons adorned the formal caps of the imperial family or specially honored subjects.

If the well-rope is long enough, why should it not be used to draw water?

"A thousand lî by one thread are pulled" describes the force of karmic affinity, believed to control destiny and relationships due to actions in previous incarnations.

In the epic novel Westward Travelogue—*inspired by Táng monk Xuánzàng's (599–664) solo expedition to bring Buddhist Tripitaka sûtras from India—magic Monkey Sun, "Awakened to Void," Wùkong, converted to the cause, tames libidinous monster Pigsy Zhu "Eight Precepts," Bajiè. He leads him to his master the Táng Monk, who is really Golden Cicada, Jinchán, a disciple of the Buddha, reincarnated for not paying attention during a sermon.[250] [No. 5] Cicadas, which re-emerge from hibernation shedding their chrysalises, symbolize rebirth.*

TUG: 8 dynamics

Treasure swords chop apart, two pairs of hands.
*(Double Chop dynamic: two little-fingers use force, downward
slashing—No. 12, preceding.)*
On his neck a cord is firmly, firmly fastened:
(This body dynamic: pluck firmly two ears, once gripped.)
Straight as a crimson zither-string, in trembling motion:
(Press firmly the wrists. Forward once plant.)
Soft as red velvet ribbons, in bunches suspended.
(Left side, again once plant. Use drop to Finish.)

A long well-rope—how can it be all day tied?
*(Know-sign [Nos. 3, 18] hands: left grabs face. Rising Spring
dynamic.)*
A thousand lî by one thread are pulled.
(Dodge past, two hands plucking, hands forward press.)
Monkey Wùkong pulls tight Pigsy Bajiè, *(Two hands once
drop. Nod head and retire.)*
One step, one trip, to see Gold Cicada Monk.
*(Grip firm his head, once plant. Over crown, flying past go.
Again once sit in den.)*

a) Tug—Main Dynamic

Two hands both lateral. Energy drops to the ten fingertips, inward
once clasp. Elbow-points' force into bosom once retracts. Body
downward once sits, Energy retracts to buttock-points. Grab arms.

b) Tug—Subsidiary Dynamic: Fierce Tiger Backed into Corner

Both hands catch hold of wrists. Head downward once ducks.
Forehead downward once topples. Energy collects in rear-buttock.
Grab wrists.

No. 14: Both Hands Push Mountain

Hands issue from below the heart. Upward press the chest cavity. Energy urges hand-hearts *[i.e., the hollow center of the palms]*. Right foot in front, left foot behind.

Moved but unmoving:
"Steady as Grand Mountain."
Both hands push it:
Fiercely upward lift.

圖 推 雙
像 山 手

Notes: The techniques resemble the squeeze and press of Tàijíquán pushing hands [cf. Qi Jiguang, Long Spear no. 22, Push Mountain to Fill-up the Sea].[256]

"Grand Mountain," Tàishan in Shandong, is the sacred peak of the east, near the home of Confucius.

In ancient myth, demon Gònggong, battling to control the world, butted Heaven's Pillar—"Incomplete Mountain," Bùzhou Shan. This myth was used to explain the tilt of the world's axis, which contributes to the alternation of seasons. The mountain is identified with Mt. Kunlún in Tibet, and the story resembles the Hindu myth of Mt. Sumeru (in the same area) as world axis.

The story of the climactic stand-off between Xiàng Yû and Liú Bang at the Hóngmén banquet is told above. [Nos. 10, 12; 70:II-ii; 72:23]

The Yuè Family Army, led by Yuè Fei (1104–1142), heroic general of the Southern Sòng dynasty, won victories over Jurchen Jin, which had conquered north China. Nevertheless, his government decided on a policy of appeasement, and Yuè Fei was executed. His tomb at Hángzhou subsequently became a national shrine. History records his prowess in

archery and spearmanship. Styles of boxing, notably Xíngyìquán, are
attributed to him. His subordinate's purported preface to Bodhidharma's
Change Sinews Classic *credits the secrets of that book for Yuè Fei's*
"divine strength." Yuè Fei, canonized as Wûmù, "Martial Reverence," is
remembered in Shàolín boxing for his double push:[251] *Palm law practice*
takes its lineage from Yuè Wûmù's Double Push Hands.

> *Overall you should from armpits project force,*
>   *connecting to palm-hearts ...*
> *Palms control the opponent by contact,*
>   *entering the chest-ribs' heart-cavity....*

PUSH: 8 dynamics

Two hands tug along, Heaven's Pillar snaps:
(Tug Rope dynamic: fiercely forward plant—No. 13, preceding.)
Its foot root without a thread, how will it be supported?
(This body dynamic: double-hand one push.)
Push over one generation's champion hero:
(Left side catches upper arm, leading Sink and Finish.)
Open out myriad ages' heartfelt thoughts.
(Right-side push chest cavity; combined palms once separate.)

Who says Grand Mountain is unshakeable?
(Tiger Pounce dynamic: right burst, left press.)
Leaning like a withered tree, how can it stand?
(Reverse body, grip and cut. Hit Flying Fairy Palms.)
At Hóngmén charge the camp, armored knights topple; *(Left*
  palm straight pushes. Right palm backward unrolls.)
Yuè Family Army orders directly may instruct.
(Rotate steps. Both hands rapidly push him.) [cf. No. 15 "Direct"]

a) Push—Main Dynamic

Two hand-backs adhere to chest-front. Forward one squeeze.
Energy issues from the heart.

b) Push—Subsidiary Dynamic: *[Princess]* Iron Fan Shuts Gate

Two hands both lateral. Catch hold of shoulders. Forward one
squeeze. Energy drops to the ten fingertips.

Notes: Iron Fan Princess is a Râkshasa girl, wife of Bull Demon who, like Râvana, sports ten heads, and mother of fiery Red Boy. She slams her cave door against Monkey in Westward Travelogue.[252] *[Nos. 8, 22; 70:I-iii] Iron Fan Shuts Gate first features in Chéng Chongdôu's (1616)* Shàolín Staff. *"Fan" (shan) also means "door."*[253]

提　用　抱　鉄扇　▲
捉　槍　琶　哈　鉄扇關門
進　順　琵　似
　　步

FIGURE 20: *Iron Fan Shuts Gate in Shàolín Staff*
Chéng Chongdôu 1616 remarks: "*Iron Fan* is roughly similar to *Hold Lute* [in Qi Jìguang's spear]. Use the staff-tip, with compliant steps, to raise, grab, and advance." (Xú Hèlíng 1930 no. 53 Tiêshan Guanmén. Matsuda 1975: 49 *Wûbèizhì lxxxix* no. 55 Tiêshan Jînbìmén)

No. 15: Directly Tallied and Delivered Letter

Two hands cross-fork. Duck head. Entire force once dispatched, Energy Finishes in middle-fingers. Left foot in front, right foot behind.

A strange gate, who knows?
Direct Tallying follows timing.
Punctually delivered, there arrive
Sunny and Shady—two letters.

Notes: This move has kinship with Seven Stars [No. 1], named after the Northern Dipper, whose profile it resembles, in Qi Jiguang's Boxing Classic *and* Tàijíquán. *This is Yú Dàyóu's title for the eighth move in his* Sword Classic *on staff-fencing. [70:I-ii]*

Oppose is a dynamic of counter-attack, aimed directly along and inside the line of the incoming attack. A direct thrust is hard to detect and hard to deflect. It is straight, but cross-forked to catch or respond to the opponent's attack with left and right. [27; 31; 70:I-ii]

Tally sticks were broken into two halves. An official letter was delivered only after matching tally halves to verify the identity of the recipient. Tallying here is a metaphor for keying in to and following the line of the opponent's incoming force.

OPPOSE: 8 dynamics

An Invisible Letter is a letter that may be suspect:
(Push Mountain dynamic: body forward stretches, to read letter—No. 14, preceding.)
Of this centrals mystic marvel—who has knowledge?
(This body dynamic: two hands once forked, forward push.)
On a lucky day, you suddenly encounter a Direct Tally arrival:
(Left side, one push.)
At its rear-side another direct message follows.
(Right side, one push.)

Shady and Sunny, compliant or opposed, show Two Extremes:
(Advance step, one scissors: Two Dragons Enter Sea dynamic.)
[No. 9]
Sun, Moon, and Star light divide into Triple Extraordinaries.
(Light-sign (guangzì 光字)'s three dynamics: Left, Right, Center.)
At leisure, a tranquil Mind with minute details plays:
(Right palm is on edge, left palm extended; eyes nearby observing.)
Reckoning up, demons and gods even will hardly deceive it.
(Fork hands, once butt. In the void's center, show your face.)

Notes: "Tally" also has the meaning of magic charm or secret spell in esoteric Daoism. An "Invisibility" (dùnjiâ) letter is a magic charm of invisibility.

"Triple Extraordinaries" (san-qí)—Sun, Moon, and Stars—are three odd numbers that figure in fortune-telling numerology. Here they imply the triple alignment of Foot, Hand, and Nose points, along which to urge energy in a single direction.

a) Oppose—Main Dynamic

Two hands Shady. One crosses, one forks, straight extending to head-top. Forward once burst. Energy drops to the wrists' two bone-joint tops. Hit his chest and abdomen.

b) Oppose—Subsidiary Dynamic: Gallop Horse, Push Saber

Two hands both Shady: tiger-mouths *[the jaw-like opening of the hands between thumb and fingers]* catch firmly inward, once across. Thumb-energy forces in parallel urge, to grapple his wrists.

FIGURE 21: *DIRECTLY DELIVERED LETTER* IN YÚ DÀYÓU'S FENCING

Míng General Yú Dàyóu's *Sword Classic:* stick fencing no. 10. (Qi Jiguang c. 1562, 1966: 76.)[261]

No. 16: Fierce Tiger's Reaching Claws

Hands rotate, body receives. Hands downward, Finish force once presses. Energy thrusts to hand-hearts. Two feet in side-by-side stance.

Fierce tiger turns his body:
Of force using the complete range.
Down he thrusts, entering the earth:
Immediately from a stand he pounces.

圖 探 猛
像 爪 虎

Notes: This leap includes hand, elbow, hip, and knee attacks. [72:34] Cf. Qi Jiguang: Long Spear, no. 5. Green Dragon Extends Claws.

The tiger was revered as spirit of Earth and guardian of its sacred mountains. In folk culture it was the epitome of martial courage, and as mysterious and magical a beast as the dragon. Mountain gate is also a term for the entrance of a monastery, which the tiger was believed to protect. "Golden bowl" here is evidently a metaphor for the tiger's ravenous maw, ready to devour victims just as naturally as it drinks water.

DEVOUR: 8 dynamics

Of Earth's hundred beasts, the tiger is honored; *(Dispatch Letter dynamic: with crossed hands, forward once enter— No. 15, preceding.)*
Hungry he catches prey, guarding the mountain's gate.
(This body dynamic: hands extending straight, press down.)
Furiously he chases deer, extending jade claws; *(Two fists, one Shady, one Sunny. Oblique burst.)*
Thirstily drinks from pure springs, revealing a golden bowl.
(Two hands, one Shady, one Sunny, separately stretch.)

His back against crags in wide wilderness, men lose courage.
(Rotate body, spear elbows. Left hand flexed, collects down.)
With twitching tail, he withdraws to cave; all are scared senseless.
(Backward sit in den. Right hip once rests.)
His strength disperses a herd of goats, all ducking heads:
(Two hands grip head, left knee upward butts.)
More than this a wandering lad does not dare to speak.
(Hands once draw in, making an "inviting men" attitude. It is still Extending Claws dynamic.)

a) Devour—Main Dynamic

Parallel foot stance. Two hands both Shady. Thumbs upward once receive; four fingers downward once roll-up, just like iron pillars. Grab wrists.

b) Devour—Subsidiary Dynamic:
White Snake Entwines Creeper

Once Shady hands. With tiger-mouths grapple firmly: thumbs control his thumbs. Hands, Liver Energy (wood) once entering, feet once dropping: their force is ten-fold. Pincer (grab) his wrists.

No. 17: Zhongkuí Rubs His Brow

Right fist faces upward. Left fist rests against the heart. Energy drops to the crown. Right foot in front, left foot behind.

Zhongkuí guards the home,
Two hands chafe and polish.
His divine brow, once rubbed,
Scares away evil demons.

闔　抹　鍾
像　額　馗

Notes: Hands are raised to protect the head and neck, while also positioned to attack the opponent's head and neck. To Head Cannon and Tiger Hold Head figure in Qi Jiguang's Boxing Classic *and Chén Style Tàijíquán.*

Zhongkuí [No. 12, above; 71:36, below] is the chief demon-catcher. The name "Zhongkuí" fortuitously combines the word for an ancient exorcism mallet (zhongkuí > chuí) with kuí, chief star in the northern Dipper, and "examination." He is said to have been an ugly scholar who came first in the Táng palace examinations, but committed suicide after rejection by the emperor on grounds of looks. Years later, appearing in a dream to Daoist Emperor Mínghuáng (r. 713–755), he recovered from Waste Vermin Demon (Xuhàoguî) the emperor's lost jade flute and scented bag. Zhongkuí's portrait was then imperially commissioned from maestro Wú Dàozî.[254] He was canonized and became also God of Literature. He is depicted in twisted pose, "kicking the Dipper" while brandishing a sword or writing brush. The Dipper's box, in the shape of a grain-measure, implies the harvest. Its apparent rotation around the Pole was believed to govern the seasons.

STICKING: 8 dynamics

He guards the Central Palace, Idea and Energy rampant:
(Reach Claws dynamic: angry eyes, staring pupils—No. 15,
  preceding.)
A stalwart frame, extraordinarily unique, reveals divine light.
(This body dynamic: one hand is above, one hand below.)
Running round the golden steps, he extirpates Waste Vermin,
  (Left hand vertically rises, right hand across ribs.)
To recover the jade flute with the scented bag.
(To Head Cannon dynamic.) [Nos. 11, 18, 19, 21, 24; 72:35]

Once, ascending the empyrean to pay court at God's Gate, *(Rub*
  Brows dynamic: body prone, left is above, right below.)
You were enfiefed as Hades' Ruler, and Laureate Scholar.
(Kuí Star Lifts Dipper dynamic.)
In green robes, arrayed below, your Lean on Sword dynamic.
(Sway body, both hands rise over head-top.)
Certainly teaches evil demons to hold their heads and hide.
(Tiger Hold Head dynamic.) [Nos. 12, 19]

a) Sticking—Main Dynamic

Two hands, both lateral, adhere to the two ears. Hands backward once lead, head upward once supine. Right hand upward, once uproots, resting on head-top. Left hand adheres to right-ribs.[255] Head upward once advances, adhering to arms' interior.

b) Sticking—Subsidiary Dynamic: Vajrapâni Twists Lock

Two hand-palms mutually combine: one above, one below. Upper-hand little-finger inward once leads, adhering to armpit. Rear-hand thumb outward, into bosom-interior once retracts.[256] Left and right alternate, without a break. Barge pulse-channels.

Notes: Vajrapâni in Buddhist temples are heavenly adamantine guardians. Lâo Zî forges adamantine locks and chains and a contractible head-fillet, on the Jade Emperor's orders, to restrain the rebellious Monkey.[257]

No. 18: Hidden Crossbow Shoots Eagle

Right hand downward rolls, left hand upward bursts. Energy retracts to pulse-channels. Right foot in front, left foot behind.

Space midst, flying birds:
Only the eagle is hard to shoot.
Hidden crossbow's one shot:
To fend off, it is unable.

Notes: This move resembles Jade Girl Threads Shuttle in Tàijíquán. Upper hand covers or holds, while lower hand attacks the upper body. Bend Bow to Shoot Tiger is familiar from Tàijíquán, deriving from Qi Jìguang's Boxing Classic "Ambush" Dynamic: In Den with Bow Await Tiger. [No. 19] Great Roq Unfurls Wings figures in Baguàzhâng.[258] *[72:5]*

The mechanical crossbow (nû) is an invention of the Warring States, c. 300 B.C.

The mythic Great Roq (dàpéng) is a giant bird, immortalized by Zhuang Zî's parable of greatness; its wings create typhoons and whirlwinds.[259] *For "flying tiger," see White Tiger Barges Mountain. [No. 19]*

Lî Kuí, "Black Whirlwind," rebel hero of the Water Margin epic of Northern Sòng, c. 1100, wielding an axe in each hand attacked Daoist "True Man," Luó Zhenrén, whom he suspected of treachery, in his shrine.[260] *Axes Chop Lâojun's Hall may refer to this.*

Change Classic, *hexagram 40, Deliverance* (Xiè: ䷧), *line six: "The duke acts to shoot a hawk on a high wall top."* Confucius comments: *"A gentleman conceals a weapon on his person, awaiting the time to move. What unfavorable is there? He moves and is not constrained. Consequently he issues forth and has success."*[261] Confucian tradition upholds a duty to fight evil, even in high places, and in particular to avenge parents.

FOLLOW: 8 dynamics

Rig up a cool tent, peep out to watch:
(Rub Brow dynamic—No. 17, preceding.)
Space midst, touching Heaven, is a black roq.
(This body dynamic: with groove-hand laws upward shoot.)
Right hand releases arrows, the arrows as if breaking:
(Bursting Sky Cannon: left grips, right hits nose.) [Nos. 11, 17, 19, 21, 24; 72:35]
Left hand pushes the bow: the bow is then strung.
(Axes Chop Lâojun's Hall dynamic: right chops, left pushes chest.)

"The great roq unfurls wings" but cannot escape; *(In Den with Bow and Cannon: advance right step. Hit bursts to face.)*
"On high wall, a shot hawk" drops colored feathers.
(Again advance step. Hit with covered hands.)
Ten fingers, on continuous crossbows, together release rising:
(Turn head. Fierce Tiger Flips Body dynamic: Know-sign hands.) [Nos. 3, 13]
Even flying tigers find it hard to get away.
(To bosom center, once retract: still Return to Prime dynamic. With it hit Fire Arrow Through Heart.)

a) Follow—Main Dynamic

Two hand-hearts face inward. One middle-finger tip, upward one butt. One elbow-tip Energy, downward once pulls. Thrust to chin-underside.

b) Follow—Subsidiary Dynamic: "Crimson Cloak" Nods Head

Front hand seizes firm his hand. Flying body, scissors rise. Let rear hand, aiming firmly at *Crown-gate,* once peck. Energy drops to five fingertips. Hit temples.

> *Notes: During the Sòng dynasty, Ouyáng Zhi, awaiting the results of public examination, noticed an official in a crimson cloak, Zhuyi, repeatedly nodding. After his success was posted, Zhi looked around, but the man was nowhere to be seen.*[262] *Crimson Cloak has since been venerated as a companion of the God of Literature.*

FIGURE 22: QI JÌGUANG'S IN DEN WITH BOW AWAIT TIGER
Míng General Qi Jìguang's Thirty-two Boxing Dynamics: no. 10.

No. 19: White Tiger Barges Mountain

Two palms once unfold. Body backward supine. Energy flashes to back's rear. Left foot in front, right foot behind.

White tiger washes face:
Discarding body, backward rotate.
Two palms, once supine:
"Grand Mountain Crushes an Egg."

圖 象 白
像 山 虎

Notes: Dodge backward to spring in and attack low. Qi Jìguang's Long Spear no. 17 says: "Grand Mountain Crushes Egg dynamic is an Eagle Catching Hare law."

Qi Jìguang's Boxing Classic: 10 Ambush has "In Den with Bow Await Tiger" [No. 18 has "In Den with Bow and Cannon"], which is paraphrased here in the first line. Bestride Tiger, Ascend Mountain (cf. "Carry Tiger Back to Mountain"), Cannon Fist, and Tiger Hold Head [No. 12] are all paralleled in Tàijíquán.

White Tiger is a constellation in the West, direction of death, which it symbolizes. The flying tiger was symbolic of evil men getting power: "The Zhou Book says: Don't add wings to a tiger: it will fly into the city and pick men to eat."[263] Zhugé Liàng (181–234) applies this image to a general's "awesome dynamic."[264]

If a general can hold troops' authority, and grasp troops' essential dynamics, in approaching subordinates he is like a fierce tiger to whom is added feathered wings. He soars over the Four Seas, following whatever is encountered, to deploy them.

DODGE: 8 dynamics

Duck down, in den with bow, to await the fierce beast:
(Shoot Eagle dynamic—No. 18, preceding.)
White tiger with one leap enters the deep mountain.
(This body dynamic.)
Flipping body, it directly occupies a high boulder top;
(Two hands once flick-down, making the back once compress.)
It lowers its head, prone spying into blue water bay.
(Right foot backward thrusts, right hand cups. Hit abdomen.)

It unfurls open flying limbs and adds feathered wings;
(Body Bestride Tiger, Ascend Mountain dynamic.)
Closing firm a gaping maw, it reveals spots and stripes.
(Both hands once slap, tiger-mouths shut tight [thumbs against index-fingers].)
Baring teeth, brandishing claws, backward retiring into cave.
(Rotate body, one scissors. Left and right separate out.)
To twist its neck and "Hold its Head" is no idle matter. [Nos. 12, 17]
(Rotate body, obliquely walk, retracting Cannon Fists dynamic.) [Nos. 11, 17–18, 21, 24; 72:35]

a) Dodge—Main Dynamic

One foot ahead, one foot behind. Head is backward supine, two hands backward once dodge. Energy drops to hand-backs. Head Energy drops to occiput, *Pillow Bone.*

b) Dodge—Subsidiary Dynamic: Avalokiteshvara Presents Palms

i) Front-hand edge is vertical to armpit; rear hand extends straight, adhering to rear hip.

ii) *Cross-sign* dynamic *[20; Nos. 3, 7, 12a-b, 24; 72:12, 22]:* front-hand little-finger Energy drops into bosom; rear-hand Energy drops into fingertips towards front hip. You should use immediate steps. Strike bladder.

Notes: Avalokiteshvara, Guanyin, "Goddess of Mercy," is the most popular Buddhist bodhisattva, latterly worshipped in female form. The name is construed as "Down-Looking Lord" or "Regarder of the World's Cries." Palms are joined here, as for prayer, in the Indian namaste mûdra. [Nos. 11, 22]

FIGURE 23: GRAND MOUNTAIN CRUSHES EGG FROM QI JÌGUANG'S SPEAR

Míng General Qi Jìguang's Long Spear, no. 17. (*Jîxiào Xinshu x*: Tàishan Yaluân). The high raising of Grand Mountain (Tàishan) is followed by the crushing down to the ground of Finish (no. 18 Mêirén Rènzhen, "-nâi Jìntóu qiangfâ";[273] cf. FIGURE 14)

No. 20: Twin Peaks Tower Up

Double elbows parallel rise, towards bosom-center once butt. Energy points the elbow-tips. Right foot in front, left foot behind.

Jade Gate, ancient ford:
Twin peaks abruptly loom.
Elbow-tips vertically rise,
To hit the central heart cavity.

Notes: Elbow slashes and body barges combine with ear grab and with foot and leg sweeps. "Twin Peaks" is identical in sound to "Twin Winds," shuangfeng, whose form is evident in the succeeding dynamic, No. 21: Crab Closes Pincers, below. [60]

Tàiháng is the eastern mountain range between Hébêi and Shanxi; Jade Gate is at the western entrance to the Gobi Desert on the Silk Road. An old metaphor for the impossible goes "to carry Grand Mountain across the North Sea."[265]

Chénxiang, the "Giant Soul," jùlíng, of local legend and Yuán dynasty opera, chopped open (Shânxi) Mt. Huá, "Flower Mountain," with an axe to free his mother, the "Triple Goddess," San Shèngmû, imprisoned there by her brother Èrláng for marrying a mortal, the scholar Liú Xí.[266] The legend explains the split top of this mountain. Qi Jì-guang's Boxing Classic, under No. 4: Reverse Single Whip, has "Chénxiang Dynamic Pushes over Grand Mountain." Chéng Chongdôu's Shàolín Staff: 24 is named "Chénxiang Chops Huá Mountain."

Ban Chao invaded the Western Regions under Hàn emperor Míngdì (A.D. 58–75) and subdued over fifty states there.

The "harvest moon" of autumn is considered brightest, and in it the hare is said to pound with pestle and mortar the elixir of immortality. "Male" and "Female" (Qián, Kun: ☰, ☷), the first two hexagrams of the Change Classic, *symbolize Sky and Land, the essence of Sunny and Shady.*

SURPRISE: 8 dynamics

On your back carry Tàiháng Range towards Jade Gate:
(Barge Mountain dynamic—No. 19, preceding.)
Twin peaks face-to-face tower, in dynamics self-honoring.
(This body dynamic.)
Chénxiang chops his axe, Mt. Huá cracks; [Nos. 7, 12]
(Right hand hacks elbow, left hand bursting through hits.)
Ban Chao enters the pass, the ford is secure.
(Left elbow once bends, advance left-step close to body. Barge law.)

Moon bright in ninth-month autumn: pounding a frosty pestle;
(Advance right-step, right elbow plants and presses.)
Mountain-top at half night, shrieking heart apes.
(One scissors, spring and rise. Pluck ears, backward grip.)
Heaven's creation, Earth's foundation, leave enduring traces:
(Flick-up elbow. White Tiger Washes Face dynamic.)
Myriad ages, thousand years, Sky with Land (Qián and Kun hexagrams).
(Two elbows wave in motion. Pulley Wheel Rotation dynamic.)

a) Surprise—Main Dynamic

Two wrists flex, hook to heart-cavity sides. Two elbow-tips forward once shoot: Energy drops to two bone-joints' top. Hit short ribs.

b) Surprise—Subsidiary Dynamic: Golden Hooks Hang Jade

Two hands once pull down. Rotate body. Rear foot one sweep. Energy takes the five fingers. Kidney Energy (water) urges Heart Energy (fire). Sweep out heel. Alternatively, a stamp to ankle bone is possible.

No. 21: Crab Closes Pincers

Two hands circle outside, combining to hit temple acupoints. Energy pushes middle-fingers. Right foot in front, left foot behind.

Crab folds hands in salutation:
Golden pincers, one pair.
Combining at center:
A skull is smashed.

Notes: Combined fists close in, hitting the temples. It is comparable to Twin Winds Pierce Ears, shared by both Yáng Tàijíquán[267] and Jintái's Subdue Demons Boxing.[268]

The bow metaphors of horn and round full moon of autumn are used in No. 2: Rhinoceros Gazes at Moon, above. The compound bow, of spliced horn, was the most formidable weapon of horsemen from the central Asian steppes.

Shady and Sunny here refer to "female" cavity and "male" protuberance in mortar mills. In martial terms, they describe the anvil and hammer action of fixing and crushing forces. Crab pincers show this imbalance between the bigger right claw and smaller left claw. The same principle of opposing yet complementary functions underlies the Tàijíquán's theory of movement, which condemns "double-weighting."

HOOK: 8 dynamics

The crab spits bubbles, not exposing its head:
(Twin Peaks dynamic—No. 20, preceding.)
A life of lateral walking, quite at liberty.
(Doubled hands greatly battling, to the right enter.)
On the right, carry a wolf-toothed, eagle-feather arrow;
(Right hand chops, one penetrating chop.)
On the left, saddle a horn-bow, like the moon of ninth-month autumn.
(Advance left-step, cover hands. Again, once draw bow.)

On the inside, cannon balls first strike the ears; *[Nos. 11, 17–19, 24; 72:35]*
(Left hand hits left; right hand hits right.)
Shady and Sunny, mortar stones rotate, on and on.
(Unleash palms to hit ears and cheek. Returning, clip nose and mouth.)
Encountering opponents, in parallel salute hands:
(Both fists combine to hit head and ears.)
Your whole body, mail-armored, generally has no worries.
(To extract men's heart-cavity, it is still Closed Pincers dynamic.)

a) Hook—Main Dynamic

Two hands both Shady. From outside, inward hook. Energy drops to ten finger-joints. Hit temples' *Grand Sunny* acupoints.

b) Hook—Subsidiary Dynamic: Tug Ox Across Hall

Two hands are both Shady. Ten fingers downward cup, elbows flex. Catch firmly his legs and foot-tips, thumbs securing his toes, knees at his calves, one sweep.

> Notes: *The subsidiary dynamic describes a pull-up leg tackle.*
>
> *King Xuan of Qí (r. 342–329 B.C.) observed a man "tugging an ox across the hall" for sacrifice to consecrate a bell. Feeling that the ox bore an expression like an innocent man being led to execution, he ordered the ox exchanged for a sheep.*[269]

FIGURE 24: *TWIN WINDS PIERCE EARS*

This technique is shared by Yáng Tàijíquán and Jintái Boxing. It is absent from Qi Jiguang and Chén Tàijíquán. (Chén Yánlîn, 1936: 116)

No. 22: Boy Bows to Buddha

Rolling hands, thrust at nose and mouth. Both hand-backs mutually close in. Energy butts fingertips. Right foot in front, left foot behind.

> **Goodly-Wealth (Sudhâna) Boy**
> **Worships Avalokiteshvara.**
> **Hail to Amitâbha Buddha!**
> **Red fire issues from forest.**

Notes: Both palms together slam the opponent, and separate to hit or throw. You kneel down to punch the foot, and spring up to hit or head-butt the face.

In the epic novel Westward Travelogue *(c. 1600), son of a Râkshasa demoness [Nos. 8, 14], Red Boy can deploy "samâdhi true fire." He is converted by bodhisattva and mahâsattva, "great being," Avalokiteshvara (Guanyin) [No. 19b] to become the Buddhist Sudhâna (Shàncái), "Goodly Giver" or "Goodly Wealth."[270] The story of Sudhâna's pilgrimage in search of enlightenment is told in Gandavyûha, Heroic Array, at the end of the Avatamsaka "Garland" Sutra. Red Boy and his Râkshasa mother have affinity with the Indian legend of the child-stealing goddess Hârîtî, whose own son is held hostage by the Buddha until she agrees to convert.[271]*

Manjushri, "marvellous fortune," bodhisattva of wisdom, rides a lion. Samanthabhadra, bodhisattva of "universal goodness," rides an elephant. The Buddha, to whom prostrations are made, is seated on the Lotus Terrace. "Twenty-four prostrations" match the Twenty-four Dynamics of Cháng Boxing.

Amitâbha Buddha is the Buddha of "Infinite Brilliance" in the Western "Pure Land" paradise. The Amitâbha Sutra asserts that one will be reborn there by calling on his name, reciting: "Namu Amitâbha Buddha" (nánwú amítuófó). The hands are placed together in the Indian "namaste" (namu) greeting. [Nos. 11, 19b]

CONNECT: 8 dynamics

Râkshasa Girl's son is Red Boy:
(Closed Pincers dynamic—No. 21, preceding.)
Mahâsattva converts him into Goodly Wealth.
(Two palms combine firmly. Hit Kow-tow dynamic.)
Kneel down with prone head: Earth's door shuts;
(Hands below separate. Doubled fists down-thrust. Knees and feet, right kneeling, left standing. Right fist pounds foot-surface.)
Rising time, crowned with pearls: Heaven's gate opens.
(Rotate body, combine palms. Burst to hit face.)

Leftward glance: Manjushri to left side runs;
(Follow-sign dynamic [No. 18]. Left rotate body, combine palms.)
Rightward look: Samanthabhadra from right side comes.
(Right rotate body, combine palms.)
One sheet of fire and cloud, in space midst dances;
(Combined palms: upward one separates, downward one separates.)
Twenty-four prostrations, prostrate at Lotus Terrace.
(Separate palms: Rapid Nodding Head dynamic.)

a) Connect—Main Dynamic

Two hands combine palms, "like a Buddhist monk worshipping Buddha." Upward, one butt. Energy drops to the ten fingertips. Upward butt nose-tip.

b) Connect—Subsidiary Dynamic:
Zhang Fei's Trick Horsemanship

i) Two hands are both Sunny. Flex elbows, compress his forearms. Front foot arches up, once drops across his heel.

ii) Hands rotate to Shady, aiming at his face, once press. Rear hand scoops his occiput *"Pillow Bone."* Alternatively, *[to pull]* head-hair is also possible.

Notes: Zhang Fei is a chivalric lancer in the Three Kingdoms saga. [Nos. 11, 12; 70:II-i; 71:21; 72:8, 25]

No. 23: Butterflies in Pairs Fly

Hand-backs close in firm, extend fingers, pound the chest. Energy urges fingertips. Right foot in front, left foot behind.

Penetrating flowers, butterflies
Flitting and fluttering come.
Zhuang Zhou's one dream:
A pair plays among plum blossoms.

Notes: This is a dynamic of single and double thrusts and slaps. [72:28]

Proto-Daoist philosopher and satirist Zhuang Zhou (c. 300 B.C.) dreamt that he was a butterfly. On waking, he wondered whether he might be a butterfly dreaming he was a man.[272]

ADVANCE: 8 dynamics

Don't despise butterflies' Energy force slight:
(Combined palms hit the chest—No. 22, preceding.)
All day they pick among the greenery with golden flippers.
(Forked hands, once enter.)
When Spring enters the Yellow River north, flowers begin to fill;
(Right hand grips, left hand flicks-up: right hits abdomen.)
As rains hit the autumn Yangtze, leaves just fatten.
(Advancing right-step, chop hit.)

Little boys in silly games together clap hands;
(Advancing left-step: into ear, right palm slap-hits.)
Feathery wings flit and flap, in themselves forgetful of traps.
(Rotate body. Double palms slap-hit.)
Only Zhuang Zhou's pure dream is good;
(Hands from heart-center outward separate.)
Each hour, each minute, sharing in the never-never.
(Downward grasp. Combine hand-backs: one thrust.)

a) Advance—Main Dynamic

Two hands close in backs, downward once unload. Upward one butt. Hit throat.

b) Advance—Subsidiary Dynamic: Secretly Ford at Chéncang

Front-hand edge dynamic: to groin, one kick. Rear hand straight drills lower abdomen. You need to advance, alternating feet.

Notes: Liú Bang made a show of reconstructing the cliff-face scaffold road that he had burnt to secure his retreat, but stealthily forded the Wèi River at Chéncang (Shânxi) with his army to surprise Xiàng Yû. This story gave its name to one of the Thirty-Six Stratagems.

No. 24: Gold Cat Catches Rat

Whirlwind, alternating legs. Doubled hands outward hook. Energy flows to both eyes. Duck body, fork stance.

You are a true rat;
All day you dread the cat.
When his golden tail thrice twitches,
With your life you'll be lucky to escape.

Notes: This is a twirling finish of kicks and pull-downs, with leap and head attack. Qi Jùgnang's Long Spear 16 Magic Cat Seizes Rat dynamic has this poem:

> *This is a "nothing midst generated something" spear law.*
> *Advance steps, feint low, pounce and wrap.*
> *Trick his spear to move, deploying Pear Blossoms [spear-tip fireworks]:*
> *If you encounter pressure, flick up to Heaven, burst and hit.*

Cháng's Twenty-four Dynamics conclude, like Tàijíquán, with retiring and spin steps: Bestride Tiger, Aimed at Head Cannon (= Bend Bow Shoot Tiger), and triple turn (= Swing Lotus Kick), ending with Cross-sign Hands. [Nos. 7, 12, 19] Compare Wáng Shùjin's Whirlwind Palms' final Baguàzhâng change. (see FIGURE 26)[273] Thirteen Dynamics Exercise refers to "spirit like a catching-rat cat."

RETIRE: 8 dynamics

Golden cat, golden tail, golden pupils yellow:
(Paired Flight dynamic—No. 23, preceding.)
Golden eyes catch rats, the rat gang panics.
(Double hands vertically rise: hit left ear.)
Cross-sign Chop comes: chests and bosoms break; *[Nos. 3, 7,
12a–b, 19b; 20; 72:17, 22]*
(Double hands once sweep. Again, once hit ribs.)
Compliant dynamic's embrace goes: shoulder and back are hurt.
(Grab right shoulder, downward once drop.)

Flip body, straight jump into west neighbor's garden:
*(Rotate body, one jump. Look at Fruits dynamic.) [Nos. 5,
13, 24b]*
Claw tips again sweep east house wall.
(Bestride Tiger. Right foot once sweeps.)
To the head, exerting strikes, a host of vermin die;
(Bend body. To Head Cannon hit.) [Nos. 11, 17–19, 21; 72:35]
At leisure retire to feed, at will stroll around.
(Thrice rotate step. Move-sign dynamics. Retract firmly.)

a) Retire—Main Dynamic

Both hands parallel flying, backward rotate. Two legs once twist. Two hands separate to Shady hands. Outward once separate, wrists and elbow-tips all flex. Energy drops to *Crown-gate*, foot-tips, hip-tips, elbow-tips, toe-tips, and fingertips. Contrive a watching strategy.

b) Retire—Subsidiary Dynamic:
On Flower Mountain, Look at Fruits

Two hands, rotate body, once sweep. Again one rotation; again one sweep. One shoulder high; one shoulder low. One hip uplifts, one hip drops. Flip body, supine look. Two hands both flexed, as one adhere to ears' underside.

Notes: Monkey King lives with his tribe on "Fruit and Flowers Mountain," Huaguôshan.[274] Look at Fruits is akin to Monkey Presents Cup [Nos. 5, 13] and Monkey Presents Fruits in Baguàzhâng. Chén Xin describes Tàijíquán's Elbow-neath Fist:

Just like a Monkey's image,
A fairy peach elbow-neath hanging:
You dare look, don't dare eat.
In tranquility, nourish your nature's Central Heaven.[275]

FIGURE 25: QI JÌGUANG'S SPEAR'S MAGIC CAT SEIZES RAT

Surprise tactics from Míng General Qi Jìguang's Long Spear, no. 16. (*Jîxiào Xinshu x:* Língmao zhuóshûshì).

FIGURE 26: WÁNG SHÙJIN'S BAGUÀZHÂNG *WHIRLWIND PALMS*

This is the start of the eighth and final change in Wáng Shùjin's Baguà Connecting Palms. (1978: 93)

VI

70. I. Spear Laws: Twenty-four Explanations
槍法二十四說 Qiangfâ Èrshísì Shuo

[INDENTED PREFACE]

Without *i) Guiding Principles [four]*, the great root
cannot stand.

Without *ii) Great Items [eight]*, marvellous applications
cannot be implemented.

When the body stands, and applications are implemented,
yet there is lack of *iii) Variations [twelve]*, then you
will be obstructed and scarcely penetrate.

These "Twenty-four Explanations" are therefore in need
of urgent interpretation.

Furthermore, if you can with spirit illuminate them, as
things come smoothly responding, then you will see
regeneration to infinity's marvels.[276]

i. Four Great Guiding Principles 四大綱領 Sì-Dàganglîng

a) Steps and Eyes

Step laws, if uncoordinated,
Are the entire body's encumbrance.
If twisted aslant, or obliquely skewed,
It is hard to advance or retire.

Wide or tight suitably centered,
"T" or "V" steps in goose formation,
Front vacuous, rear substantial:
Motion then magically penetrates.

b) Hand Laws

The two hands' applications
Need to separate the "dead" from "living':
Front and rear retract and release,
Flex and extend in zig-zag.

The front grips the road to run,
The rear grips, following it.
The entire body having Energy,
Hitting and thrusting have force.

c) Body Way

Body is commander-in-chief,
Five organs are generals.
If you cannot in order deploy them,
You seek self-destruction.

Body Energy urges deployment of
Head, eyes, hands, and feet.
Motion and stillness are one house,
Magic in speed, heroic in stature.

d) Head and Face

Of four limbs and a hundred joints,
The head is leader.
If this place is not coordinated,
The whole body altogether halts.

Compare it to the troops' general:
Only the head is followed.
If the head does not reach,
Of multitudes, what is the use?

ii. Eight Great Items 八大條目 Ba-Dàtiáomù

a) Opposing Stabs (dízha)

Don't fend off, don't block:
Charge ahead to enter.[277]
Meet the moment, straight ascend:

This is the correct road;
To drag open is the far road.

Slight force is ineffective;
Shooting late does not reach.

Notes: Qi Jiguang's Boxing Classic *first records the key maxim: "Don't block and parry, it's just one blow. If you block and parry there will be ten blows." This is the principle of direct attack prevailing over circuitous interception. [27; 31; 69:15]*

b) Surprise Battle (jingzhàn)

Dream midst, taken by surprise,
Unconscious combustion.
I do not see there are Men,
How to know there is a "Me"?

Nourish to completion an "Expansive Energy,"
Sensitive Perception body:
Make contact and immediately shoot.

Notes: The dream and Sensitive Perception (Magic Penetration) body (língtong-zhi tî) suggests Buddhism and Daoism. This appears to draw on latent powers of the sub-conscious. Again we see Mencius' "Expansive Energy" (hàorán-zhi qì).[278] *[29; 32; 34; 58; 69:21b; 70: II-i] "Surprise Battle" as discussed above. [53]*

c) Sticking and Following (niánsuí)

Like glue, like lacquer:
When he arrives, I arrive.
Even if you shed your shell,
You will not escape me.

If Energy's Moment is not efficient,
Body laws do not follow:
If "firing time" is insufficient,
How can one get them?

Notes: Spear "sticking and following" is still practiced in Tàijíquán and is the vital component in its "pushing hands" techniques. "Firing time" is a metaphor for self-cultivation; it derives from metal smelting and alchemy. [69:17 Stick, 18 Follow]

d) Slide Away (huátuo)

Seeing hard, soften;
Seeing motion, rotate.
He, like a tiger great in force,
In vain goes forth, in vain retires.

If Form and Energy are unable to combine as one,
While men already unify with the Prime,
How can you perform skillfully?

Notes: These are the techniques of escape from and avoidance of superior force. "Prime" refers to the body center, below the navel, where body Form and Energy unite.

e) Rise and Duck (qîfú)

Thrusting spear laws
Are not all at mid-level:
Abruptly high, abruptly low,
Cunning as a swimming dragon.

Without high and low,
Shady and Sunny do not rotate.
Without opening a road,
Doors and gates are not cleared:
At their center, a golden needle resides.

Notes: Here we see the vertical dimension, high and low, employed as a stratagem to penetrate the center. "Golden needle" is a metaphor from acupuncture.

f) Advance and Retire (jìntuì)

Knowing the Moment,
            knights never rigidly clash.
Who dares to jab Energy?
            Yáng Family Sixth Lad.

Knowing to advance, knowing to turn back:
Lively in motion he was unencumbered.
Ample, with room to spare,
He didn't enter blind alleys.

Notes: Yáng Yánzhao is the formal name of outstanding lancer general, "Yáng Family Sixth Lad," Yángjia Liùláng. He was the son of Yáng Yè (d. 986), who died heroically in battle against the Khitan tartars. The Yáng family upheld this tradition of northern border defense against the Khitans for three generations, and they are celebrated both in history and fiction.[279] Yáng Family Spear (no relation to Yáng Family Tàijíquán) is named as a leading school by Qi Jiguang.

g) Blast and Hit (bengdâ)

Spear's rise and drop,
If not up, is down.
Go forth and return, not in vain:
Low blast, high hit.

When you dissolve obstructions,
Then the whole body is all spears.
When the entire body is claws and teeth,
The enemy has extreme difficulty laying hands.

h) Uplift and Push (títui)

If he raises, I uplift.
If he blasts, I push.
According to his plans, adapting plans
Indeed is a marvellous ploy.

Exploitation of dynamics can economize force.
If the enemy does not alter his Moment,
His active Energy will be borrowed steadily.
One shot, his life goes home to the west.

Notes: "Borrowing energy" is "borrowing force" in Tàijíquán.[280] [38; 53; 70:II-ii] West is the direction of death in ancient Chinese religion.

iii. Twelve Variations 十二變通 Shí'èr-Biàntong

a) Follow Center (Suízhong)

He thrusts, I deflect.
He passes, I pass.
If he does not get to flip the body,
In sum he has no remedy.

As if sticking, not sticking;
As if detached, not detached.
In contact and separation midst,
He cannot feel it out.

Notes: Here the relationship of sticking spear to Tàijíquán pushing hands is immediately apparent.

b) Employ Center (Shîzhong)

At my passing time,
He has not yet seen it.
Furiously forceful, the thrust comes,
Precisely centered on the Moment's trigger.

When his thrust comes,
My pursuit has already arrived.
Eyes are bright, hands quick,
Dharma's Force profound and marvelous.

c) Conclude and Press (Zông'àn)

Front palm applies force,
Detached shoulder downward sinks.
Straight drop contrives Press;
Shrugging then contrives Conclusion.

Conclusion bursting forward runs,
Press straight facing down.
Their central Finishing Energy
Is not a fraction out.

d) Flick-up and Deflect-down (Tiâoliâo)

Surge through void, to arise
At his shaft underside.
Flicking-up, do not leave his shaft;
Deflecting-down, then blast and explode.

If he Flicks-up, then follow him,
If he Deflects-down, then leave open.
Once hard, once soft,
The imperative shooting time has come.

e) Pluck and Scoop (duótuo)

Two shoulders together shrug,
Twin elbows downward sink.
"Proffer tray" and enter
Within a tenth of an inch.

Flip supine and arise:
One lift, one follow.
Of one kind are Jabbing Laws;
Finish Energies are not the same.

Notes: This technique combines downward pulling with upward lifting. Proffer Tray is one of the Twenty-four basic open-handed techniques, above. [69:4] Note two occurrences of Finish Energy in c) and e) above. [15; 17; 18; 22; 50; 54; 57; 69:9, pass.]

f) Intercept and Barge (Jiékào)

Shoulder blades apply force,
"Iron Fan" shuts the gates.
One then vibrates open,
One then hard thrusts.

Sulphur-yellow rapid fire,
Even men are carried along.
To break in doors and enter,
Sink and loose are first.

Notes: Lady Iron Fan is a cave-dwelling fiery demoness, wife of the Ox Demon King, encountered by the mystic pilgrims in Western Travelogue. *[69:14] "Iron fan" (tiêshan) can also mean "iron door." Barge is also a Tàijíquán close-range technique, to breach defenses and explosively attack the opponent's body.*

g) Stall and Lead (Dùnlîng)

Guard the ground unmoving:
Entice him to enter the orifice.
Inside there is a pitfall,
How could he know?

Force that cannot be intercepted
Is enticed to enter the battlefield.
Moments move, dynamics rotate:
He is cast into the meshed net.

h) Hook and Hang (Gouguà)

Hook divides into high and low;
Hang differs by inside and outside.
Front- and rear-hands alternate:
Supine or prone, they twist and reel.

Hard Hooks, supple Hangs:
Shady and Sunny divide clearly.
Hands and wrists, palms and shoulders,
If mixed up won't work.

i) Combined Palms (Hézhâng)

Shady hands downward sink,
Sunny Energy supporting them.
Urge force to straight advance,
Don't let him arise.

If not Shady, they are not heavy;
If not Sunny, they are not lively;
Mutually complementary in use,
They are named Sink and Scoop.
[13; 18; 30; 41; 57; 70:II-i]

Notes: Tàijíquán Theory has: "When Shady and Sunny mutually complement, it is called understanding power." This key phrase has been ascribed to Cáo Cao (155–220).[281] Shady hands are face-down, sunny hands face-up.

j) Grasp and Flip (Lôufan)

Sunny enters, Shady advances;
Shady rotates, Sunny pursues.
Flipping rivers, stirring seas,
Vibrate and shake Sky and Land.

Grasp uses fierce pull-ins,
Flip uses fierce drops.
Abruptly rise, abruptly drop:
Shady and Sunny divide.

k) Rein and Crush (Lèya)

Not retreating, as if retreating;
As if advancing, not advancing:
Centered Energy, downward accumulating,
Sinks to fell his shaft.

Shady rein-in:
> scoop-up front shoulder, sink rear shoulder; *[pivot up]*

Sunny rein-in:
> sink front elbow, stand rear elbow. *[pivot down]*

l) Pull-out and Roll (Choujuân)

Long can use short,
Straight can use crosswise.
Follow the Moment, respond to change:
Mind magic (sensitive), body pure.

If you can pull-out, then excellent:
The intimidator, conversely, is endangered.
If you can roll-up, then excellent:
The controller, conversely, is injured.

一之法揮扎黏沾形圓體立人雙（1）

（式肩剃）法揮扎黏沾圓平人雙（1）

二之法揮扎黏沾形圓體立人雙（2）

（式腿剃）法揮扎黏沾圓平人双（2）

FIGURE 27: YÁNG TÀIJÍQUÁN STICKING SPEARS

This is the spear equivalent of pushing-hands, "Touch and Stick Thrusting Shafts" (zhannián zhagan), from Yáng family Tàijíquán. (Chén Yánlín 1936: 233ff)[282]

II. Scoop and Subdue Spear

i. Scooping Spear Postures 托槍式 Tuoqiang shì

Oblique body divides void from substance:
Concentrate the spirit, Energy like a rainbow.
Left relaxes, right retracts fully:
Shaft slightly downward hangs.

In stillness, you can make Triple Tips align: *[head, hand, foot]*
In motion, then Six Coordinates equalize. *[68:11]*
Spirit lively shatters the hard and rigid:
Hard and soft, by nature, mutually complement.
[13; 18; 30; 41; 57; 70:I-iii]

Notes: Void and Substance in Tàijíquán Theory define the principle of single-weighting, clearly differentiating weighted from unweighted feet. Thirteen Dynamics Exercise says: "There is nothing hard and rigid that is not shattered … hard and soft mutually complement."

ii. Subduing Hand 降手 Xiángshôu

You need to *borrow* activated *Energy* to be marvelous. Otherwise, if I subdue, he rotates to arrive at my spear-top! Some say: Subduing Hand, and Finish dynamic's dropping to a point are the same. You must ten out of ten devour his shaft, so he cannot rotate. Only then may it be applied.

> In Spear Laws, only Subduing Hand is difficult:
> Sweep, Tap, Knock, and Hack (shua, qiao, ke, kân), all
>   men repeat.
> When you know it thoroughly, then slightly smiling,
> Just take his prior dynamic back to its source.

Notes: To borrow energy is to "borrow force" in Yáng Tàijíquán's Discharge and Release Maxims.[283] *[38; 53; 70:I-ii]*

A poem says:
> From above, downward, is called Subduing:
> High mountain falling rocks are irresistible. *[Sun Zi: V]*
> Energy's dynamics return to source, body law advances,
> Cut through the pass, seize the defile: demons and gods
>   panic.

> To be one man's match, do not consider an achievement:
> At Gaixià, battle Xiàng the "Double-Eyed";
> On Chángbân Slope, Zhào Zîlóng.

Notes: Hegemon King Xiàng Yû, the "Double-Eyed," had the strength to "lift a tripod-cauldron" and boasted of "pulling up mountains." He gave up study of sword fencing to be "one man's match" in order to become a "myriad men's match." His rival Liú Bang finally surrounded him at (Anhui) Gaixià. After a desperate break-out, Xiàng Yû cut his own throat in 202 B.C.[284] *[69:10, 12, 14; 72:23]*

Cáo Cao attacked Liú Bèi at (Húbêi) Chángbân, where hero Zhào Zîlóng single-handedly rescued his wife and son from the enemy.[285] *[69:11, 12, 22; 71:21; 72:25]*

> A million-strong army are like schoolboys:
> One spear shaft, like an aquatic dragon.
> Drop on top, shoot Energy from below to attack.
> "To strike west, sound in the east."

Below, sweep the hall; above, against clouds butt.
Blast, Shake, Deflect, Push, Flick-up, and Surprise.
(beng, yáo, bâi, tui, tiâo, jing)
Waist, shoulders, and hips outdo the whirlwind.
Appear and disappear, transmuting shadows without
    trace.

Void and substance, substance and void, who can
    determine?
What need to "knock over mountains" or "lift tripod-
    cauldrons"?
Wait until you sight the great enemy to display heroism:
Only when you know this may you be considered expert.

Notes: To "knock over mountains" and "lift tripod-cauldrons" refer to feats of brute force by primeval rebel Gònggong, and Hegemon King Xiàng Yû. [69:10] "Sound in the east, strike in the west" (shengdong, jíxi) is a tactical proverb from the Táng dynasty, utilized by Máo Zédong in his theory of guerilla warfare.[286]

III. Short and Long Range Weapons

i. Saber and Sword 刀劍 Daojiàn

Saber and Sword are neither two nor one:
If you wish to succeed, then be good at concentration.
At leisure use the hard, when busy use soft.
Steps should follow, weapons should stick.

Head, Hands, Feet connect in mutual succession;
Waist, Shoulders, Hips strive for efficient convenience.
Until near to the body, in general do not block:
He will naturally be busy, I naturally at ease:

If acquainted with transmutation's exercise, there's never
    any difficulty.
If you ask the Central Mystery's wondrous logic,
It is still at oblique walking and Single Whip:
Do the myriad differences to one root connect, or not
    connect?

The husbandman always in himself has truth:
"Expansive Energy" in his chest is concealed.
I urge you, sir: nourish to complete a steely great body,
　Filling up space-time, for myriad ages strong.

Notes: This song is full of resonance with Tàijíquán Theory "hard and soft," "follow and stick," and "a myriad to one root connected." It likewise urges use of all body-parts holistically. Single Whip [69:8, 9; 72:9, 13, 19, 30] is a technique familiar from Tàijíquán. "Expansive Energy" is again a quotation from Mencius.[287] *[29; 32; 34; 58; 69: 21b; 70:I-ii]*

ii. Spear and Fists 槍拳 Qiangquán

Spear and Fists put Spirit and Energy first;
Moment's dynamics come next;
Just to speak of Force's quantity is lowest!
Every man has a road to reach the Mysterious Pass,
To be sprightly and lively is easy, to transmute is hard.

Men have void places, I have none;
At men's turning-back time, I back turn.
Chop, Uplift, Blast, and Hit are like gunpowder;
Hands, feet, shoulders, hips are as smoke and fire.

Beyond this are the Pénglái [*Triple Island*] immortal guests:
Three is One, oh! One is Three.
Long against Short, no need to struggle;
Short against Long, no use to panic!

Notes: Tàijíquán pushing hands, which embodies the essence of Tàijíquán martial applications, is closely related to sticking spears. Chop, Uplift, Blast, and Hit (pi, tí, beng, dâ) may be compared to the four powers of Tàijíquán. The three magic islands of Pénglái are placed by legend in the Yellow Sea, north of the Shandong peninsula. The belief in their existence may derive from a mirage, which is reported from the area. "Three is One" refers basically to the triple alignment of head, hand, and foot.

71. Monkey Pole
猿猴棒 **Yuánhóu Bàng**

[48 Techniques]

1. Clasp Hands, Mid-Level. 2. Ape Beast Opens Lock. 3. Cover Hit. 4. Oblique Pole. 5. Scissor Leap. 6. Mid-Level. 7. Back Throw. 8. Rear Cover Hit. 9. Su Qín *[69:3, 12; 71:26]* Shoulders Sword. 10. Draw-up, Chop Mountain. *[69:7, 12, 20; 71:15, 36]* 11. Left Cut. 12. Right Cut. 13. Suspend Leg, Pull Hit. 14. Raise Pole, Hit Face. 15. Reverse Hand, Chop Mountain. *[69:7, 12, 20; 71:10, 36]* 16. Covered Hit. 17. Twist Pole. 18. Push Hit. 19. Greet Face-bone. 20. Returning Pole, Hit Brain-Rear. 21. Zhang Fei Backward Climbs Bridge. *[69:11, 12, 22b; 70:II-i; 72:8, 25]* 22. Hurl Pole. 23. Again Hurl. 24. Lower-Hand. 25. Mid-Level. 26. Su Qín Laterally Shoulders. *[69:3, 12; 71:9]* 27. One Span Bridge. 28. Extract Step. 29. Measure Heaven Rod. 30. Great Bridge Spear. 31. Return-Body Cover Hit. 32. Double-Twist Pole. 33. Jade Girl Threads Shuttles. *[Cf. Tàijíquán]* 34. Steal-Step Cover Hit. 35. Lower-Body. 36. Draw-up Pole, Chop Mountain. *[69:12; 71:10]* 37. Fairy Points out the Road. *[69:3; 72: 16; Qi Jìguang, Rattan Shield and Broadsword 3.]* 38. Four Gate-gods Fight. 39. Above, Hit Cloudy Summit. *[69: 10; 72:5, 13, 19, 24, 26, 31–34]* 40. Below Hit, Sweep Hall. 41. Woodcutter Shoulders Firewood. 42. Scissor Flick. 43. One Shake, Chop Mountain. *[69:7, 12, 24; 71:10, 15; 72:24]* 44. Advance Left-Step, One Jab. 45. Advance Right-Step, One Wheel Hit. 46. Mid-Level Scoop. 47. Herd Sheep Staff. 48. One Pull-back.

FIGURE 28: TRUE MARTIAL GOD IN CHÁNG'S MONKEY POLE

Cháng Family manuscript: True Martial (Zhenwû) represents the element of Water and the North. He is the chief deity worshipped at Húbêi's Mt. Wûdang:

> Heavenly One produces Water, North Pole's True Martial:
> Both hands press a sword, Myriad Things all submit. *[Cf. 72:1]*

FIGURE 29: MONKEY KING IN CHÁNG MONKEY POLE

Cháng Family manuscript: Monkey King is Sun Wùkong from the epic *Westward Travelogue* of Táng monk Xuánzàng's pilgrimage to India. Monkey makes himself immortal by forging himself in Lâo Zî's Eight Trigrams furnace.[288] The pill of black and white is the tàijí ball of Shady and Sunny, yin and yáng forces.

> I have one pill of black and white, mutually harmonized.
> In the Eight Trigrams furnace interior,
> I refined to completion the elixir drug.

72. Double Sword Catalogue
雙劍名目 Shuangjiàn míngmù

[36 Techniques]

1. *Zhenwû Presses Sword*

   Note: *"True Martial" is Daoism's god of war and the North. [Cf.* FIGURE *28]*

   Lateral body stance, both hands hold swords. Cross and fork downward, once press.

2. *Waves Roll up Floating Duckwood*

   To head-top parting, push twice.

3. *Rain Knocks Down Flowers*

   To body-sides parting, sweep once.

4. *Wáng Láng Hacks the Ground*

   Note: *Wáng Láng was defeated by Liú Xiù (4* B.C.–A.D. *57), who became Emperor Guangwû, founder of Eastern Hàn.*

   Spring up, drop down doubled swords. Squat body, hack the ground.

5. *Great Roq Unfurls Wings [69:18]*

   Spring up. Left and Right *Cloudy Summit* dynamic. *[69:10; 71: 39; 72:13, 19, 24, 26, 31–34]*

6. *Lone Goose Exits Flock*

   Backward, once scissor. Right hand to head-top, once slash.[289]

7. *Two Dragons Play with Pearl [69:4]*

   Left and right turn and hack. One sword at forearm-top, one sword at ribs-underside.

8. *At Mángcháng Bisect Snake [69:12, 22]*

   Let swords once retract. *[Zhang Fei's] Trick Horsemanship* dynamic. *[69:11, 12; 70:II-i; 71:21; 72:25]* Chop groin, hacking downward.

9. *Golden Bridge Rainbow*

   Level fling down one *Single Whip* dynamic. *[69:8, 9; 70:III-i; 72:13, 19, 30]*

10. *Thrice Recover Luòyáng*

    Note: *In* A.D. *9 usurper Wáng Mâng overthrew Hàn. Later the Red Eyebrow sect captured Luòyáng but withdrew, and, in* A.D. *25, Luòyáng was inaugurated as capital of Eastern Hàn.*

Cover and Grind Triple Fist dynamic. *[cf. Pounding Mortar fist of Chén Tàijíquán]*

11. **Chén Péng Presents Saber**
    Note: Chén Péng helped Liú Xiù, future Emperor Guangwû (r. 25–47), to found Eastern Hàn.
    Deflecting Hand, Punching Fist dynamic.

12. **Oblique Wind Blows Swallows**
    Oblique Walk, Back-foot Step dynamic.

13. **Black Clouds Cap Summit** *[69:10, 12; 71:39; 72:5, 19, 24, 26, 31–34]*
    Once again, *Cloudy Summit*, with *Single Whip*. *[69:8, 9; 70: III-i; 72:9, 19, 30]*

14. **Cinnabar Phoenix Preens Plumage**
    Geese Part Golden Plumes dynamic.

15. **Beautiful Lady Retires to Cavern** *[69:8]*
    Backward retire, parting clasp. Right hand makes sword laterally depress his shaft. Left-hand dynamic is high.

16. **Fairy Points out the Road** *[69:3; 71:37; Qi Jiguang's Rattan Shield and Broadsword 3]*
    Backward one chop. Rotating body dynamic.

17. **Refine Earth into Steel**
    Cross-sign step. *[20; 69:3, 7, 12, 19, 24; 72:22]* Turn swords downward, once point. Left hand hangs over head-top; right hand downward thrusts.

18. **White Snake Spits Out** *[cf. Tàijíquán]*
    Right hand flips up, one jerk. Scissor step. Left sword to bosom center, one jab.

19. **Paired Wings in Tandem Fly**
    Yet again, one *Cloudy Summit*. *[69:10; 71:39; 72:5, 13, 24, 26, 31–34]* Roll open *Single Whip*. *[69:8, 9; 70:III-i; 72:9, 13, 30]*

20. **Kunwú Cuts Jade**
    Note: This sword, which could cut jade, was presented by barbarians to King Mù (trad. r. 1001–947 B.C.) of Zhou on his legendary westward expedition.[290]
    Left hand, once sweeps. Right hand, stealing a step, once chops. Again, advance a step, both swords level unroll.

21. *Rhinoceros Gazes at Moon [69:2]*
    Two hands to left side circling, push. Let swords rise to head-top, reverse to back-rear, head upward looking.

22. *Golden Scissors Snip One Branch*
    Downward once push. Then cross-fork, once part from groin downward. Both parting, flick up. Cross-sign *[20; 69:3, 7, 12, 19, 24; 72:17]* step law.

23. *Hegemon King Inspects Ranks [69:10; 70:II-ii]*
    Backward once rotate body. Left-hand sword rises above head-top. Right hand is horizontally across chest. Stretch body in *Look-out* dynamic.

24. *Èrláng Chops Mountain [69:7, 12, 20; 71:10, 15, 36]*
    Note: *Èrláng, "Second Lad," is a god, identified with Lî Bing, first Qín governor c. 300 B.C., who opened Sìchuan's first major irrigation canal. In* Westward Travelogue, *Èrláng, with the aid of his faithful hound, captures the rebel Monkey King.*[291]
    Once *Cloudy Summit. [69:10; 71:39; 72:5, 13, 19, 26, 31–34]* Left-hand sword vertical, right-hand sword is raised to head-top. Downward *Chop Mountain* dynamic.

25. *Alone Battling Cáo Cao's Troops [69:11, 12, 22; 70:II-i; 71: 21]*
    Both swords to left side, once push. Again to right side, once push.

26. *Level Sweep Sandy Desert*
    One *Cloudy Summit. [69:10; 71:39; 72:5, 13, 19, 24, 31–34]* Rotating body, slice away their heavenly souls.

27. *Disrobed, Stab Zhû*
    Note: *Xû Zhû, "Tiger Crazy" (hûchi), a warrior of "tyrant" Cáo Cao (155–220), stripped naked in the heat of battle. He was wounded and almost impaled by the lance of his opponent, Mâ Chao.*[292]
    Left hand forward, once hacks, once turns. Again once hack. Advance right step. Compliantly jab to ribs-rear.

28. *Obliquely, Butterflies Play in Plum Blossoms [69:23]*
    Both hands reverse hack. Right hand once follows, left hand flips and rises. Right hand to breast center one thrust, one

drop. Left hand again turns, one jab. Right hand again once hooks and pulls. Both swords roll open.

29. *Yakshas Patrol the Sea* [*Qi Jiguang's* Long Spear no.1]

> Note: Yakshas are demons from Hindu mythology, recruited by Buddha to protect the Law (dharma).

Both swords separately hack. Left hand, once clasps right hand. Extending body, downward once thrust, sword tip jabs into the ground. Right leg kneeling on the ground is still more marvellous.

30. *Tài'A Out of its Scabbard*

> Note: Tài'A is the legendary sword forged by Ganjiàng of Wú, c. 500 B.C.[293]

Turn head, toe-kick once right; twice raise slicing feet. Enter one *Single Whip*. [69:8, 9; 70:III-i; 72:9, 13, 19] Again, supine hands cross and retract. Bring feet together. One [sword] unrolls, one [sword] releases: twice.

31. *Gray Dragon Drags Tail* [*Qi Jiguang's* Long Spear no. 19, *Gray Dragon Shakes Tail*]

Left and right *Cloudy Summit* drop dynamic. [69:10; 71:39; 72:5, 13, 19, 24, 26, 32–34] Left hand upward flips and stirs. Right hand downward stirs and hacks.

32. *Great Fire Scorches Heaven*

Cloudy Summit drop dynamic. [69:10; 71:39; 72:5, 13, 19, 24, 26, 31, 33–34] Both hands from the center burst and flick-up.

33. *Green Dragon Waves Head*

Cloudy Summit drop dynamic. [69:10; 71:39; 72:5, 13, 19, 24, 26, 31–32, 34] Both hands sweep to deflect.

34. *Fierce Tiger Extends Claws* [69:16; *Qi Jiguang*: Long Spear 5, *Green Dragon Extends Claws.*]

Cloudy Summit drop dynamic. [69:10; 71:39; 72:5, 13, 19, 24, 26, 31–33] Both hands part from clasp, forward extend and thrust.

35. *Yellow Dragon Rotates Body*

Left and right, thrice butt with the commonplace is not the same. Basically, it is *Flip Flowers, Cannon* dynamic [69: Nos. 11, 17–19, 21, 24]. Drop to a point, both swords from below upward flick. Push with body.

36. *Zhongkuí Ducks Swords* [FIGURE 32. 69:12, 17]

Left and right apart sweep. Left[294]-leg is slightly suspended. Left sword vertically stands, at front-knee inside. Right sword, high raised, over head-top retracts, awesomely quivering. Then you get its true secrets.

These sword catalogue items are not too numerous. Dancing through them, I feel wind arise behind my ears. Though they cannot compare to Sun Great Dame's marvels [*whose sword dance was celebrated by Táng poet Dù Fû (712–770)*], if you practice them a long time, they indeed may protect your person. Thus you will not miss out on the ancients' qín [*zither*] and sword recreational diversions!

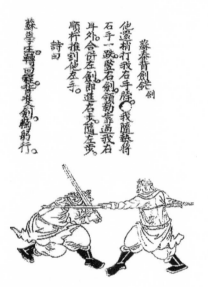

FIGURE 30: CHÁNG DOUBLE SWORD

Cháng Family manuscript: Su Qín became an itinerant alliance broker traveling between the Warring States in the third century B.C. [71:9]

Su Qín the student turns back home;
Shouldering double swords, bowing his body, he goes.

FIGURE 31: CHÁNG DOUBLE SWORD AGAINST SPEAR: *DAOIST PRIEST WATCHES STARS*

Cháng Family manuscript: double swords forked catch the attacking spear. *[69:3]*

> An old hawk, observing stars, he comes;
> Supine face looking up, head high raised.

FIGURE 32: CHÁNG DEMON POLE: ZHONGKUÍ THE DEMON CATCHER

Cháng Family manuscript: Zhongkuí makes obeisance. Táng emperor Mínghuáng, rescued by Zhongkuí in a dream, first ordered Wú Dàozî to paint his portrait. *[69:12, 17; 72:34]*

> The Center (Palace) has demon sprites,
> They fear the wielded sword.
> Zhongkuí, with one scissoring,
> Routs them westward fleeing.

FIGURE 33: CHÁNG DEMON POLE: LIGHTNING STRIKES

Cháng Family manuscript: a demon guardian, hair on end, wearing leopard skin cummerbund, strikes like lightning.

> Inner sparkling, not at one fixed,
> Like lightning it flies.
> Stone sparks, water bubbles,
> How fast they are annihilated!

APPENDIX I
Cháng's Correspondences
with *Tàijíquán Classics*

Cháng shows little of the self-conscious literary polish, classical quotations, and compression of the *Tàijíquán Classic* author, yet there are a host of echoes. Wile (1996: 186–189) lists twenty-one parallels, of which I include here only seven, marked by * (serial numbers 4; 32; 34; 35; 45; 46; 47, below). My own list here of fifty parallels, exact or close, while by no means exhaustive, applies criteria of similarity of content, as well as formulaic similarity in style of expression and language. The italicized Roman letters represent Cháng's six books, and italicized Arabic numbers his seventy-two chapters.

I.
1: Zhongqì Lùn
　　1. **not partial nor leaning.** -bùpian –bùyî.
　　2. **Grand Polarity,** Tàijí.
4: Rùyáng Fúyin, Rùyin Fúyáng shuo
　　3. **Lifted and pushed, backward toppling worries.** xiantui, hòudâo-zhi you.
　　4.* not partial nor leaning; without excess and insufficiency. -bùpian –bùyî, wúguò -bùjí.
　　5. flexion, return it with extension. qu-zhê huán-zhi –yî shen
　　6. ... are all thus. –wú-bù -jie rán.
9: Yinrù, Yinfú; Yángrù, Yángfú shuo
　　7. **not partial nor leaning.** -bùpian –bùyî.
10: Yinyáng Luàndiân Rùfú shuo
　　8. **suddenly in front, suddenly behind...** -huqián, -huhòu...

229

9. **Although application laws are unlimited...** –sui yòngfâ –wúqióng.

10. **Energy necessarily is clogged and obstructed.** qì -bì rúzhì.

11 (25): Lùn Tóu

11. **not partial nor leaning.** -bùpian -bùyî.

II.

12 (27): Lùn Shôu

12. **Grand Polarity, Tàijí.**

13 (26): Lùn Zú

13. **still as the mountain ranges.** jìng –rú shanyuè.

14. **left vacuous and right substantial; right vacuous and left substantial.** zuôxu –ér yòu shí-zhê, yòuxu -ér zuôshí-zhê...

15 (11): Yinyáng Zhuânjiê Lùn

15. **stillness at its Pole becomes motion... Motion at its Pole becomes stillness.** jìngjí -ér dòng..., dòngjí -ér jìng...

16. **high, and higher, till you can go no higher.** -ruò gao, -ér -gènggao, wúkê gao.

17. **low, and lower, till you can go no lower.** -ruò di, -ér -gèngdi, wúkê di.

18. **... are all thus.** -wú-bù -jie rán.

19. **at midpoints without intervening breaks.** -zhong –wú jiànduàn.

16 (12): San-jian wéi Qì-zhi Gânglîng Lùn

20. **Although there be a thousand or myriad threads... all go home by one track...** –sui yôu qian-tóu, wàn-xù... zônggui yi-zhé.

21. **Energy's leader...** qì-zi tônglîng.

17 (16): Guòqì Lùn

22. **Energy goes, but is tugged and dragged...** qì qù, -ér qianchè.

23. **Left Energy is at the right, so retain the idea at right...** zuôqì -zài yòu, liúyì -yú yòu...

20 (13): San-jian Zhào Lùn

24. **still as the mountain ranges.** jìng –rú sanyuè.

25. **Every time I see a common student, in motion and stillness both unsteady, it is surely because he has not researched...** –Mêi jiàn súxué, dòngjìng –jù –bùwêntuô, -gài –wèijiù...

21 (14): San-jian Dào Lùn
26. In pushing (destroying) men, not to be hard and steely is all from this fault.
Tui (cuî) ren, -bùjiangang, -jie shì cî shi.
27. ... minute by minute to pay attention. kèkè liúyì.

23 (21): Xíngqì Lùn
28. ... are all thus. -wú-bù -jie rán.
29. If he moves, I instantly move. Ta dòng, wô –jí dòng.
30. does not admit a hair. -bùróng háofâ.

25 (20): Jujing Huìshén, Qìlì Yuanyuán Lùn
31. Without essential spirit, there is no Energy and force! -wú jingshén, -zé -wú qìlì...
32.* Inwardly consolidate the essential spirit. nèi shí jingshén.

26 (23): Démén -ér Rù
33. he whose hands are fast... he whose hands are slow... shôujié-zhê... shôumàn-zhê.
34.* stick and connect inseparably. niánlián –bùlí.

27 (24): Tóushôu, Èr-shôu, Qiánhòushôu Lùn
35.* discarding the near and going afar... shêjìn jiùyuân...
36. stick and connect... niánlián
37. Every time I see one use this and get hit, it is invariably because he has not seen this fault. -Mêijiàn yòng cî, -ér yíngrén-zhi dâ-zhê, gài –wèijiàn –qí yôu cî shi –yê.

28 (22): Diânqì Lùn
38. not partial nor leaning. –bùpian –bùyî.
39. Concentrate central Energy—spirit coalesced, Energy filled. Like opening a bow... Ju zhongqì, shénníng. -Rú kaigong...

III.
30: Héliàn Zhong èrshísi-Shì [commentary]
40. Grand Polarity... Grand Polarity... Infinity. Tàijí... Tàijí... Wújí.

34 (31): Yângqì Lùn
41. Grand Polarity. Tàijí.

35 (32): Liànqì Jué
42. Central Energy is *extremely hard and rigid.* Zhongqì shèn jianyìng.

36 (41): Chéng, Ting, Qíng
43. not partial nor leaning. –bùpian –bùyî.

38 (43): Lâo, Shâo Xiangsuí
> 44. **Hands fast hit hands slow.** Shôukuài dâ shôuchí.

44 (64): Dâfâ Zôngjué
> 45.* **If he does not move oh! I do not move.** bî -bùdòng -xi, wô -bùdòng.
>
> **If he is about to move oh! I first move.** bî yùdòng -xi, wô xiandòng.

46 (57): Jiâng Chushôu
> 46.* **Inwardedly consolidate the essential spirit, outwardly show peaceful ease.** nèishì *[=shí]* jingshén, wàishì anyì.

47 (58): Jiâng Diânqì
> 47.* **Before Energy moves oh! Mind first moves.** qì –wèidòng –xi xin xiandòng,
>
> **After Mind moves oh! Energy then bursts.** xin –jìdòng –xi, qì –jí chong.

IV.

68 (66): Chuxué Tiáomù
> 48. **a left movement must have a right response...** zuôdòng –bìyôu yòuying...
>
> 49. **... there is nothing rigid unbroken.** –wújian-zhi –bùpò.

VI.

70 (71): Qiangfâ: I-iii Shí'èr Biàntong
> 50. *Shady... Sunny... mutually complementary.* Yin... yáng... -jìjì *[cf. II.13; 18; III.30; 41; 57; VI.70:II-i]*

APPENDIX II
The Tàijíquán Classic
(Hébêi) Lî Yìyû (1832–1892) manuscripts[295]

a) Great Polarity Boxing: the Theory
attributed to (Shanxi) Wáng Zongyùe (?-?)

"Great Polarity (Tàijí) without poles (of Infinity) is born":
   [I.1; II.12; III.30]
Of Shady and Sunny (negative and positive), the mother:[296]
In motion dividing, in stillness joining. *[cf. II.15]*
"Without excess or insufficiency":[297]
Following flexion, it proceeds to extension. *[I.4]**

If men are hard, I am soft—
It is called "running away" (zôu);
When I comply, at men's backs—
It is called "sticking" (niân).
Move fast and the response is fast;
Move slowly and the response is slow.
Though its metamorphoses are myriad,
"One principle pervades them."[298] *[cf. I.10; II.16]*

From familiarity with the moves,
You gradually awaken to understanding power
   (dôngjìng).
From understanding power,
You by stages reach spiritual enlightenment (shénmíng).
"Without application of force for a long time,
You cannot thoroughly penetrate this."[299]

Vacuously draw up the crown's power;
Let breath-energy sink to the dantían *[below the navel]*.
"Not partial, nor leaning,³⁰⁰ *[I.1; 4; 9; II.11; 28; III.36]**

Suddenly concealing, suddenly revealing: *[cf. I.10]*
Left weighted, then left vacuous;
Right weighted, then right ethereal. *[cf. II.13; IV.68]*

"Look up, it's still higher"; *[cf. II.15]*
Look down, it's still deeper.³⁰¹ *[cf. II.15]*
If he advances, draw out longer;
If he retreats, press in closer.

One feather may not be added;
A fly may not drop.
"Men don't know me, I alone know men."³⁰²
The hero, "wherever he goes, irresistible, ³⁰³
Surely entirely derives from this.

This skill has many side-schools.
Although each has its distinctive postures,
As a rule, they don't go beyond
Strong oppressing weak, slow yielding to fast. *[II.26; III.38]*

Have-strength beating lack-strength,
Hands-slow yielding to hands-fast, *[II.26; III.38]*
Is all from innate, natural ability
Unconnected to studied force.

Refer to the phrase:
"Four ounces deflect a thousand pounds"—
This is clearly not force's victory.³⁰⁴
Regard the image of the old man able to hold off a
    crowd—
How could this by speed be accomplished?

Stand like a level balance,
Lively as a carriage wheel—
Depress one side and the other follows.
When both are weighted, it is impeded.

Every time I see someone of several years' pure practice,
Unable to manoeuvre and adapt,
Inevitably causing himself by men to be controlled,
It is because the fault of double-weighting has not been
    realized. *[cf. II.20; 27]*

To avoid this fault, you must know Shady from Sunny:
"Sticking" is "running," "running" is "sticking";
"Shady does not separate from Sunny,
Sunny does not separate from Shady."[305] *[cf. II.26; 27]**
When Sunny and Shady complement each other,[306]
    [VI.70:I-iii cf. II.13; 18; III.30; IV.41; 57; VI.70:II-i]:
This then is "understanding power."

After understanding power,
The more practice, the more skill.
Quietly studying and experimenting,
You gradually arrive at "following what the heart
    desires."[307]

Its root is: "to discard self and follow men."[308]
Many mistakenly "discard the near and seek afar."[309]
    *[II.27]**
This is called: being "out by a hair's breadth, wrong by a
    thousand miles."[310] *[cf. II.23]*
Students may not but carefully distinguish.
This is the theory.

b) Thirteen Dynamics Exercise: Mental Analysis
attr. Wû Yûxiang (c. 1812–1880)

With the mind circulate the breath-energy,
Striving to make it sink firm,
Then it can be absorbed into the bones.

With the breath-energy manoeuvre the body,
Striving to make it follow compliantly.
Then it can readily obey the mind.

If the essential spirit can be lifted up,
Then you will be without slowness and heaviness'
    concerns. [cf. I.4]
This is what is meant by "keeping the crown suspended."

Idea and breath-energy must be converted sensitively,
Then there is a feeling of roundness and mobility.
This is what is meant by "inter-changing empty and full."

In shooting forth power, one must sink firm and loose
    clean,
Concentrating in one direction.
Stand the torso centrally erect and at ease,
Held up on eight sides.

Circulate the breath-energy as if "threading the nine-
    bend bead," [311]
Leaving no cranny unreached.
Deploy power like a hundred times tempered steel,
Leaving nothing rigid undestroyed. [IV.68]

Its form is like a hawk seizing a rabbit,
Its spirit is like a cat catching a mouse,
Still as the mountain ranges, [II.13; 28]
In motion like Yangtze and Yellow Rivers.

Store power as if drawing a bow, Shoot forth power as if
    loosing an arrow. [cf. II.28]
In the bent, seek the straight:
Store up and then shoot forth.

Force is from the spine shot forth,
Steps following the torso alternate.

Drawing in is letting loose,
Cut off and then reconnect.
To and fro must have a folding action.
Advance and retreat must interchange.

Extremely soft and supple:
Only then extremely hard and strong. *[II.35]*
If you can inhale and exhale,
Only then can you be sensitive and mobile.
"Energy by straightness is nourished without harm,"[312]
Power by bending is stored in abundance.

The mind is the commander's ensign,
The energy is the flags, *[cf. II.16]*
The waist the banner.

First seek opening out,
Later seek tight concentration.
Then you can attain the close-knit.

First in the mind, afterwards in the body.
Abdomen relaxed, breath-energy absorbed into the
    bones.
Spirit at ease, body at rest.

Minute by minute bear in mind, and remember: *[cf.
    II.21]*
Once in motion, everything in motion.
Once at rest, everything at rest.
Tugged into motion, back and forth. *[cf. II.17]*
The breath-energy adheres to the back,
And is absorbed into the spine.

"Inwardly concentrate the essential spirit,
Outwardly show peaceful ease."[313] *[II.25; III.46]* **
Make steps like a cat walking,
Deploy power like unwinding silk.

The whole body is concentrated at essential spirit, not at
    energy. *[II:25; 28]*
If at energy, it is impeded. *[cf. I:10]*
He who has energy lacks force;
He who nurtures *["lacks"]* energy is pure adamant. *[cf.
    II:25]*

Energy is like a carriage wheel,
The waist is like a carriage axle.

"If he does not move,
Yourself does not move.
If he moves slightly,
Yourself has moved first."[314] *[II.23; III.44; 47]**

The power is as if relaxed, yet not relaxed.
About to open but still unopened.
Power may be interrupted, idea is uninterrupted.

First in the mind,
Then in the body.
Once movement is commenced,
The whole body must be light and sensitive.
Above all, it must be coordinated.

Let energy expand freely,
The spirit inwardly absorbed.
Do not allow deficient places,
Do not allow protruding or caved-in places.
Do not allow disconnected places.

Its root is at the feet,
It is shot forth at the legs,
Governed at the waist,
Formed at the hands.
From feet and legs and waist,
It should always be entirely one energy.

Advancing forward, retreating backward,
You can then get the moment and get the dynamic.
If unable to get moment and get dynamic,
The body then becoming uncoordinated and disordered,
The fault should be sought at waist and legs.
Upwards, downwards, forwards, backwards, left and
    right:
Are all thus. *[I.4; II.15; 23]*

All this is idea,
Not at externals.
Where there is high, there is low.
Where there is forward, there is backward.
Where there is left, there is right. *[cf. IV.68]*

Should your idea be upwards,
First lodge a downwards idea. *[cf. II.17]*
It is like, when scooping up an object,
To add the idea of crushing it,
So that its root will automatically be broken.
Then its destruction will be speedy and without doubt.

Vacuity and substance should be clearly distinguished,
Each place has each place's vacuity and substance.
The whole body's every joint is coordinated,
Allowing not a hair's breadth interruption. *[cf. II.15; 23]*

Long Boxing is like the Long Yangtze or Great Sea,
Surging on and on without a break.

Uproot, Pull, Squeeze, Press;
Grab, Cut, Elbow, Barge:
These are the Eight Trigrams.

Advance, Retreat, Left Look, Right Turn, Center Fixed.
These are the Five Actions.

Uproot, Pull, Squeeze, Press:
are the Four Sides.
Grab, Cut, Elbow, Barge:
are the Four Corners.

Advance, Retreat, Left Look, Right Turn, Center Fixed:
Are Metal, Wood, Water, Fire, Earth.

Together they make Thirteen Dynamics.

Appendix III
Xú Zhèn's 1932 Preface

Xú Zhèn 1936: Textual Notes

- This book's text is entirely according to the Shânxi Education Library Co. (Jiàoyù Túshushè) moveable type edition. From within it, erroneous words have been separately collated in an appendix to signal caution.
- This book formerly had commentary in the upper margins. Now these have all been moved to the end of each article, and are marked by one column identation.
- Illustrations are reproduced from the originals *[drawings]*, so as not to lose authenticity.
- The sequence of articles has been re-arranged. The original sequence is shown in an appended table.

The prefaced account of Chúnchéng's *[= Cháng Nâizhou]* works is based on Yuán Yûhuá's preface. Mr. Cháng's anecdotes *[omitted below, since they duplicate those in* Introduction: xii Local Histories, *above]* are based on *Physical Education periodical* articles by Chái Zhuorú: "Scholar Boxer Cháng San; *Black Tiger Extracts Heart*, Chái Rúzhù *[Sìshuî Gazetteer writes: Rúguì]*." The periodical is the January 1921 *Physical Education Journal, a Bêijíng Physical Education Research Co. (Tîyù jìkan*, Bêijíng Tîyù Yanjiùshè) publication.[315]

Xú's Preface, 1932

Mr. Cháng's Martial Skills Book is (Qing) Cháng Nâizhou's composition. The old edition was divided into *Developing and Nourishing the Central Energy Theory*, and *Martial Defense Reference*, two kinds. Altogether there were one hundred and thirty-one pieces, the pieces were disordered and the spelling corrupt. I don't know whether the manuscript was improperly arranged or miscopied. Now I have excised repetitions and ordered the sequence. This corrected text is re-written as six chapters. In all there are seventy-four pieces. I re-named it *Mr. Cháng's Martial Skills Book* from its matter. The table of contents is as above.

Cháng Nâizhou, styled Chúnchéng, Pure Sincerity, was a Hénán Province Sìshuî man. In the Qiánlóng reign (1736–1795) he received the Míngjing "Illuminated Classics" degree. He composed *Zhou Changes Expounded, Zhouyì Jiângyì*, one book. *[Xú Zhèn is mistaken here: this book on the* Change Classic *was written by Nâizhou's elder brother Cháng Shìzhou.]*[316] Being from youth up intrigued by martial skills, during writing and recital's leisure he practiced hand-fighting and fencing. After ten years he met (Hénán) Luòyáng's Yán Shèngdào and his skills greatly progressed. Finally, from these he won a great name.

Among his works are:
1) **Central Energy Theory**
2) *Twenty-four Energies*
3) **Martial Defense (Preparedness) Reference**
4) *Martial Defense Essentials*
5) *Green Dragon Enters Sea*
6) *Arhat (Luóhán) Boxing*
7) *Black Tiger Boxing*
8) *White Tiger Boxing*
9) *Cannon (Pào) Boxing*
10) *Small Red (Hóng) Boxing*
11) *Twenty-four Great Battle Boxing*
12) *Six Coordinates Pole*
13) **Monkey Pole**
14) *Six Odds Spear*
15) *Flying Cloud, Eight Dynamics Spear*
16) *Seventeen Spear*
17) *Spring-Autumns Halberd (Chunqiudao)*

18) *Single Sword Against Spear*
19) *Double Swords Against Spear [cf. Figures 30, 31]*
20) *Double Swords Paired Off*
21) *Sword Pointing to Seven Stars*
22) *Tiger-Tail Éméi Sickle*

> Notes: The three boldfaced items above, namely **Central Energy Theory**, **Martial Defense Reference**, *and* **Monkey Pole**, *occur as titles in Cháng's work, translated above. Twenty-four Energies is probably the "Twenty-four Words, above. Other unpublished items listed match those in the Eight Sets still practiced in the Cháng family. (Appendix IV) The three underlined items, namely Cannon Boxing and Red Boxing, are known to have been practiced both at Chénjiagou and Shàolín, while* Spring-Autumns Halberd *is known both from Chén archives and from a fragmentary attachment to Mr. Wáng of Shanxi's* Shady Tally Spear *manuscript, found in a Peking market c. 1930 by Táng Háo. These shared items evidence significant cross-influences betwixt Cháng, Chén, and Shàolín traditions.*

On account of his being a literary gentleman, yet loving the martial, men nicknamed him Scholar Boxer. Some say Mr. Cháng first studied with Yû Ràng, [17] and later met Yán Shèngdào. His skill becoming ever more expert, he roamed all over the four quarters. What he heard and saw then being extensive, his studies having attained great completion, he traveled to Kaifeng. Kaifeng men at the time were suffering from a violent bandit, Wáng Lún. One evening, Lún placed his coat on the governing mansion's pillar base and attached a message: "When the coat goes, then Lún goes." *[Cháng]* Nâizhou heard of it, took the coat, and hung it on a high rod, announcing, "If Lún in three days is not gone, I will take and denounce him." Lún thereupon fled.

Nâizhou's wife came from the Qín family, a Héyin (Mèngjin) hereditary clan. *[xii:b), above:* Sìshuî Gazetteer *says Lî clan of Xingyáng's Cáolî]* Their manor was grand and imposing. The porch stone steps had a thickness over two feet. Qín family boys, seeing Nâizhou arriving, playfully raised a stone. Nâizhou raised his hand and flung it. The stone immediately broke into pieces. Qín family boys again pressed him to break the stone steps. Nâizhou climbed them and the stones all split in the middle. Further, he could walk on the surface of water, and his body could stick to walls. Such curious and abnormal techniques are related in a plethora of tales and may not be completely rationalized.

On the other hand, his books speak of boxing skills based on nourishing Energy, striving to cause Energy to be stored in the abdomen, essence and spirit to combine into one, so Energy and force are completed. Energy force is essence and spirit ability to overcome things. He says that, in response to an opponent, it is important for empty and solid to be mutually complementary. He says: when exercising, both arms should be soft and flexible, not employing force. He says that to knock down a man, it is necessary for the front leg rapidly to advance to the opponent's body rear, either at the man's legs inside or outside. He says that refinement laws [training methods] must adapt to dynamic spontaneity, striving to make the external form [body] into one house; further, to make it rounded and fluent, allowing sinews and joints to relax and open. He is altogether subtle, marvelous and profound, and gets the pivot key!

His theory, under *Hitting Laws [44]*, says:
> If he does not move, I do not move. If he is about to
> move, I first move.

His theory, under *Issuing Hands [45]*, says:
> Inwardly consolidate the spirit, outwardly display
> peaceful ease.

This is Tàijíquán's essential meaning, yet Mr. Cháng also got it. They suffice to demonstrate his exceptional expertise.

Among Nâizhou's disciples, Chái Rúzhù *[the* Gazetteer *writes: Rúguì]* is the most famous. In the Sìchuan and Southern Sectarian Rebellion *[White Lotus sect 1795–1804]* campaigns, he constantly led a brigade and trained them to defend the neighborhood. The Sectarian Rebels feared him.

Master Cháng's sons and grandsons also had those who were able to transmit his teachings, down to Nâizhou's fifth-generation descendent Dépû, who used his skills to teach Sìshuî's Yuán Yûhuá. After Yûhuá in

1921 (tenth year of the Republic) was appointed to Mt. Song Garrison
[by Shàolín] as boxing and fencing coach, this book was first published
in Shânxi Province. Mr. Féng Chaorú obtained a copy to show me.
Nâizhou's works on martial skills, with each book's essentials, are
quite complete in this compilation. The remainder is superfluous detail.
If one gets to see this compilation, one may see his skilled techniques in
entirety. So I put it in order and made it consistent.

(signed) 1932, July, **Xú [Zhèn] Zhédong**.

Appendix IV
Cháng Family Boxing

Cháng Yìjun demonstration photograph (2002): Blasting Heaven Cannon Chongtian Pào (from Eight Sets: 2. Xiâo Luóhàn, below)

Cháng Yìjun in 2002 showed me illustrated manuscripts, which he kindly permitted me to photograph, including sample pages of Monkey Pole, Yaksha Demon Pole, Double Swords Against Spear (Shuangjiàn díqiang, dated Qiánlóng 45-nián, 1780), and Energy breathing (qì) theory with diagrams. *[FIGURES 28–33]*

Cháng Yìjun also listed for me the Cháng Family system of Eight Sets, with Monkey Pole, which he said altogether takes two hours to perform, as follows:

Ba-tào Eight Sets
1) Dà Luóhàn, **Great Arhat** (Buddha's Disciples)
2) Xiâo Luóhàn, **Small Arhat**
3) Qinglóng chuhâi, **Green Dragon Out of the Sea**
4) Pàoquán, **Cannon Fist**
5) 24-shì; 24-pianshì, Twenty-four Dynamics, Twenty-four
   Subsidiary Dynamics

6) Báihû quán, **White Tiger Fist**
7) Heihû quán, **Black Tiger Fist**
8) Yînzhàn quán, **Hidden Battle Fist**

Weapon: Yuánhóu Bàng, **Monkey Pole**

Appendix V
Xú Zhèn's Sequence of Articles

My restored sequence of Cháng's 72 articles, with Xú Zhèn's corresponding sequence of 74 articles

Ch	1	2	3	4	5	6	7	8	9	10	11	12	13	14	15	16	17	18	19	20
Xú	1	2	3	4	5	6	7	8	9	10	25	27	26	28	11	12	16	17	15	13
Ch	21	22	23	24	25	26	27	28	29	30	31	32	33	34	35	36	37	38	39	40
Xú	14	19	21	18	20	23	24	22	29	30	65	74	67	31	32	41	42	43	61	44
Ch	41	42	43	44	45	46	47	48	49	50	51	52	53	54	55	56	57	58	59	60
Xú	59	60	62	64	56	57	58	33	35	40	36	35	38	39	63	46	37	45	48	54
Ch	61	62	63	64	65	66	67	68	69	"	";	70	71	72						
Xú	55	47	49	51	50	52	53	66	68	69	70	71	72	73						

Xú Zhèn's sequence of 74 articles, with my corresponding restored sequence of 72 articles

Xú	1	2	3	4	5	6	7	8	9	10	11	12	13	14	15	16	17	18	19	20
Ch	1	2	3	4	5	6	7	8	9	10	15	16	20	21	19	17	18	24	22	25
Xú	21	22	23	24	25	26	27	28	29	30	31	32	33	34	35	36	37	38	39	40
Ch	23	28	26	27	11	13	12	14	29	30	34	35	48	52	49	51	57	53	54	50
Xú	41	42	43	44	45	46	47	48	49	50	51	52	53	54	55	56	57	58	59	60
Ch	36	37	38	40	58	56	62	59	63	65	64	66	67	60	61	45	46	47	41	42
Xú	61	62	63	64	65	66	67	68	69	70	71	72	73	74						
Ch	39	43	55	44	31	68	33	69	"	";	70	71	72	32						

Notes: The sequence of **1–10** and **29–30** is identical in both. At the original positions of **22, 39, 43** duplicate articles were removed by Xú. I follow Xú in the repositioning of **72** (Xú's 73) Double Sword from its received position at 29. I combine Xú's 68–70 Twenty-four Words, Twenty-four Word Illustrations and Twenty-four Word Subsidiaries as **69**, under one article, as in Cháng's received schema.

Cf. Xú Zhèn 1936: 145–146, showing Cháng's received table of contents.

Bibliography

Bâo Xiântíng 寶顯廷 prefaced 1931, 1936: *Xíngyì Quánpû Zhèngxùpian*, re-issued Huálián chubânshè, Táibêi, 1972.

Chái Zhuorú 柴桌如 1921: "Scholar Boxer: Cháng San: Cháng San Rúquánshi Cháng San 儒拳師萇三; "Black Tiger Extracts Heart: Chái Rúzhù" 黑虎掏心柴如柱 [= Rúguì 桂]; in *Physical Education periodical (Tîyù jìkan)*, Bêijíng Tîyù Yanjiùshè, January 1921. (present availability unknown)

Cháng Nâizhou 萇乃州: *Chángshì Wûjì shu, Mr. Cháng's Martial Skills Book*, 萇氏武技書, Cháng-shì Wûjì shu, ed. Xú Zhèn (Zhédong) 徐震 (哲東), prefaced 1932, 1936, after Shânxi Jiàoyù Túshushè moveable type edition, illustrations photographed from originals; re-issued 1969, Liánhuá chubânshè, Táibêi; Zhonghuá Wûshù chubânshè 1973, Táibêi.

Chén Pànlîng, see: Léi Xiàotian.

Chén Wànqing 陳萬卿: "The Martial Forests rare flower—Cháng family boxing" Wûlín qíba, recent unpublished television address.

Chén Xin 陳鑫 1919, Chén Pànlîng inscribed 1964, 1968: *Tàijíquán túshuo*, Zhenshànmêi, Táibêi.

Chén Yánlín 陳炎林 1936: *Tàijíquán Zhenzhuàn*, Huálián chubânshè, Táibêi, 1980.

Chén Zengzhì 陳增志, Chén Wànlî 陳萬里 2001: "Chángjiaquán qîyuán kâo," *Wûhún 2001–2 (152)*: 40–41.

Chéng Chongdôu, Zongyóu ("Lineage of Yu Dáyou"?) 程沖斗, 宗猷 1616: *Shàolín Gùnfâ Chánzong*; 1621: *Gengyú Shèngjì*; *Shàolín Gùn tújiê* 少林棍圖解 Reproduced Matsuda 1975; Xú Hèlíng 1930.

(Hàn) Dàdài: *Ritual Record Lîjì*.

Déqián 德虔, Sùfâ 素法, Shàolín monks, 1989: *Shàolín Dâlêi Mìjué*, Bêijíng Tîyùxuéyuàn chubânshè, Bêijíng.

Dudbridge, Glen 1970: *The Hsi-yu Chi*, Cambridge University Press.

Guodiàn Chûmù Zhújiân, Jingménshì Bówùguân 1997, Wénwù chubânshè, Bêijíng.

(Qing) Hú Xû 胡煦 (1655–1736): *Zhouyì Hánshu*; essay in *Zhou Zî Quánshu*, 1757, Jiangxi.

(Jìn) Huáng Fûmì 皇甫謐 (215–282): *Jiâyî Jing* 甲乙經, *Alpha-beta Classic* of medicine.

(Hàn) Huáng Shígong 黃石公: *Sanlyuè Three Stratagems.*

(Míng-Qing) Huáng Zongxi 黃宗羲 (1610–1695): *Obituary for Wáng Zhengnán* (1617–1669); son Huáng Bâijia: *Internal Boxing.*

(*Tàishàng*) *Huángtíng Jing, Yellow Court Classic* 太上黃庭經, attr. Lady Wèi (c. 300), (Xiyúnshan) Wùyuán Zî, Liú Yiming 劉一明's commentary, reissued 1966, Chóngguang Shudiàn, Táinán.

(Qing) Jî Yún 紀昀 (1724–1805) 1789–1798 written, 1800 published: *Yuèwei Câotáng Bîjì* 閱微草堂筆記. Wang Xiándù 1979 preface; 1980, Shànghâi Gûjíchubânshè, Shànghâi. Cf. *Sì-kù Quánshu.*

Jintái Boxing Tablature 金台拳譜, Huang Shuîyuan 黃水源 ed. 1929: Zhongxi Shujú, Shànghâi. Courtesy Allen Pittman.

Jung, C.G. and C. Kerényi 1950: *Essays on a Science of Mythology*, tr. R.F.C. Hull, New York.

Kang Gewu (Géwû) (1948–) (of Zhaotong, Yúnnán) 1995: *The Spring and Autumn of Chinese Martial Arts—5000 Years*, Plum Publishing, Santa Cruz, California.

Léi Xiàotian 雷嘯天 1979: *Chén Pànlíng's* 陳泮岭 *Xíngyìquán Shîèr-Xíng*; *Baguàzhâng*; Zhenshànmêi chubânshè, Táibêi.

Lî Chéng 李誠 1991: *Xíwû Bìdú*, Bêijíng Tîyù Xuéyuàn chubânshè, Bêijíng.

    1995, with Lî Guangjié 李光捷, Lî Bó 李勃: *Wû-zhi Hún: Zhongzhou Wûlín míngrén dà xiêshí* 武之魂: 中州武林名人大寫實, (reprint from 1986, *no. 11, Zhonghuá Wûshù:* "Cháng Nâizhou, Chéngou jié zhìyôu"), Guójì Wénhuà chubânshè, Bêijíng.

Lî Tianjì 李天驥 prefaced 1980, Lî Déyìn 李德音, 1981, 1982: *Xíngyìquán sù*, Rénmín Tîyù chubânshè.

Louis, Francois 2003: "The Genesis of an Icon: The *Taiji* Diagram's Early History": 145–196, *Harvard Journal of Asiatic Studies*, June 2003, Vol. 63, No. 1, Harvard Yenching Institute.

Matsuda Ryûchi 松田隆治 1975; 1979 (Korean version) *Chungguk Musulsa* "*History of Chinese Martial Arts*," tr. Cho Eunhun, Seorin Munhwasa, Seoul.

    1986 (Chinese version): *Zhongguó Wûshù Shîlyuè*, Huálián chubânshè, Táibêi.

    1993: "Cháng Sanzhâi 1724–1783, Xingyáng, Hòu Xincun (Sìshuî-xiàn)," *Bûjitsu* 武術 *Martial Skills* periodical, autumn 1993, Fukuchôdô 福昌堂, Tôkyô.

Mèng Zî 孟子, 軻 (c. 300 B.C.): (eponymous author of *Meng Zî*) Dialogues of the Confucian philosopher, Mencius.

Pointing to Moon Record, see: *Zhîyuè Lù.*

(Qing) Pú Songlíng (c. 1640–1715) of Shandong: *Liáozhai Zhìyì Leisure Studio Record of the Unusual.*

Qi Jiguang 戚繼光 c. 1562, 1966, Lî Ying'áng ed.: *Mr. Qi's Martial Arts, the Complete Book, Qishì Wûyì quánshu,* Huálián chubânshè, Táibêi. *Sì-kù Quánshu* 728–576: *Jîxiào Xinshu.*

San-guó Yânyì, see *Three Kingdoms Romance.*

Sawyer, Ralph D. tr. 1993: *The Seven Military Classics of Ancient China,* Westview, Boulder.

Shady Tally Classic, Yinfú Jing 陰符經, attr. Yellow Emperor (attr. c. 2000 B.C.), commentary by Zhugé Liàng q.v. et al.

Shahar, Meier 2000: "Epigraphy, Buddhist Historiography, and Fighting Monks: The Case of the Shaolin Monastery," *Asia Major,* 3rd Series xiii-2: 15–36, Academia Sinica, Taiwan.

Shàolín Quánshù Mìjué, Zunwôzhai zhûrén 尊我齋主人 "Respect Me Studio Master": 1936, augmented version of *Shàolín Zongfâ* qv., Shànghâi; 1971 Wûshù chubânshè, Táibêi.

Shàolín Zongfâ, Shàolín Lineage Law, gûbên, Zunwôzhai zhûrén "Respect Me Studio Master": Chén Tiêxîng (Tiêsheng) 1914, text only, Shànghâi; Jiang Xiáhún 1922 with illustrations, re-issued Lî Yingáng, 1963, 1968, Qílín Túshu gongsi, Hong Kong. Cf. *Shàolín Quánshù Mìjué.*

Shàolínsì Ziliàojí xùbian, Wúgû, Yáo Yuân comp., 1984, Shumù Wénxiàn chubânshè, Bêijíng.

Shîjî, Historians' Records, see: Simâ Qian.

Sì-kù Quánshu, Qindìng "Four Archives" Complete Books, imperially authorized 四庫全書, 欽定 ed. Jî Yún q.v. from 1772, under Qing Emperor Qiánlóng, mammoth compendium of Chinese literature of every category.

(Hàn) Simâ Qian 司馬遷 (d. c. 85 B.C.): *Shîjî* 史記, *Historians' Records.*

(Qing) *Sìshuî Xiànzhì* 汜水縣志 *Sìshuî District Gazetteer,* Zhào Dongjie 趙東階 redaction.

Sun Zî, Wû 孫子武 (c. 500 B.C.): (eponymous author of *Sun Zî*) *Arms' Laws, Bingfâ* 兵法, *The Art of War.* Cf. Sawyer.

Szymanski, Jarek 2002: website *FromInsideChina* on Cháng Boxing.

Tàigong, Lyû Shàng 太公望, 呂尚 (c. 1100 B.C.), attr.: *Liù-Tao Six Satchels.*

Táng Háo (Fànsheng) 唐豪 1930, 1969: *Shàolín, Wûdang kâo,* Huálián chubânshè, Táibêi.

1935, 1971: *Nèijiaquán d yanjiù,* Liánhuá chubânshè, Táibêi.

1963: Gù Liúxing 顧留馨 ed., prefaced 1963, Shànghâi: *Tàijíquán yanjiù,* (undated, c. 1980) Yixin shudiàn, Hong Kong.

1971: Zhu Qìngzhong 朱慶忠, ed. *Wáng Zongyuè, Tàijíquán Jing*

yanjiù, Huálián chubânshè, Táibêi.

1978, with Xú Zhèn, Dèng Shíhâi: ed. *Tàijíquán kâo*, East Asia Book Agency, Hong Kong.

1986: Yú Cíyùn 俞慈韻 ed.: *Shénzhou Wûyì (-shàngcè)*, Jílín Wénshî chubânshè, Chángchun.

Three Kingdoms Romance, San-guó Yânyì 三國演義, Yuán dynasty romance by Shi Nâi'an, based on the history of the collapse of the Hàn dynasty into three warring kingdoms of Shû, Wèi, and Wú.

(Sòng) Wáng Anshí 王安石 (1021–1086): *Jinggong Lùnyì*.

Wáng Shùjin 王樹金 1978: *Baguà Liánhuán Zhâng*, Táizhong, Táiwan.

Water Margin, Shuîhú zhuàn 水滸傳, attr. (Yuán) Shi Nâian 施耐庵, a prose epic of rebel outlaws, based in the marshes of western Shandong in the Northern Sòng dynasty (c. 1100).

(Hàn) Wèi Bóyáng 魏伯陽, (Qing) Zhu Yuányù 朱元育 1669 ed.: *Cantóngqì: chányou* 參同契闡幽, Zhenshànmêi chubânshè, Táibêi.

Westward Travelogue, Xiyóujì 西游記, attr. (Míng) Wú Chéngen 吳承恩, humorous and lyrical fantasy based on legends of the overland pilgrimage of Táng monk Xuánzàng to bring back Buddhist sutras from India.

Wile, Douglas 1996: *Lost Ta'i-chi Classics from the Late Ch'ing Dynasty*, SUNY, New York.

1999: *Ta'i Ch'i's Ancestors: The Making of an Internal Martial Art*, Sweet Chi Press, New York.

(Yuán) Wú Chéng 吳澄, 文正: *Wú Wénzhènggong Quánjí*. Confucian philosophy.

Wû-deng Huìyuán, "Five Lamps Meet at the Prime" 五燈會元, ed. (Sòng) Shî Pûjì/Huìmíng 釋普濟/慧明 1258, reissued 1976, Déchang chubânshè, Táibêi. A classic collection of Chán Buddhist masters teaching from the five major schools.

Wú Jingxián, Wú Bîngxiào 1990: *Yinbâqiang*, Rénmín Tîyù chubânshè, Bêijíng.

(Qing) Wú Shu, Pike 吳殳 prefaced 1678, 1970: *Shôubeì lù* 手臂錄 *"Hand and Arm Record,"* Huálián chubânshè, Táibêi. The classic of spearmanship.

Xí Yúntài 習云太, Hú Xiâofeng 胡曉風 1985: *Zhongguó Wûshùshî*, Rénmín tîyù chubânshè, Bêijíng. Chinese martial history.

Xiyóujì, see *Westward Travelogue*.

Xú Hèlíng 徐鶴齡, of Chéngjiang, prefaced 1930 at Shànghâi: (Míng) Chéng Chongdòu: *Shàolín Gùn tújiê*, "Shàolín inner disciple: (Jînjiang ['hóng']) Mr. Chén's secret copy (mìcángbên)," re-published 1968, Guóshù Cóngbian-2, Huálián chubânshè, Táibêi.

Xû Yûsheng 許禹生: *Guóshùguân Jiângyì*: "Chángjiaquán-zhi chuàngshîngshî, Wúgû, Yáo Yuân ed. 1984, *Sháolinsí Ziliàojí-xùbian*: 281–286, Shumù Wénxiàn chubânshè, Bêijíng.

Xú Zhèn, Zhédong 徐震, 哲東 prefaced 1935, 1936: *Tàijíquán Pû lîdông, biànwèi: hébian*, 1965, Zhenshànmêi chubânshè, Táibêi.

> 1936: *Chángshì Wûjìshù*, preface 1932, 1969 Liánhuá chubânshè, Táibêi; cf. Cháng Nâizhou 1969.

> 1936 preface, 1965: *Tàijíquán Kâoxìnlù* Unicorn Press, Hong Kong.

> 1936: *Tàijíquán Pû lîdông*; *Tàijíquán Pû biànwèi*; *Tàijíquán Kâoxìn lù*; see Táng Háo 1978.

Yìjîn Jing 易筋經, *zhenbên, mìbên Xîsuíjing*, attr. Bodhidharma [d. 536], (Táng) "Paramiti's translation," 1979, Zìyóu chubânshè, Táibêi.

Yinfú Jing, see *Shady Tally Classic*.

(Míng) Yú Dàyóu 俞大猷: *Zhèngqìtáng yújí: iv Jiànjing*, "*Correct Energy Hall additional collection: Sword Classic*," 1565, see also: Qi Jìguang.

(Qing) Zhang Kôngzhao 張孔昭, Cáo Huàndôu 曹換斗 prefaced 1784; Tányînlú 1930 ed.: *Quánjing, Quánfâ Bèiyào* "*Boxing Classic, Boxing Laws*" *Essentials*" 拳經拳法備要.

Zhang Yàozhong 張耀忠 1989: *Tàijíquán Gûdiân Jinglùn Jízhù*, Shanxi Rénmín chubânshè, Tàiyuán.

(Hàn) Zhào Yè 趙曄: *Wú-Yuè (Chunqin*, "*Annals of Jiangxi and Zhèjiang.*") 吳越春秋.

Zhîyuè Lù 指月錄 "*Pointing to Moon Record*," (Míng) Qú Rûjì 瞿汝稷 (1548–1610) ed. 1602; 1976, Xinwénfeng chubânshè, Táibêi. Teachings of Chán Masters up to the Sòng dynasty.

Zhongguó Xìqû Qûyì Cídiân "Chinese Dramatic Arts Dictionary" 1981, Shànghâi Yìshù yanjiùsuô.

(Three Kingdoms) Zhugé Liàng, Kông Míng 諸葛亮, 孔明 (181–234): 1960, 1974 ed. *Zhugé Liàng jí*, Zhonghuá shujú, Bêijíng.

Zunwôzhai zhûrén "Respect Me Studio Master," see: *Shàolín Zongfâ*; *Quánshù Mìjué*.

Endnotes

1 Xú Zhèn 1936: 145–146.

2 Chén Wànqing personal discussion (8/21/03). A synopsis of Cháng Shìzhou's work *Zhouyì Jiângyì* 周易講義 on the *Change Classic* is given in *Sì-kù Quánshu: Zôngmù: x Jingbù Yìlèi cúnmù iv* (1: 243).

3 *Zuôzhuàn: Lû Chénggong 16th year.*

4 Yû Ràng 禹讓. Xú Zhèn 1936, 1965 -shàng: 11 attributes the statement on Yû Ràng being a teacher of Cháng Nâizhou to Chái Zhuorú 1921.

5 Zunwôzhai zhûren "Respect Me Studio Master" 1915: *Shàolín Lineage-law*: 13.

6 (Sòng) Zhào Yànwèi: *Yúnlàn Mànchao*.

7 Louis 2003: 166–169.

8 Xú Zhèn prefaced 1935: *Tàijíquán Pû lîdông*.

9 Chén Wànqing (8/21/03)) advised me the date of Cháng's death is unknown, and merely deduced from his latest recorded date as 1783. Lî Chéng 1991: 177; 1995: 392; and Chén Zengzhì, Chén Wànlî 2001: 40 give his dates as 1724–1783. *Bujitsu* 武術, autumn 1993, accepts "Chang Sanzhâi 1724–1783." Wile 1999: 202 voices skepticism, though he accepts the period is correct.

10 Táng Háo 1986: 10 cites Wáng Xianqiàn (1842–1917): *Donghuá Lù* on Yongzhèng's 1727 anti-boxing edict. Wile 1999: 5–6 on edict; 56 on Wáng Zhengnán.

11 Chén Zengzhì, Chén Wànlî 2001: 40–41.

12 Liáng Dào 梁道, Yû Hóngqí 禹鴻起.

13 Gûsuí, Wáng Xinxiàng 古隨王新象.

14 (Míng) Qi Jìguang: *Jìxiào Xinshu. Sì-ku Quánshu* 728: 574–575.

15 Xú Zhèn 1936, 1965 *Tàijíquán Kâoxìnlù –shàng*: 10–11 Wénxiutáng 文修堂 manuscript. "Transmission" liúchuán 流傳 is Xú Zhèn's reconstruction of the nonsensical near-homophone "leak drill" lòuzuan 漏鑽:

此槍法圖係記[氾]水縣禹槍家漏鑽係張飛神至倀禹家. Manuscript note: 倀家外生[甥].

16 Táng Háo 1986: 23 "Jiâng Fa." Lî Chéng 1991: 148 "Chén Wángtíng."

17 *Lúnyû ix*: "Yán Yuan heartily sighed, saying: I look up (supine), it is still higher; drill in, it is still harder; spy it ahead, suddenly it is behind."

18 Wile 1996: 80–83 (147–148) *Yang Family Forty Chapters 30, 34.*

19 (Míng) Qì Jìguang c. 1562, 1966: 74 "Xianrén Pêngpánshì."

20 Wile 1996: 24, 43, 46, 101, 104–105, 113 "The insertion of the Ch'eng-ch'ing "Postscript" in the Wu Hsin-ku and Ch'en Ts'eng-tse prefaces to Sun Lu-t'ang's [1861–1932] *T'ai-chi ch'uan hsueh* establishes that this text cannot be later than 1919...."

21 Zhang Kôngzhao, Cáo Huàndôu preface 1784: 3. Wú Shu 1684, 1970: 3.

22 *San-guó Yânyì lxxi "gangróu jìjì."* Instructions of Cáo Cao to his general Xiàhóu Yuan, whose head was later taken by Huáng Zhong.

23 Xú Zhèn 1936: 221 dismissed an ascription to Zhang Sanfeng by a "Yáng school manuscript" as a forged accretion. Wile 1996: 37, 109 etc accepts as authentic the Mâ Tóngwén manuscript, "dated 1867," "copied by Lî Yìyú," which assigns authorship to "Zhang Sanfeng." Yet Wile 1999: 196 now classes the Mâ Tóngwén "edition" among "spurious or highly suspicious works posing as authentic...."

24 Táng Háo, Gù Liúxing preface 1963, c. 1980: 161–162.

25 Wú Jìngxián, Wú Bîngxiào 1990.

26 Xú Zhèn 1936, 1985 *Wáng Zongyuè Kâo*: 61–65; *Tàijíquán Kâoxinlù*: 179–180. Táng amends "went out of the lodge" chuguân 出館 to "brought out his draft" chugâo 出稿.

27 Táng Háo 1935: 72. Táng Háo, Zhu Qìngzhong 1971 *Wáng Zongyuè kâo*: 11–12. Wile 1996: 107.

28 Xú Zhèn 1935: 10–18 Wû Yûxiang's "jointly signed."

29 Xú Zhèn 1936: 127ff.; 138 poem; 144–145 *Jîshôu liànfâ, chéngfâ.*

30 Xú Zhèn 1935: 20 *preface, 1881.11.6* "reverently signed," 25 *postscript, 1881.11.3* Lî Yìyú "copied."

31 Xú Zhèn 1935: 20 *preface*; 25 *postscript.*

32 Wile 1996: 7, 110, 117.

33 "Salt shop" yándiàn 鹽店 is close in sound to "opium shop" yandiàn 煙店, an alternative term for "opium den" yanguân 煙館.

34 Xú Zhèn 1936: 120–122. Wile 1996: 17.

35 Wile 1996: 16–20.

36 Wile 1996: 101.

37 Xú Zhèn 1936 *Tàijíquán Pû biànwèi* passim. Wile 1996: 36–38.

38 *Wú Wénzhèng jí: iii Dáwèn: 2, Sì-kù Quánshu.*

39 Táng Háo, Gù Liúxing 1963: 184 *Zhou Zî Quánshu,* (Qing) Hú Xû 胡煦: Yinyáng -bùxiang lí, yôu -xiangxu, -xianghù-zhi miào.

40 Xú Zhèn 1935: 11 Lî Yìyú manuscript.

41 *Zhou Yì Jiângyì. Sì-kù Quánshu: Zôngmù: x Jingbù Yìlèi cúnmù iv* (1: 243). cf. Matsuda 1986: 43.

[42] *San-guó Yânyì lxxi "gangróu jìjì."*

[43] Louis 2003: 181ff.

[44] This is confirmed by (Hàn) Wáng Chong (27–c. 100) who in *Lùnhéng: Biétong* lauds the sword fencing of "Quchéng, Yuè maiden's school."

[45] Xú Zhèn 1936: *Tàijíquán Kâoxìnlù*: 127ff.

[46] (Míng) Yú Dàyóu: *Zhèngqìtáng yújí: ii: 7–10.*

[47] *Yìjîn Jing: Nèizhuàng Shényông:* 16, 127. (Qing) Pú Songlíng: *Liáozhai Zhìyì: xi Tiêbùshan fâ.* Sha Huíz' is a Moslem name. Wú Jìngzî: *Rúlín Wàishî: xlix:* 475, *lii:* 495, Rénmín Wénxué chubânshè, 1958, Bêijíng.

[48] Déqián, Sùfâ 1989: 13–14 *Xinyìbâ, Liùhé Quánpû, Liùhé Qiangpû, Liùhé Daopû.*

[49] Táng Háo 1986: 34–37 *Xíngyìquán bízû -yû pû.* Matsuda Ryûchi 1975, 1979: 199–202. Lî Chéng 1991: 175. After the "General Hitting" section are the dated signatures of four Hénán residents: 1735.1 (Xin'an) Wáng Zìchéng; 1754.7 (Rûzhou) Wáng Chenlín; 1779.10 (Rûzhou) Mâ Dìngzhèn; 1733.3 (Hénánfû = Luòyáng) Lî, unknown. The work itself is reported no longer extant.

[50] *Shàolínsì Ziliàojí xùbian* 1984: 257–258.

[51] (Míng) Qi Jìguang c. 1662, 1966: *x Chángbing duânyòng shuo:* 30. (Qing) Wú Shu 1684, 1970: *Shôubì lù: iv:* 144 *San-jian Bù-zhào,* 1970.

[52] Táng Háo 1935: 72. Táng Háo, Zhu Qìngzhong 1971 *Wáng Zongyuè kâo:* 11–12.

[53] *Shàolínsì Ziliàojí xùbian* 1984: 257–258.

[54] Déqián, Sùfâ 1989: 4–5.

[55] Wile 1996 *13:* 70; *xxxix:* 151.

[56] Lî Tianjì 1980: 201.

[57] Bâo Xiântíng 1931: 46.

[58] "Bactrian camel" tuó 駝; "ostrich" tuó 鴕.

[59] J.G. Fraser 1922: *The Golden Bough* (abbr.), Macmillan, *lxvi; lxvii.*

[60] *"Documents Classic" Shujing: Yushu,* Kuí 夔. The limping shaman's dance was anciently called "Yû step" Yûbù 禹步, after legendary Emperor Yû, who became lame after his cyclopic works in channeling China's rivers. "Zhongkuí kicks the Dipper" is a classic phrase, echoed in an application of *69:17.*

[61] (Hàn) Ban Gù, Zhao: *Hànshu: Wûxíng Zhì-shàng.* Cf. (Sòng) Wáng Anshî: *Jinggong Lùnyì: iv Hóngfàn zhuàn* "Tianyi shengshuî." 天一生水. Zhu Xi commentary on *Zhou Li* 嬚 i: 12–13.

[62] *Guodiàn Chûmù Zhújiân* 1997: 123.

[63] C.G. Jung and C. Kerényi 1950.

[64] Cf. (Qing) Pú Songlíng: *Liáozhai Zhìyì: iv Qítian Dàshèng.*

[65] *Shîjì: cix Lî Jiangjun lièzhuàn.* "Flying General" Lî Guâng of Hàn, a

great archer, was said to have "monkey arms." Rúchún, an early commentator (pre 500), explains that monkey arms (bèi) interconnect (tong) through the shoulders.

66 Déqián, Sùfâ 1989: 3.

67 Táng Háo 1986: 166–169 *"Long Boxing's development."*

68 Táng Háo 1931: *Shàolín Wûdâng Kâo*: 44–45 Wáng Shìxìng 王士性.

69 (Qing) Lín Qìng 麟慶 1828: Hóngxuê yinyuán tújì 鴻雪因緣圖記. Táng Háo 1930: 43.

70 Zhang Kôngzhao, Cáo Huàndôu prefaced 1784.

71 Wile 1996: 119.

72 Chén Xin 1919: 140–143.

73 Chén Xin 1919: 146–147 *Tàijquán quánpû*: Zhongqì "Central Energy" 162ff *fù Zhongqì biàn.* Wile 1996: 119; 1999: 81.

74 Chén Xin 1919: 212 Bùshì éméiyuè, mólái xiào bizhen? Gongwan hébùfa? Yi-fa Bèi jingshén. 不是娥眉月摩來肖逼真弓灣何不發一發倍精神.
cf. Wile 1995: 52 Lî Yìyú: "Eight-Character Secret Transmission: The ward-off [pêng] arm is extended at an angle like the crescent moon…"

75 Chén Xin 1919: 86–88.

76 Chén Xin 1919: 146 *Tàijíquán Jingpû.*

77 Chén Xin 1919: 156.

78 Chén Xin 1919: 97, 171, 192, 202, 441.

79 Wile 1996: 47, 129.

80 Chén Xin 1919: 440–441: Shanqióng, shuî jìn, yí -wúlù: Fûjian yi-kào può tóngqiáng. Bùdào shen-yûshen -xiangkào, -Suiyôu bâozhu nán fàngguang. 山窮水盡疑無路府肩一靠破銅牆不到身與身相靠雖有寶珠難放光.

81 Chén Xin 1919: 251, 253.

82 Déqián, Sùfâ 1989: 40–45.

83 Wile 1999: 82–188; 1996: 186–188.

84 Du Mù 都穆 (1459–1525), who visited Shàolín in the 11th month of 1513, is the first writer to note the Shàolín martial tradition. He remarks of the stone that appeared to reflect Bodhidharma's image: "So they say, Essential Sincerity may penetrate metal and stone." Gû wèi: jingchéng -kê tong jinshí. 故謂精誠可通金石 *Bâoyàntáng Mìjí*, pûjí -dì-4: *Yóu Míngshan* jì, iv: 4–5. cf. Shahar 2000: 15ff.

85 *Dàxué: vi Shì Chéngyì.*

86 At Xingyáng 滎陽 on 8/21/03.

87 *Qing Shî*, 1961, Guófáng Yanjiù, Táibêi: 3083ff names Xú Ji 徐積 as governor of Hénán 1774–1778. Xú Ji's interest in martial arts is verified by Kang Gewu 1995: 68.

88 Wile 1996: 118–120.

89 Lî Chéng et al.: *Wû-zhi Hún*: 343: *Chángjiaquán chuánrén d' fengcâi*. Matsuda Ryûichi, in *Bûjitsu "Martial Skills,"* autumn 1993. Liú Yìmíng 劉義明; Gao Qinglián 高青蓮; Chén Shàowû 陳少武.

90 Zhang Yìzhong 張一中. Zhu Tianxî 朱天喜; Shì Dégen 釋德根; "big knife" dàdao 大刀. Chéng Rìmào 程日Z, teacher of Cháng Family Boxing at Zhèngzhou Shàolín Wûshù xuéyuàn, Jinshuî-qu 金水區, Xishî Zhàocun 西史趙村.

91 Shàolín monks take the surname Shì "Shaka" of the Buddha, and first name by their generation, here: Eternal > Virtue > Action. Shì Déjiàn 釋德建 "Virtue Established," lay name Xú Yi 徐一; Shì Xíngjia 釋行嘉 "Action Excellent"; Shì Xíngtao 釋行韜 "Action Strategy"; Yônglì 永立 "Eternal Stance," lay name Ding Hóngyì 丁紅義 "Red Justice"; Shì Xíngxìng 釋行性 "Action Nature."

92 Hénán Province, between the provincial capital Zhèngzhou, and Sìshuî 汜水, at Xingyáng xiàn: Wángcun xiang, Hòu-xinzhuangcun liù-zû 滎陽縣王村鄉後新莊村六組. Cháng Yìjun 萇毅軍, Cháng Hóngjun 萇紅軍 "Red Army, sons of Cháng Shanlín 萇山林 "Mountain Forest."

93 Zhèng Tianxióng 鄭天雄. Hóng Yìmián 洪懿綿.

94 Chén Xin 1919 *fùlù Chénshì Jiachéng*: 478 (i) Chén Jìxià: Cháng Sanzhâi 萇三宅.

95 Preface to the 1973 Táibêi Zhonghuá Wûshù edition of Cháng Nâizhou, *Qinglóng chushuî*.

96 "Flying" General Zhang Fei, hero and adherent of Liú Bèi, founder of the Minor Hàn dynasty (A.D. 221–263).

97 *Sìshuî Xiànzhì: 8 Rénwùzhì* 汜水縣志: *8 人物志*: 48 Xú Quán 徐銓. "Zhào village" Zhàocun 趙村 may be Zhàobâo, across the Yellow River, near Chénjiagou.

98 Táng Háo 1986: 23 attests that Chénjiagou tradition gave the name of Chén Wángtíng's retainer, who had been a commander under rebel Lî Jìyù, as Jiāng Ba "Eight." *Sìshuî Xiànzhì: 8 Rénwùzhì*: 47ff. For further local traditions and legends, see: Chái Zhuorú 1921. Xú Zhèn 1978: 118–120 "Jiâng Fa is he whom Chénjiagou calls Jiâng Bâshì. He is a Qing Qiánlóng period [1736–1795] man, as Chén Xin's writing may attest." Wile 1996: 114–115 "Chiang Fa."

99 Chén Xin 1919: 477. Chén Wángtíng/Zòutíng 陳王廷/奏庭, Lî Jìyù 李際遇.

100 Xú Zhèn 1936, 965: *Tàijíquán Kâoxìnlù-shàng*: 12. Jiâng Ba, "Bâshí/shì."

101 Xú Zhèn 1936, 1965 *Tàijíquán Kâoxìnlù* -zhong: 9–10. This picture is reproduced on the cover of the 1985 edition. Táng Háo 1986: 23. Lî Chéng 1991: 148, 156 on Chén Wángtíng and Jiâng Fa.

102 (Yuán) Shi Nâi'an: *Shuîhú zhuàn*: xiii Jíxianfeng Dongguo zhenggong, Qingmiànshòu Bêijíng dòuwû.

103 General Yuè Fei (1104–1142) of Southern Sòng (1127–1278), patriotic hero and victorious general, executed under pressure from the appeasement faction, for his uncompromising opposition to the Jurchen Jin, who had conquered north China. Fei, "flying," as in "flying general," was the personal name of both heroes.

104 Baron Huán is the posthumous title conferred on Zhang Fei (fl. c. 200), heroic general of the Three Kingdoms period. "Cassock and bowl" is metaphor of lineage, borrowed from Chán Buddhism.

105 Chái Rúguì 柴如桂 [Rúzhù 如柱].

106 Chén Tianjuàn 陳天卷.

107 Cháng Kèjiân 萇克儉.

108 Xú Zhèn 1932 preface. Matsuda 1986: 43. Yuán Yûhuá 袁宇華; Cháng Dépû 萇德普.

109 *Yìjing: Xící "Appendix": I-xi.*

110 (Sòng) Zhu Xi: commentary on *Zhongyong, "Central Norm."*

111 (*Tàishàng*) *Huángtíng Jing: Nèijîng Jing*, 1966, (Xiyúnshan) Wùyuán Zî, Liú Yiming's commentary: 10–11.

112 (Hàn) Wèi Bóyáng: *Cantóngqì: xxix Xíngdé Fânfù.*

113 Lâo Zî: *Dàodé Jing: vi.*

114 Chén Xin 1919: 214, cites *Língshu Wèiqìxíng pian* on "50 circulations" per day.

115 The text here of this passage shows signs of corruption. I restore it from the medical text.

116 *Yìjîng Jing: Nèizhuàng Shényông; Liànshôu Yúgong.*

117 *Dàzàng Jing 375: Dàban Nièpán Jing iii: Jingangshen pîn, v: 622.*

118 *Mèng Zî: iia-2 Gongsun Chôu: Hàorán-zhi qì.*

119 I amend "upper posterior" to "**lower** posterior," complementary to "upper anterior."

120 I read "**prone**" for "supine" here in order to maintain the contrast.

121 (Sòng) Zhu Xi: commentary on *Zhongyong.*

122 Chén Xin 1919: 162.

123 (Sòng) Zhu Xi: commentary on *Zhongyong.*

124 The received text repeats: "Sunny, Sunny." Cf. *Yellow Emperor's Internal Classic: Soul Trunk, Huángdì Nèijing: Língshu, 13 Jingjin.*

125 I reconstruct this sentence whose text appears corrupt.

126 *Wú Wénzhèng gong Quánjí*, 1448. I am unable to find this quotation in the *Sì-bù Cóngkan* edition.

127 *Yìjing: Xící a: ix.* I amend four "Earth's Five" [#Earthly Five... #Heavenly Five... #Earthly Five... #Heavenly Five], and "Heavenly Three generates Wood [#Water]." Wile 1999: 108 does not amend. Cf. S.V.R. Camman: "The Evolution of Magic Squares in China," *Journal of the*

American Oriental Society 80 (1960): 116–124; "Old Chinese Magic Squares," *Sinologica* 7 (1962): 14–53.

[128] The received text appears to confuse "straight-on" zhèng 正 and "oblique" zé 仄, which I correct.

[129] (Sòng) Zhou Dunyí: *Zhou Liánqi xiansheng quánjí, i: Tàijítúshuo.*

[130] Chén 1919: 196.

[131] I read "close" for "open," in contrast with next.

[132] *San-guó Yânyì: lxxi "bùbù wéiying."* cf. (Qing) Wèi Yuán 魏源: *Shèngwûjì: vi.*

[133] (Hàn) Wèi Bóyáng: *Cantóngqì: xxvii.*

[134] *Yìjîn Jing: Nèizhuàng Shényông; Liànshôu Yúgong.*

[135] (Míng) Qi Jìguang 1966 ed.: 30. (Qing) Wú Shu 1684, 1970: 144 *"Three Points Not Aligned" San-jian Bù-zhào.*

[136] (Jìn) Huáng Fûmì 皇甫謐 (215–282): *Jiâyî Jing, "Alpha-beta Classic"* of medicine: *i–15 Wu-sè "Five Colors."*

[137] I adjust the order "Form, Nature, Color," from "Nature, Form, Color," to conform with what follows.

[138] Xú Zhèn restores four missing phrases after "Wood Energy at birth" up to the next line "his Form is pointed and sharp."

[139] (Hàn) Simâ Qian: *Shîjì: lxv Sun Zî lièzhuàn:* "avoid the solid, pound the vacuous" (bìshí dâoxu).

[140] *Sun Zî: i Jì.*

[141] *Sun Zî: i Jì; vi Xushí.*

[142] Xú Zhèn 1935 *Tàijíquán Lîdòng:* 18 *Dâshôu Safàng* "Eight Sounds"; *Tàijíquán Biànwèi:* 6 *Gejué* "Song 3." Chén Yánlín 1936: 294, *Dâshôu:* "Song 3" (of 7).

[143] (Hàn) Zhào Yè: *Wú-Yuè Chunqiu: ix.* Cf. (Hàn) Wáng Chong (27– c. 100): *Lùnhéng: Biétong* attributes her art to a town named Quchéng.

[144] To enter Buddha's gate is a byword for ordination. The subject concerns "entering the gate," and the next section *[27]* refers to "gates outsiders" ménwài as uninitiated laymen, "outside the gate fellows" ménwàihàn. Sòng dynasty Chán master Hùguó Cî'an Yuán used this expression to Nánzong Bîzhi of eminent layman Su Dongpo's gatha of enlightenment. *Wû-deng Huìyuán: vi -Wèixiáng Fâsì:* 39. To restore the sense, I read "life" huó as fó "Buddha"; insert an "enter" rù before the second "outer" wài; "and" jí as "then" jí: Fó[huó] yôu wàimén. -Fei rù wàimén, -jí[jí] ménwài -yê. 佛[活]有外門非入外門即[及]門外也.

[145] Confucius: *Lúnyû "Analects": xi Xianjìn.*

[146] *Chén Yánlín 1936: 294, Qiánlóng Old Copybook Tàijíquán Classic:* song 4 of 7. Rèn ta jùlì lái dâwô... Zhan, nián, lián, suí: -bù diudîng.

[147] Cf. (Hàn) Huáng Shígong: *Sanlyuè "Three Stratagems"*: *iii Xiàlyuè "Lower Stratagem."*

[148] (Hàn) Dàdài: *"Ritual Record" Lîjì*: *xlvi Lî chá* quotes the *Change Classic.*

[149] *Shîjì*: *lxv Sun Zî "biography" lièzhuàn.*

[150] *Sun Zî: i Jì*

[151] Tàigong, Lyû Shàng (1100 B.C.) attr.: *Liù-Tao "Six Satchels"*: *xxvi Junshì "Armies" Dynamics.* (Míng) Qi Jìguang: "Boxing Classic" *Quánjing.* Wile 1999: 18.

[152] (Míng) Chéng Chongdôu 1616: *Shàolín Gùnfâ Chánzong* passim.

[153] *Sun Zî: vii Junzheng.*

[154] *Zuôzhuàn: Lû Chénggong* 16th year.

[155] Chén Yánlín 1936: 300 four words: qíngyîn songfàng. Wile 1996: 100–101.

[156] *Sun Zî: Bingfâ: v Shì.*

[157] (Qing) Jî Yún, 1800: *Yuèwei Câotáng Bîjì: xix Shàoyáng xùjí*: 480–481, citing (Hébêi: Nánpí) Zhang Fóucuo, Jîngyùn: *Qiupéng Xinyû.*

[158] *Mèng Zî: iva-12 Lílóu: Ju Xiàwèi*: "Utmost sincerity that does not move has never been." (Zhìchéng, -ér –bùdòng-zhê, -wèi-zhi yôu-yê.) *Dàxué: vi Shì Chéngxià..*

[159] The line "If there is utmost sincerity, then metal and stone for it will open" is attributed to Yáng Xióng (53 B.C.–A.D. 18) by (Hàn) Liú Xin *Xijing Zájì: v-7* who retells the same tale of heroic early Hàn "flying general" Lî Guâng. cf. *Shîjì: cix Lî Jiangjun lièzhuàn.*

[160] (Hàn) Liú Xiàng: *Xinxù iv: 24–25* follows (Hàn) Hán Ying: *Hánshi Wàizhuàn: vi.*

[161] *Xún Zî: xxv Jiêbì.*

[162] (Míng) Du Mù: *Bâoyàntáng Mìjí*, pûjí -dì-4: *Yóu Míngshan* jì, iv: 4–5. Gû wèi: jingchéng -kê tong jinshí.

[163] (Míng) Chéng Chongdôu 1616: *Shàolín Staff Laws*: 2. Middle Four-Level dynamic:

> Middle Four-Level dynamic is truly a wonder.
> Gods appear, demons vanish: it is not easy to know.
> Closing or opening, vertically or horizontally, at will transmute.
> All dynamics do it homage, for ever unmovable.

[164] *Mèng Zî: vib-2 Gào Zî: Câo Jiao wèn.*

[165] Chén Zengzhì, Chén Wànlî 2001: 40–41 cite a comprehensive system of "ten levels" of Cháng boxing. Among these, the central Twenty-four Fists in mid-stance belong to the fifth level; in floating high-stance the sixth; and in sinking low-stance the seventh.

[166] A popular saying goes "familiarity can produce skill," shóu néngsheng qiâo.

[167] *Zhànguó Cè "Warring Kingdom Stratagems"*: *Chûcè*.

[168] Chén Xin 1919: 477 pijian zhíruì 披堅執銳.

[169] (Sòng) Zhou Dunyí: *Tàijítú*.

[170] *Lankâvatâra Sûtra*, tr. D.T. Suzuki 1932, London: *III, lxxvii*, 207–208, 179 "impermanency of form."

[171] *Zhuang Zî: xxvi Wàiwù*.

[172] Chén Xin 1919: 94. *Prajna Pâramitâ Hridaya "The Heart" Sûtra*.

[173] *Sun Zî: v Shì "Dynamics"*: "Dynamics are like bending a crossbow, Moment like shooting the trigger."

[174] *Mèng Zî: iia-2 Gongsun Chôu: Hàorán-zhi Qì*.

[175] *Poetry Classic: i Zhounán: 1*: a wedding song "Guan-guan go the Ospreys..."

[176] *Zhuang Zî: xxxiii Tianxià*: a paradox of the dialectician Huì Shi.

[177] Zeng Zî, attr.: *Zhongyong: xii*: "The gentleman's Way is pervasive yet hidden..."

[178] *Mèng Zî: iia-2 Gongsun Chôu: Hàorán-zhi Qì*.

[179] *Yìjîn Jing: Nèizhuàng Lùn* 1979: 6; 105.

[180] (Míng) Yú Dàyóu 1565: *Zhèngqitáng jí: Jiànjing*, Correct Energy Hall Collection: "Sword Classic." Reproduced in Qi Jiguang: *Jixiào Quánshu: xii*: 70–72.

[181] (Míng) Qi Jìguang: *Jìxiào Quánshu xii "Short Weapons' Long Application"*: 70–72.

[182] Cf. Zhang Ba's biography, in Introduction, above.

[183] (Hàn) Huáng Shígong: *Three Stratagems, San-Lyuè: Xiàlyuè*.

[184] Chén Xin 1919: 477.

[185] *Mèng Zî: iia-2 Gongsun Chôu: Hàorán-zhi Qì*.

[186] (Sòng) Lí Jídé comp.: *Zhu Zî Wénlèi xviii: Dàxué 5 huòwèn-xià*: 415, Zhonghuá Shujú 1983, Peking. *Autumn Day Casual Composition*; cited by Zhu Zî, *Yûlèi xviii: Dàxué "Great Learning"*: "...Wànwù jìngguan –jie zìdé; Sìshí jiaxing –yû rén tóng. Dào tong Tiandì yôu xíngwài, Sìrù fengyún biàntài-zhong..."

[187] *Sun Zî: v Shì*.

[188] *Sun Zî: vii Junzheng*.

[189] Xú Zhèn 1935: 15, on Wû Yûxiang. Chén Yánlín 1936: 300 *Safàng Mìjué*.

[190] (Hàn) *Wú-Yuè Chunqiu: ix* on "South Forest Virgin" Nánlín Chùnyû.

[191] *Sun Zî: Bingfâ: xi Jiû-dì, "Nine Grounds."*

[192] *Yìjîn Jing: Nèizhuàng Shényông; Liànshôu Yúgong*.

[193] (Míng) Chéng Chongdôu 1616: *Shàolín Gùnfâ Chánzong, no. 39*. (Qing) Wú Yì: *Shôubì lù: iv Mâjia Qiang kâo*: 216 *Jìntóuqiang*, 1970, Huálián chubânshè, Táibêi.

194 *Sun Zî: vii Junzheng.*

195 Chén Yánlín 1936: 300 *Safàng Mìjué.*

196 *Sun Zî: vii Junzheng:* "Of triple armies, you may seize the Energy..."

197 *Sun Zî: i Jì; v Shì; vii Junzheng.*

198 *Yìjing: Hexagram 64 Jìjì.*

199 *Mèng Zî: iia-2 Gongsun Chôu: Hàorán-zhi Qì.*

200 (Hàn) Wèi Bóyáng: *Cantóngqì: xxvi, "Lead and Mercury mutually resort."*

201 (Hàn) Simâ Qian: *Shîjì: Xiàng Yû zhuàn.*

202 (Míng) Chéng Chongdòu, 1616 no. 42. Matsuda 1975: 47 *Wûbèizhì lxxxix* no. 44; 58 *Wànbâo Quánshu* [Seikadô Library, Tôkyô].

203 Confucius: *Analects: xix.*

204 *Zhîyuè Lù "Pointing to Moon Record"* (1602), VII–7.

205 Chén Xin 1919: 225.

206 *Yìjing: hexagram 4: Méng,* judgement, attr. King Wén c. 1150 B.C.

207 *"Shady Tally Classic" Yinfú Jing* standard text, which I show in square brackets, differs slightly from Cháng's citation. Confucius' *"Analects" Lúnyû: xv* has: "Gentlemen are firm **in adversity (gùqióng);** small men then become **dissolute.**"

208 Confucius: *Lúnyû "Analects": vii.* "Great Elegance" is the title of the *Poetry Classic* chapter which hymns the great achievements of dynastic founders.

209 *Zhongyong "Central Norm": xx.*

210 *Yàn Zî Chunqiu: ii Jiàn-xià.*

211 *Hàn Wûdì Nèizhuàn.*

212 (Míng) Wú Chéng'en attr.: *Xiyóujì: v.*

213 (Qing) Zhang Zhòngcái 張仲才: *Wénshî Zhenjing* 文始真經.

214 (Hàn) Simâ Qian: *Shîjì: xcvi supplement.*

215 (Hàn) Ban Gù: *Hànshu: lxxiv.*

216 (Hàn) Simâ Qian: *Shîjì: lxiii.*

217 *Chunqiu Zuôzhuàn: Lû Xuangong* 2nd; 15th year.

218 *Jìnshu: Wen Jiào zhuàn.*

219 (Warring States c. 300 B.C.) "Pheasant-Cap Master" *Héguan Zî: v Huánliú.*

220 *Zhîyuè lù xi:* 15.

221 Qi Jìguang: *Jîxiào Xinshu xii Duânbing Chángyòng shuo* [Yú Dàyóu]: 67 "Èr-lóng zhengzhu."

222 I amend "hair" máo 毛 to "flower" hua 花.

223 *Sòng Shî: Yînyì: Chén Tuán zhuàn.*

224 I amend "right-hand" to "left-hand" here.

225 Wáng Shùjin 1978: 89ff, *No. 7.*

226 *Xiyóujì: v.*

[227] *Shijing: Guófeng: Wèi: Zhìgû.*

[228] (Qing) Jin Shèngtàn 金聖嘆: *Sanshísan Bùyìkuàizai* 三十三不亦快哉.

[229] (Qing) Wú Shu 1684, 1970:*Iv Mâjia Qiang kâo:* 217–218.

[230] Léi Xiàotian 1979: 235, 246.

[231] *Kaitian Yíshì.*

[232] Chén Xin 1919: 269.

[233] (Táng) Lî Bái's poem: "Shanyin Daoist [Wáng Xizhi], if I should meet, Must write the *Yellow Court* in exchange for white swans."

[234] *Huángtíng Jing.*

[235] Chén Xin 1919: 95–96, 199–200.

[236] Léi Xiàotian 1979: 224.

[237] *Analects ix.*

[238] *Chunqiu Zuôzhuàn: Lû Xigong* 16th year.

[239] *Hànshu: Ban Chao zhuàn.* Trevor Leggett, *The Tiger's Cave.*

[240] Chén Xin 1919: 167.

[241] Hàn: Simâ Qian, *Shîjì:* vii *Xiàng Yû Bênjî;* xcii *Huáiyinhóu,* "hissing roar, chìzhà.

[242] (Míng) Wú Chéng'en: *Xiyóujì: i.*

[243] *San-guó Yânyì: xlii.*

[244] I amend "wrist center" zhongwàn 中腕 to "solar plexus" zhongguàn 中脘. Chén Xin 1919: 127, like Cháng, writes "zhongguàn" as "zhongwàn." See: 2, acupuncture chart, above.

[245] Huáng Zongxi 1680: *Nánléijí;* Huáng Bâijia: *Nèijia Quánfâ.* Táng Háo 1935, 1971: 41ff. Wile 1999: 65 "the coiling chop, which enables one to counter a chop with a chop."

[246] Chén Xin 1919: 337ff.

[247] *San-guó Yânyì: xli.* "Blue Mercury" Qinggong 青釭=?汞.

[248] *San-guó: xliv.*

[249] *San-guó Yânyì: liv.*

[250] *Xiyóujì: xix.*

[251] *Shàolín Lineage Law: Illustrated Explanations* 1915: 13.

[252] *Xiyóujì: lix.*

[253] (Míng) Chéng Chongdòu, 1621: *Shàolín Gùn tújiê: liii.* "Secret edition" Xú Hèlíng 1930, 1968.

[254] (Míng) Chén Yàowén: *Tian-zhong Jì* 天中記.

[255] I amend "left-ribs" to "right-ribs" here, following the sense of the picture.

[256] I amend "upper-hand little-finger" and "rear-hand thumb" to "lower-hand little-finger" and "upper-hand thumb" in interests of sense.

[257] *Xiyóujì: vi.*

[258] Wáng Shùjin 1978: 83ff, *No. 6.*

[259] *Zhuang Zî: i Xiaoyáoyóu.*

260 *Shuǐhú zhuàn: lii.*

261 *"Changes" Zhouyì: Xící-shàng 5.*

262 (Sòng) Zhào Lìngzhì, *Hóuzhenglù.*

263 *Hán Fei Zî: xl Nànshì.*

264 *Zhugé Liàng jí: Jiàngyuàn—Bingquán: 77.*

265 *Mèng Zî: ia-7: Liáng Huìwáng: Qí Huán, Jìn Wén,* "jia Tàishan, -yî chao Bêihâi."

266 *Zhongguó Xìqû Qûyì Cídiân,* 1981: 5 93. The play is also called *Bâolián Deng, Mángcháng Shan,* or *Pishan jiùmû.*

267 Chén Yánlín 1936: 116.

268 Jintáiquán 1929: 14. This work, claiming Sòng dynasty lineage, illustrates "Eight-trigram Boxing," Baguàquán (no relation to circular Baguàzhâng) in 64 moves; "Subdue Demons Boxing," Xiángyaoquán in 24 moves; and "Monkey Boxing," Hóuquán in 24 moves.

269 *Mèng Zî: ia-7 Liánghuì Wáng: Qí Huán, Jìn Wén.*

270 *Xiyóujì: xli–xlii, lix–lxi.*

271 Dudbridge 1970: 16.

272 *Zhuang Zî: ii Qíwùlùn.*

273 Wáng Shùjin 1978: 93ff, *No. 8.*

274 *Xiyóujì: i.*

275 Chén Xin 1919: 263.

276 I reposition this introduction from the end of *72 Double Sword Catalogue.*

277 I amend chuàngrán "charge like" to chuàngqián "charge ahead."

278 *Mèng Zî: iia–2 Gongsun Chôu: Hàorán-zhi Qì.*

279 *"Sòng History," Sòngshî:* Yáng Yè zhuàn. (Míng novelist) Qínhuái Mòkè: *Yángjiajiàng Yânyì zhuàn.*

280 Chén Yánlín 1936: 300 *"Discharge and Release Secrets" Safàng Mìjué.*

281 *San-guó Yânyì lxxi "gangróu jìjì."*

282 Chén Yánlín 1936: 232–235.

283 Chén Yánlín 1936: 300 *Safàng Mìjué.*

284 Simâ Qian: *Shîjì: vii Xiàng Yû Bênjì; xcii Huáiyinhóu Lièzhuàn.*

285 *Three Kingdoms Romance, San-guó Yânyì: xli.*

286 (Táng) Dù Yòu: *"Encyclopedia" Tongdiân: 153* "Soldiering" *Bing vi.*

287 *Mèng Zî: iia–2 Gongsun Chôu: Hàorán-zhi Qì.*

288 *Xiyóujì: vii.*

289 I read the word "cloud" yún 雲 as shuâ 耍 = "sweep" shua 刷.

290 *"Ten Continents Record," Shí-zhou Jì.*

291 *"Westward Travelogue," Xiyóujì: vi.*

292 *Three Kingdoms Romance, San-guó Yânyì: lix.*

293 (Hàn dynasty) *"Record of Treasure Swords." Yuèjué shu: xiii Wàizhuàn: Jì Bâojiàn.*

[294] I amend "left" to "right" for reasons of sense.

[295] Xú Zhédong (Zhèn) preface 1936, reissued 1965: *Tàijíquán Kâoxìn Lù-xià*: 46–54. cf. Táng Háo, Zhu Qìngzhong 1971: 1–7. Zhang Yàozhong 1989 passim.

[296] (Sòng) Zhou Dunyí (1017–1073):
> Without poles, and so it is the Grand Polarity:
> Grand Polarity begets negative and positive.

[297] Confucius: *Analects, Lúnyû: xi*: "Over-reaching is like falling-short."
> *Doctrine of the Mean, Zhongyong: iv*:
> The Way is not implemented. I know why!
> The clever over-reach, the foolish fall-short.

[298] *Analects: iv*: "My way has One, that pervades it."

[299] Zhu Xi (1130–1200) commentary on the *Great Learning, Dàxué: v* "*Investigate Things to Extend Knowledge,*" *Géwù Zhìzhì*.

[300] *Documents Classic, Shu Jing*: "*Vast Plan*" *Hóngfàn*: "Neither one-sided, nor leaning."

[301] *Analects: ix*: "Look up at it, and it's still higher. Bore into it, and it's still harder."

[302] *Analects: i*:
> I don't worry about men not knowing me;
> I worry about not knowing men.

[303] (Three Kingdoms) Zhugé Liàng: "*Mind Book*" *Xinshu: Jiàngyuàn—Bingshì*: 91 (*Zhugé Liàng jí*, 1960, 1974 Zhonghuá shujú, Bêijíng):
> The good general
> Adapts to Heaven's timing,
> Proceeds with Earth's dynamics,
> Accords with Men's profit:
> **Then wherever he goes, he is irresistible,**
> Whatever he strikes is a hundred percent secured.

[304] cf. *Pushing Hands Song,* transmitted in the Chén family at Chénjiagou:
> Let him with gigantic force come to hit me:
> Pull into motion four ounces to deflect a thousand pounds.

[305] *Zhou Zî Qúanshu* 1757, Hú Xû (1655–1736): "Sunny and Shady do not leave each other." Táng Háo, Gù Liúxing preface 1963 Shànghâi: *Tàijíquán yanjiù*: 184.

[306] Cf. *San-guó Yânyì lxxi "gangróu jìjì."*

[307] *Analects: ii*: "At seventy, I **follow what my heart desires** and did not transgress the rules."

[308] *Documents Classic: Great Yû's Council*: "Examine the multitude: **discard self, follow men.**" *Mencius: iia–8 Gongsun Chôu: Shàn –yû Réntóng*: "**Discard self, follow men.**"

309 (Qín-Hàn) Huáng Shígong: *Three Stratagems: Lower Stratagem*: "Those who **discard the near to** scheme for **the far,** labour without result. Those who discard the far to scheme for the near, at leisure attain their end." cf. *Later Hàn History: xviii Biography of Zhang Gong.*

310 *Changes Apocrypha Yìwêi: Tongguà yàn juàn-shàng* (Hàn: Zhèng Kangchéng zhù): 205 "Correct their root and myriad things are rationalized, lose it by a hair's breadth, err by a thousand lî." Zhèng -qí bên, -ér wànwù lî; shi-zhi háolî, chà-yî qian-lî. *Dàdài: Lîjì: xlvi Lî chá: "Yì."* (Hàn) Jîa Yì: *New Book 10: Embryonic Teaching: Changes* says: Correct the root, and Myriad Things are rationalized.

Lose it by a hair's breadth, go wrong a thousand lî.

cf. (Hàn) Simâ Qian: *Shîjì 130 Postscript.* (Hàn) Ban Gù: *Hàn History: Biography of Simâ Qian.*

311 (Sòng) Buddhist priest, Mù'an: *Zútíng Shìyuàn.*

312 *Mèng Zî: iia–2 Gongsun Chôu: Hàorán-zhi Qì.*

313 (Hàn) Zhào Yè 趙曄: *Wú-Yuè Chunqiu: ix.*

314 (Hàn) Zhào Yè 趙曄:*Wú-Yuè Chunqiu: ix.*

315 (Qing) Chái Zhuorú 柴桌如: "Scholar Boxer Cháng San" Rúquánshi Cháng San 儒拳師萇三 "Black Tiger Extracts Heart" Heihû Táoxin: Chái Rúzhù [Rúguì] 黑虎掏心柴如柱 [如桂].

316 *Sì-kù Quánshu: 1–243 Zôngmù: x Jingbù Yìlèi cúnmù iv.*

317 (Qing) Yû Ràng 禹讓. Xú Zhèn 1936, 1965 -shàng: 11 attributes this data on Yû Ràng to Chái Zhuorú 1921.

Index

About the Author

Marnix Wells graduated in classical Chinese at Oxford under Professor David Hawkes in 1967. In 1968, at the height of the Vietnam war and China's "Great Cultural Revolution," he arrived in Hong Kong and began to practice taijiquan, Chinese calligraphy, and musical instruments. Since Beijing was then in turmoil, Wells traveled to Taiwan, Japan, and Korea. He learned internal martial arts from Zhang Yizhong in Tokyo, and later from the legendary Wang Shujin in Taiwan. He became general manager of a shipping office and helped plan the "Way of the Warrior" feature on the Hong brothers of Taipei for the BBC. In 2001 Wells earned a PhD in ancient Chinese philosophy from SOAS, London University. He teaches internal martial arts and lectures widely on Chinese art, music, and philosophy. He has one daughter and lives in London.